V

DATE DUE

APR 1 8 2005	

BRODART   Cat. No. 23-221

BLAKE RECORDS SUPPLEMENT

Pl. 1 Oil portrait of William Blake by Thomas Phillips (April 1807), from the original in the National Portrait Gallery (London). Note the elegant dress, the watch fob, the poised pencil, and the prominent eyes. While Phillips painted the portrait, Blake told him of a dazzling argument with the archangel Gabriel (see pp. xxiii–xxiv).

Blake Records
Supplement

Being New Materials Relating to the Life of

WILLIAM BLAKE

Discovered Since the Publication of
Blake Records (1969)

by

G. E. BENTLEY, Jr.

CLARENDON PRESS · OXFORD
1988

Oxford University Press, Walton Street, Oxford OX2 6DP

Oxford New York Toronto
Delhi Bombay Calcutta Madras Karachi
Petaling Jaya Singapore Hong Kong Tokyo
Nairobi Dar es Salaam Cape Town
Melbourne Auckland

and associated companies in
Berlin Ibadan

Oxford is a trade mark of Oxford University Press

Published in the United States
by Oxford University Press, New York

British Library Cataloguing in Publication Data
Bentley, Gerald Eades
Blake records supplement: being
new materials relating to the life
of William Blake discovered since
the publication of Blake records (1969).
1. Blake, William, 1757–1827—Biography
2. Poets, English—Biography
I. Title
821'.7   PR4146
ISBN 0–19–812853–3

Library of Congress Cataloging in Publication Data
Bentley, G. E. (Gerald Eades), 1930–
Blake records supplement.
Includes index.
1. Blake, William, 1757–1827—Biography—Sources.
2. Poets, English—19th century—Biography. 3. Artists—
England—Biography.   I. Title.
PR4146.B374 1988   821'.7 [B]   87–23983
ISBN 0–19–812853–3

Set by Joshua Associates Ltd., Oxford
Printed in Great Britain
at the University Printing House, Oxford
by David Stanford
Printer to the University

TO
E.B.B.

semper eadem

CONTENTS

LIST OF ILLUSTRATIONS

ACKNOWLEDGEMENTS

I AM grateful for generous personal assistance, usually in the form of drawing my attention to unnoticed Blake references, to Mark Abley, John Beattie, John Bidwell, David Bindman, Martin Butlin, the late Edward Croft Murray, Raymond Deck, Detleff W. Dörrbecker, Lord Egremont, Professor June Fullmer, Stanley Gardner, Roger Gaskell (of Pickering & Chatto), the late Geoffrey Grigson, James Hopkins, G. Ingli James, Mary Barham Johnson, the late Sir Geoffrey Keynes, James King, David Klausner, Jenijoy La Belle, Thomas Lange, Marion Linton, Raymond Lister, David McC. McKell, Jr., the late James Osborn, Dennis Read, R. J. Schrader, the late Ruthven Todd, Gerald Tyson, Janet Warner, Paul and Wilfred Warrington, David H. Weinglass, and Robert Woof, and especially to my dear friends Joan Linnell Ivimy and Robert Essick.

Research for this Supplement (*inter alia*) has been supported by Fellowships from the Social Sciences and Humanities Research Council of Canada in 1970–1, 1977–8, and 1984–5, and by grants from the University of Toronto for which I am deeply grateful.

The work has been crucially assisted by the librarians and staffs of

The Artists' General Benevolent Association (London)
Boston Public Library
The British Library and British Museum Print Room
Cambridge University Library (especially the Keynes Collection)
East Sussex Record Office
Fitzwilliam Museum (Cambridge)
Greater London Record Office
Keele University Library
Leeds University Library (especially the Ruthven Todd Collection)
Liverpool City Libraries
Manchester University Library
McMaster University Library
National Library of Scotland
National Library of Wales
National Portrait Gallery (London)

x *Acknowledgements*

Pennsylvania Historical Society (Harrisburg, Pa.)
Pierpont Morgan Library (New York)
Royal Academy of Arts (London)
Princeton University Library
Sheffield Public Library
University of Toronto Library
Victoria & Albert Museum Library (London)
Wedgwood Museum (Barlaston, Stoke on Trent)
Westminster City Libraries (Buckingham Palace Road, London)
Windsor Castle

and especially by those of Bodley and the Huntington Library, which are as generous in beauty and friendship as in knowledge.

This book owes most of all to the dedicatee, who shares the desk beside me wherever we do research, who selflessly does my work before her own, and who by the smile on her face and the rose in her hair lifts hearts wherever she goes, mine most of all.

Dutch Boys Landing,   G.E.B.
Mears, Michigan
23 August 1985

ABBREVIATIONS

Blake	*Blake: An Illustrated Quarterly* (the new title of *Blake Newsletter*)
BMPR[1]	British Museum Print Room
GEB	The collection of G. E. Bentley, Jr.
Gilchrist (1942); (1863)[1]	Alexander Gilchrist, *Life of William Blake*, ed. Ruthven Todd (1942); *Life of William Blake, 'Pictor Ignotus'* (1863), Vol. i
Ivimy MSS[1]	The voluminous Linnell family records in the possession of Joan Linnell Ivimy
BR	*Blake Records* (1969)
(p. 1111)	*William Blake's Writings* (1978), 1111

Modern books and articles cited without the author's name are by G. E. Bentley, Jr.

Blake's words are silently quoted from *The Writings of William Blake* (1978); bibliographical details (e.g. Mrs Bliss owned *For Children* [A]) are taken silently from *Blake Books* (1977); biographical details about Blake derive from *Blake Records* (1969), those concerning others derive from the *Dictionary of National Biography*.

[1] As in *Blake Records* (1969).

PREFACE

BLAKE RECORDS attempted 'to collect and publish as many as possible of the references to Blake made by his contemporaries' from 1737, when his father was apprenticed, to 1831, when his wife died (p. xxiii), and this was supplemented by 'Forgotten Years: References to William Blake 1831–63' in G. E. Bentley, Jr., *William Blake: The Critical Heritage* (1975), 220–69, which forms, as it were, Part VII of *Blake Records*.

In the years since *Blake Records* was published in 1969, a number of new contemporary references to Blake have been discovered, and I have tried to keep careful track of them; often my attention was drawn to them by kind friends. A number of these new references are from long after Blake's death, but they seem to be valuable when they provide testimony of individuals who knew Blake or at least were alive when he was and can provide evidence of what his contemporaries thought of him. Passages from Samuel Palmer's letters written up to half a century after Blake died, for instance, will be found scattered through the pages which follow.

Many of the new references are, of course, fairly trivial, such as Blake's opinion that a dog is preferable to a cat (see p. 81) or the vain offer by Linnell of Blake's Job engravings to a customer. A number, however, are of considerable importance, such as the new details concerning Cromek's inspired and devious dealings with Blake over the designs for Blair's *Grave* (1805–8), the business the Blake family hosiery firm did with the St James Parish School (1782–5), and the commission for Blake's great 'Ancient Britons' design by William Owen Pughe (see 1811). And some of the documents only appeared as this work was passing through the press, such as the letters of 1802–4 from E. G. Marsh offered at Sotheby's in July 1985. New documents relating to Blake's life will, of course, continue to appear, but they are likely to come from unpredictable places, as have those of the last sixteen years.

The surviving records of Blake's life are remarkably discontinuous and erratic. We still do not know where his father was born, when his sister died, what Blake's religious affiliations were for most of his life, or how he supported himself during the long period 1806–18. The table of Surviving Records of Blake sets forth briefly the sources of our information in chronological order (see pp. xv–xix). The chief omission from the table is Blake's watercolours, which do not submit readily to such an organization.

We have very little information about Blake's life up to the completion of his apprenticeship in 1779. Even thereafter there are still some years about which we have scarcely any information at all, such as 1781 and 1790. In *Blake Records* and its *Supplement*, there are only about eighty pages covering the first forty-two years of his life, from 1757 to 1799, and only six letters for this entire period, though he was writing vigorously during this time—thirty works with almost eight hundred pages in a modern edition, including *Poetical Sketches* (1783) in conventional typography, *Songs of Innocence and of Experience* (1794) and the *Marriage of Heaven and Hell* (?1790–?3) in the method of Illuminated Printing which he invented, and *Vala* (?1796–?1807) in manuscript. He also did a large amount of work for the booksellers, producing over two hundred plates for forty-seven different books. At the same time he was extraordinarily prolific in making designs in water-colour, with 543 for Young's *Night Thoughts* (*c.* 1794–7) and over a hundred for Gray's poems (1797–8).

By contrast, the years 1800—5 are very rich in materials for Blake's life, mostly because of his association with William Hayley, who kept the letters he received, including some about Blake and some from him—fifty-six Blake letters survive from these years, chiefly to Hayley. Consequently we know much more about this six-year period than we do about all his previous life put together. At this time Blake was not only busily engraving and painting for Hayley but working on his epics *Vala* or *The Four Zoas*, *Milton* (1804–?8), and *Jerusalem* (1804–?20) and designing water-colours in illustration of Milton and the Bible.

About 1805 Blake broke free of the fetters of patronage, especially the patronage of William Hayley and of R. H. Cromek, profitable in many ways though their sponsorship of him had been, and he embarked on a career marked by independence and obscurity. Much of what we know of his career then derives from the extensive publicity by Cromek for engravings of the designs for Blair's *Grave* which Blake believed had been virtually stolen from him and from the published criticism of these designs and of the pictures in Blake's exhibition of 1809.[1] Despite this publicity, most of it distressing, we still know rather

---

[1] During these years there also appeared Malkin's appreciation of Blake (1806) and Crabb Robinson's journalistic account of him in German (1811).

Surviving Records of Blake

Date	Blake Records	Blake Records Supplement	Letters¹ pages (no. of ALS)	Writings¹ pages (no. of texts)	Commercial book engravings Plates (books)²	Events in Blake's life
			Family and Milieu			
1737–55	1–4					
			The Visionary Apprentice			
1757–77	5–14					Blake born
			From Artisan to Artist			
1779	15–16				1 (1)	RA student
1780	17–20, 621–2	1			13 (4)	
1781					3 (2)	
1782	20–4				12 (6)	married
1783	24–6	1		749–99, 869–74 (3)	15 (5)	
1784	26–9			875–900 (1) 875–99 (4)	9 (1)	print shop
1785	30–1	2–8			2 (1)	
1786	31				17 (2)	
1787	31–4			900–1 (1)		
1788	34	8–9		3–21 (2)	5 (2)	

Date	Blake Records	Blake Records Supplement	Letters[1] pages (no. of ALS)	Writings[1] pages (no. of texts)	Commercial book engravings Plates (books)[2]	Events in Blake's life
1789	35–8			22–73, 902–20 (3)	1 (1)	joins New Church
1790						
1791	38–45	10	1521 (1)	800–18 (1)		
1792	46–8				29 (3)	
1793	48	10		74–169 (5)	16 (4)	
1794	48			171–283 (4)	4 (1)	
1795	48–50	11	1522–3 (1)	284–314 (3)	4 (3)	
1796	50–7	11–12	1523–4 (1)	315, 1071 (2)	28 (4)	
1797	57–9	13–14		1072–297 (1)	49 (3)	
1798		14–15			4 (1)	
1799	59–61		1524–30 (3)		6 (3)	
			Patronage and Dependence			
1800	62–78, 622		1530–49 (12)			
1801	78–87	15–17	1550–5 (5)		14 (3)	moves to Felpham

Year						
1802	88–113	17–22	1556–66 (4)	1298 (1)	15 (2)	moves to London
1803	113–37	22–7	1567–86 (8)	1299–301 (1)	12 (2)	sedition trial
1804	137–56	27–9	1586–1620 (21)	316–641 (2)	1 (1)	
1805	157–74	29–40	1620–31 (7)		8 (2)	
Independence and Obscurity						
1806	175–82, 421–31,[3] 622	40–5	1631–2 (1)	1818–19 (1)	2 (2)	
1807	182–8, 623	45–55	1636–7 (1)	1819–20, 1302–18 (2)		
1808	188–214	55–9	1637–45 (4)	642–3, 820–63 (5)	12 (1)	exhibition
1809	214–20, 623	59–60	1645 (1)		1 (1)	
1810	220–9	60–4, 132–3	1646 (1)	863–6, 1007–128 (2)		
1811	229–30, 432–55[4]	67–8		1029–53 (1)		
1812	230–1, 623					
1813	231–2	70–1				
1814	232–3					
1815	234–41	71–2	1648 (1)			

Date	Blake Records	Blake Records Supplement	Letters[1] pages (no. of ALS)	Writings[1] pages (no. of texts)	Commercial book engravings Plates (books)[2]	Events in Blake's life
1816	241–5				18 (1)	
1817	245–8	72			37 (1)	
1818	248–58		1648–9 (1)	644–61, 1054–69 (2)		meets Linnell
			The Ancients and the Interpreter			
1819	258–64, 624–5	72–6	1650 (1)		6 (1)	
1820	264–9	76		662–6 (2)		
1821	269–75	77–9		667–8 (1)	27 (1)	
1822	275–7	79		669–75 (1)		
1823	277–9	79	1650–1 (1)			
1824	279–99	80	1651[5] (1)		2 (2)	
1825	299–319	82–5	1651–4 (4)			
1826	319–37	85–7	1654–63 (12)		22 (1)	
1827	337–61	87–8	1664–70 (8)		7 (1)	Blake dies

Year			
1828	361–73, 455–76,⁶ 625–6	88–9	xxix–xxx⁷ (2)
1829	373–5	89–95	
1830	375–402, 476–507,⁸ 626	95–8	
1831	403–12	98–9	Catherine dies
1832	507–36⁹	99–100	
1833	413–18	100	

'God protect me from my friends'

¹ The text used is *William Blake's Writings* (1978). Among Blake's writings, I omit marginalia, inscriptions on designs, and most of the *Notebook*. Some dates are approximate or arbitrary; e.g. *Milton* (1804–?8) is assigned to 1804 and *Vala* (?1796–?1807) to 1797 (the dates on their title-pages).

² The information is from *Blake Books* (1977). Plates published in two books (e.g. in Kimpton's *History of the Holy Bible* [1781?] and Josephus, *Work:* [1785–6?]) are counted only once; books issued in Parts over more than one year are ordinarily counted only under the last year. No distinction is made here between plates which Blake engraved and those which he designed, except that plates engraved from Blake's designs after his death (e.g. Varley's *Zodiacal Physiognomy* [1828]) are ignored. When additional Blake plates were added in a later edition (e.g. in Darwin's *Botanic Garden* [1791, 1795, 1799]) the plates and title are entered repeatedly.

³ E. H. Malkin's prefatory account of Blake (1806).

⁴ H. C. Robinson's essay on Blake (1811).

⁵ The letter is written by Catherine Blake.

⁶ J. T. Smith's biography of Blake (1828).

⁷ See n. 5, above.

⁸ Allan Cunningham's life of Blake (1830).

⁹ Frederick Tatham's MS life of Blake (?1832).

less of this thirteen-year period of Blake's life than we do of the previous six years. There are only eleven surviving letters for this long period and only six books with his commercial engravings—at this time Blake seems almost to have given up the profession for which he was trained.

In the last ten years of his life, 1818–27, Blake was cherished and supported by a group of young men the chief of whom was John Linnell. Linnell not only commissioned Blake's great engravings for Job and Dante and largely supported him, but he meticulously kept his own papers, including his Job accounts, his Journal, and Blake's letters—twenty-three of them. In addition, through Linnell, Blake met the diarist Crabb Robinson, in whose invaluable pages Blake appears very extensively. As a consequence, we know twice as much about this ten-year period as we do about the first forty years of Blake's life.

There is a surprising amount of information about Catherine Blake during the period of her widowhood (1827–31), and during this time there appeared not only periodical obituaries of Blake but more full and extensive biographies by J. T. Smith (1828) and Allan Cunningham (1830), with Tatham's manuscript memoir being completed just after her death (*c.* 1832).

This Supplement attempts to record newly-discovered references to Blake. It is not concerned to correct typographical errors in *Blake Records* (1962)[1] or to amplify editorial matter there,[2] and only twice has it been necessary to draw attention to passages in *Blake Records* which, in light of new information, seem to have nothing to do with the poet.[3]

Blake Records and its *Supplement* are largely records of Blake as seen through the eyes of his curious or indifferent contemporaries. *Blake*

---

[1] e.g., 'sel' (p. 531) for 'self'.

[2] e.g., the source of Tatham's quotation on p. 520 ('Visions of glory spare my aching sight / Ye unborn ages crowd not on my soul') is from Gray, 'The Bard', ll. 107–8.

It may be useful to note here some duplications of accounts of Blake not remarked in *Blake Records*:

Author	Subject	Date	Page	Author Copied	Date	Page
J. T. Smith	Treasuring Blake	1845	26	J. T. Smith	1828	467
Gilchrist	Treasuring Blake	1863	39	J. T. Smith	1828	467
				J. T. Smith	1845	26
Gilchrist	Admiration for Catholicism	1863	42	Samuel Palmer	1862	321 n. 5
Ebert	German summary of Blake	1821	270	H. C. Robinson	1811	443
Ebert	German summary of Blake	1830	375–6	H. C. Robinson	1811	441
Tatham	Blake's death from 'Gall mixing with the Blood'	1833?	528	J. T. Smith	1828	475

[3] See 1802 and 1807.

Records prints a few public records, such as those of Blake's birth and marriage and death, but there are few such public records in this *Supplement*. This lack of public records would not have distressed Blake himself who wrote: 'Public Records[!] As If Public Records were True[!]' (p. 1418).

What *Blake Records* and its *Supplement* set forth are largely the exteriors of Blake's life, how he looked, where he went, all the actions which constitute almost the whole life of which most men are conscious (see the table of Important Dates in Blake's Life, pp. xlii–xlviii). They naturally omit most of that fiery inner life which smoulders, banked down and forgotten, in most of us but which for Blake was the only life which mattered. This inner life is visible in fitful glimpses in these *Records*; but they give chiefly the form of the man, the old Adam, without the substance. But Blake believed that 'Adam is only The Natural Man & not the Soul or Imagination' (p. 665). The substantial Blake, the life of the imagination and the spirit, is the only part of the man which interested Blake himself, however trying and bewildering it may have seemed to his employers and his family and friends. This imaginative and spiritual substance of the man was chiefly expressed in his drawings and engravings, his books and his songs, though it may often be heard in his conversation and seen in his letters, and it is this imaginative substance which matters to us today.

In the Introduction, I have given an outline of the imaginative, spiritual life of Blake, basing it as far as possible on the biographical records of his life to indicate how clearly even these mundane records reveal the life of the spirit. But both here and in the *Supplement*, as in *Blake Records*, I have tried to avoid speculation about Blake's politics, his sexual proclivities, his unexpressed thoughts, his religion, and the state of his soul not based in fairly obvious ways upon the surviving records. The motto here, as in *Blake Records*, is the quotation from Blake's *Descriptive Catalogue*:

Acts themselves alone are history . . . Tell me the Acts, O historian, and leave me to reason upon them as I please; away with your reasoning and your rubbish. All that is not action is not worth reading. (p. 851)

INTRODUCTION

BLAKE THE MAN: THE PUBLIC AND THE
BURIED LIFE

> My hands are labourd day & night
> And Ease comes never in my sight[.]
> My Wife has no indulgence given
> Except what comes to her from heaven[.]
> We eat little[,] we drink less[;]
> This Earth breeds not our happiness[.]
> Another Sun feeds our lifes streams . . .

> [p. 1565]

THE life of William Blake may serve to illustrate the spiritual vitality which lies buried in all of us and which may be seen most easily in the works of men and women of genius. Beneath his public roles as son, brother, husband, workman, citizen, taxpayer, and statistic, the exuberant spirit of Blake the man struggles to break forth.

Blake took the life of the spirit far more seriously than most of us do; indeed, he believed that there is no other life but that of the spirit and that all life is holy. He also took it more frivolously than most of us dare to. In the autograph album of William Upcott he wrote in 1825: 'William Blake . . . Born, 28 Novr 1757 in London & has died Several times Since'.[1]

Most of us spend our lives as strangers and afraid, in a world we never made. Blake spent his life joyously expanding his vision of the world until he learned:

> To see a World in a Grain of Sand
> And a Heaven in a Wild Flower[,]
> Hold Infinity in the palm of your hand
> And Eternity in an hour[.]

> [p. 1312]

I want to exhibit in these pages a portrait of Blake which combines the

---

[1] *William Blake's Writings* (Oxford: Clarendon Press, 1978), p. 1321, the source here-after of quotations from Blake's writings.

public man and the fiery life of the spirit buried in him, a life which he brought more and more openly into the light of day until he could write joyfully:

> I am in Gods presence night & day
> He never turns his face away[.]

[p. 965]

In a letter of January 1802, Blake wrote:

> I hear a voice you cannot hear that says I must not stay
> I see a hand you cannot see that beckons me away[.]

[p. 1558]

We must try to hear the soundless voices heard by William Blake and to see the sightless hands he saw beckoning him away.

The painting by Thomas Phillips (Plate I) is in many respects the most astonishing portrait we have of William Blake. It was made in April 1807 when Blake was fifty-one years old, in the midst of an erratic career as a minor engraver and an eccentric painter. Notice the prosperous coat, the elegant waistcoat, the watch fob or seal below his left elbow, the dapper frilled shirt at the throat; here is a man of substance and even of some fashion.

But the clothes are only incidental. Observe the right hand delicately holding a pencil, indicating that he is an artist. See the high forehead, the determined mouth, the burning, slightly protruberant eyes. This is the portrait of no ordinary man. We do not know why a successful portrait painter like Thomas Phillips should have chosen to paint Blake—certainly Blake did not commission him. We do not know how Blake happened to be wearing those fashionable clothes, for ordinarily he dressed plainly, rather like a Quaker, with a broad-brimmed black hat. But we do know the origin of the rapt expression on Blake's face.

Phillips and Blake had been talking of Michael Angelo and Raphael, and Blake had said very positively that Michael Angelo 'could paint an angel better than Raphael'. When Phillips wondered mildly how Blake could be so sure, Blake replied:

I will tell you how. I was one day reading Young's Night Thoughts, and when I came to that passage which asks, 'who can paint an angel,' I closed the book and cried, 'Aye! Who can paint an angel?'

A voice in the room answered, 'Michael Angelo could.'

'And how do *you* know' I said, looking round me, but I saw nothing save a greater light than usual.

'I *know*,' said the voice, 'for I sat to him: I am the arch-angel Gabriel.'

'Oho!' I answered, 'you are, are you: I must have better assurance than that of a wandering voice; you may be an evil spirit—there are such in the land.'

'You shall have good assurance,' said the voice, 'can an evil spirit do this?'

I looked whence the voice came, and was then aware of a shining shape, with bright wings, who diffused much light. As I looked, the shape dilated more and more: he waved his hands; the roof of my study opened; he ascended into heaven; he stood in the sun, and beckoning to me, moved the universe. An angel of evil could not have *done that*—it was the arch-angel Gabriel.

Allan Cunningham, who told the anecdote, concludes that Phillips 'marvelled much at this wild story; but he caught from Blake's look, as he related it, the rapt, poetic expression which has rendered this portrait one of the finest of the English school'.[1]

The portrait and anecdote illustrate the contrast between the public man, whether in a shabby coat or a frilled shirt, and the buried life invisible to most of his contemporaries, the buried life which shone out through his eyes and which more and more absorbed the man. The public life is easy and brief to tell—and it is not much like the man in Phillips's portrait. What is important is not our view of Blake's life, the portrait of the public man, but Blake's visions of eternity. They are what mattered most to Blake, and they absorbed him more and more, until he entered the gates of paradise singing of what he saw there with his dying breath.

Blake's public life may be quickly told. His father was a not very prosperous hosier in the London parish of St James, Piccadilly, and William Blake was born in the bedroom above the shop in 1757. He never went to school, perhaps because he would not suffer a blow in silence, and later he wrote:

> Thank God I never was sent to school
> To be Flogd into following the Style of a Fool[.]
>
> [p. 953]

He had no patience with cash or customers, but his head was full of visions, so he was apprenticed in 1772 to the successful, old-fashioned engraver, James Basire, and he spent seven years learning to transfer other men's pictures to copper.

All his life Blake made his living entirely by the work of his hands. He was a good engraver, though he was never prosperous enough to

---

[1] *BR*, 183.

take up the freedom of his guild or to have an apprentice. The print-publishers of his day largely ignored him for their most ambitious commissions, and probably only a handful of his contemporaries recognized that he became in his last years a master engraver, perhaps the greatest who has worked in England.

At the same time that Blake's career as an engraver was progressing in fairly conventional ways, he was inventing a quite unconventional way of publishing his own poetry. He called it Illuminated Printing, and the first work he published in it was probably his *Songs of Innocence* in 1789. Thereafter all his poetry was published in this medium, and every copy was coloured differently. Sometimes, for instance, the poem called 'Infant Joy' (p. 25) had its strange flame-blossom coloured red, and sometimes it was blue or pink or yellow or ochre. In these works, the text is expanded and altered by the designs, as in 'The Blossom', where the poem speaks of a robin and a sparrow but the design (p. 32) depicts only winged human figures playing in a flame-like plant which springs with supernatural vitality from the earth.

For twenty years, from the completion of his apprenticeship in 1779 until 1799, Blake was gradually making a modest name for himself as a competent engraver. He even opened a print-shop in 1784, and he exhibited a few pictures at the Royal Academy. However, the print-shop failed after about a year, and the pictures exhibited were ignored by the reviewers.

In 1800 he moved to the little seaside town of Felpham in Sussex to work under the patronage of Felpham's literary squire, the successful, liberal gentleman-poet William Hayley. At first Blake loved the sea and the villagers and his patron, but gradually he began to chafe at the worldliness of Hayley's well-meant friendship. In his Notebook he wrote of Hayley:

> Thy Friendship oft has made my heart to ake[;]
> Do be my Enemy for Friendships sake[.]

[P. 947]

What drew them finally together was a disaster. Blake was accused of sedition by a drunken soldier whom Blake had turned out of his garden. In the invasion hysteria of 1803 the danger to Blake was very real, and some of Hayley's friends thought him guilty. However, Hayley rallied to Blake nobly, paid for his friend Samuel Rose to defend him, and eventually in 1804 Blake was acquitted. But though the trial effected a reconciliation with Hayley, it left a deep mark upon

Blake's soul, and echoes of the trial reverberate through his last two epics called *Milton* and *Jerusalem*.

In 1803 Blake moved from Felpham and patronage and comparative prosperity back to London and independence and obscurity and poverty. For fifteen years we know very little of what he was doing. Only three events brought him to much public notice. One was a commission in 1805 from a hard-headed entrepreneur named Robert Hartley Cromek to design and engrave folio plates for Robert Blair's poem called *The Grave*. The commission was the occasion for both rage and triumph for Blake. The rage came because Cromek had promised Blake the lucrative commission to engrave his own designs and then, when he had seen a sample in a somewhat rugged style, commissioned the fashionable engraver Luigi Schiavonetti to engrave them instead of Blake. Blake's Notebook erupted in little pustules of savage doggerel:

> Cr[*omek*] loves artists as he loves his Meat;
> He loves the Art, but 'tis the Art to Cheat.

> [p. 940]

The triumph came because Schiavonetti's very skilful engravings, such as Phillips's portrait of Blake which was engraved for the frontispiece to the edition, helped to make Blake's art known to the widest public he ever had in his lifetime—there were two editions of the plates in 1808, one in 1813, one in 1826, and half a dozen later. Throughout the Nineteenth Century, most of those who had seen William Blake's pictures knew of him chiefly because of his twelve ambitious designs for Blair's *Grave*.

The second public event was Blake's one-man exhibition in 1809. It was held in the family hosiery shop, and scarcely anyone came—we know of only half a dozen persons who admit to having been there. The exhibition would probably be veiled in the obscurity which characterizes Blake's life at this time had it not been for the *Descriptive Catalogue* he wrote for it which attracted the attention of Leigh Hunt's brother Robert. Robert Hunt was waging a campaign in the family newspaper called *The Examiner* against what he called The Folly and Dangers of Methodism, and he thought that Blake's attempts at 'representing the *Spirit* to the eye' were alarming manifestations of these dangers. He called the Blair designs 'absurd' and even 'indecent', and when he saw the 1809 exhibition and read its catalogue he was even more alarmed. In his review he said of Blake, 'the poor man fancies

. Mahomet

Pl. 2 Blake's Visionary Head of Mahomet (c. 1819), from the original
drawing in the Santa Barbara Museum of Art (Santa Barbara, California). The attitude, hair, and rapt raised gaze are similar to those in
Phillips's portrait of Blake twelve years before (see pl. 1). This is one
of the visions which Blake recorded, often after midnight, for Varley.

himself a great master, and has painted a few wretched pictures, some
of which are unintelligible allegory, others ... [*mere*] caricature ...
and very badly drawn' (*BR*, 195, 196, 197, 216). This public rejection
too had a profound effect upon Blake; in his Notebook he wrote of
'The Examiner, whose very name is Hunt' (p. 935), and the three Hunt
brothers stalk the haunted pages of *Milton* and *Jerusalem*.

The third event which drew public attention to Blake occurred in
1819. All his life Blake saw visions and talked about them, as the anecdote about the Archangel Gabriel indicates, and about 1819 he was
persuaded to draw their portraits as well. These Visionary Heads
represented the spirits not only of the illustrious dead, such as
Mahomet (Plate II) and Edward I, but of men who were scarcely
known to history, such as 'The Man Who Built the Pyramids' and
'Blake's Spiritual Instructor in Painting', and even of spirits who had
never been men at all, such as the Ghost of a Flea. Reports naturally
began to circulate about these Visionary Heads almost at once. Most
of his contemporaries knew just what to think of them, for stories of a
similar but more famous visionary of the time had long been in circu-
lation. In his Diary for 21 May 1818, the artist Joseph Farington wrote
of him: 'Though His disorder continues He is quite clear in his mind
on subjects which occasionally have possession of it. He imagines
persons to be before Him and He speaks to their supposed presence
with all the ability He ever possessed. When He fancies the Prince of
Wales or the Duke of York to be present, He lectures them wisely.'[1]
The visionary in this case was King George III, whom Shelley
described then as 'An old, mad, blind, despised, and dying king.'[2] But
whether his subjets loved or despised their king, by 1819 they knew
that such visions indicated all too plainly his madness. Is it any wonder that few of them hesitated to conclude that Blake too was mad?

There was, however, this crucial difference between Blake's experi-
ences and those of his king: George III believed that his visions had a
real, material, external existence, palpable to others, while Blake knew
that what he saw was his own creation. One evening, when he was in
fashionable company at the house of the art patron Charles Aders,

Blake was talking to a little group gathered round him, within hearing of a lady
whose children had just come home from boarding school for the holidays.
'The other evening,' said Blake, in his usual quiet way, 'taking a walk, I came
to a meadow, and at the farther corner of it I saw a fold of lambs. Coming

---

[1] *The Diary of Joseph Farington*, ed. K. Cave, vol. xv (1984), p. 5206.
[2] Shelley, 'England in 1819'.

nearer, the ground blushed with flowers; and the wattled cote and its woolly tenants were of an exquisite pastoral beauty. But I looked again, and it proved to be no living flock, but beautiful sculpture.'

The lady, thinking this a capital holiday-show for her children, eagerly interposed, 'I beg your pardon, Mr. Blake, but *may* I ask *where* you saw this?'

'*Here*, madam,' answered Blake, touching his forehead. [*BR*, 301]

Thereafter Blake almost disappeared from public view. In 1824 Charles Lamb wrote that he had heard Crabb Robinson recite a poem by Blake beginning

> Tiger Tiger burning bright
> Thro' the deserts of the night—

which is glorious. But alas! I have not the Book, for the man is flown, whither I know not, to Hades, or a Mad House . . . [*BR*, 285]

But Blake was living then not so very far from Charles Lamb in London, and he was surrounded by a group of brilliant adolescent painters such as Samuel Palmer and George Richmond who loved him with a devotion not much this side of idolatry. And he was working at this time on his greatest artistic triumphs, his twenty-two illustrations to the Book of Job and his hundred designs for Dante. During his last years under the protection of the young painter John Linnell, Blake was loved and admired as never before, and when he died in 1827 his widow was cared for and his memory preserved with devotion by these young friends. Most of what we know of Blake after 1809 derives from the memories of John Linnell and of the circle of young disciples who called themselves The Ancients.

This is the view of Blake visible to the public of his time, and it is perhaps understandable that he was at best praised as an eccentric minor engraver and painter or at worst ignored—or dismissed, as he was by Robert Hunt, as 'an unfortunate lunatic, whose personal inoffensiveness secures him from confinement' (*BR*, 218). He was known to artists and to print-connoisseurs, but there is no evidence that Byron or Shelley or Jane Austen or Sir Walter Scott had ever heard of him. And indeed, if Blake's buried life had been known to his contemporaries, they might well have thought his real obscurity and his imputed madness all the more justified. But some might have thought differently.

In the summer of 1784 Blake's father died, and Blake may have inherited some money. At any rate, we know that about this time he moved into a house next door to the hosiery shop where he was born, he started a print-shop with his old fellow-apprentice James Parker, he may have acquired his copperplate-printing-press at this time, and he launched himself vigorously upon the sea of commerce. For the next twenty years he was comparatively prosperous, and his graphic and poetic genius were extraordinarily fertile. During these twenty years he produced no fewer than twelve books of poetry in Illuminated Printing, including *Songs of Innocence and of Experience*, *America*, *Europe*, *The First Book of Urizen*, and the *Marriage of Heaven and Hell*. But with the exception of *Songs of Innocence*, these works are concerned with a sense of betrayal, of being trapped beneath a weight of earth, and their images are of death and imprisonment. Thus in 'Holy Thursday' from *Songs of Experience*, the poem asks,

> Is this a holy thing to see
> In a rich and fruitful land
> Babes reduced to misery
> Fed with cold and usurous hand?

[p. 178]

But what the design shows is a barren tree beneath which a woman looks down in horror at a babe outstretched in death at her feet, and at the bottom right of the design, after the word 'appall', lies another dead child. They are songs of secrecy and despair, as in the poem called 'The Sick Rose':

> O Rose thou art sick,
> The invisible worm,
> That flies in the night
> In the howling storm:
>
> Has found out thy bed
> Of crimson joy:
> And his dark secret love
> Does thy life destroy.

[pp. 181–2]

And the design shows women in roses wrapped in the inhuman embrace of worms. In the poem which epitomizes 'London', we hear:

> I wander thro' each charter'd street,
> Near where the charter'd Thames does flow
> And mark in every face I meet
> Marks of weakness, marks of woe.
>
> In every cry of every Man,
> In every Infants cry of fear,

In every voice; in every ban,
The mind-forg'd manacles I hear[.]

[p. 191]

And the design shows a child leading a crippled old man through dreary slums, though neither child nor cripple is mentioned in the poem.

It is the grip of the mind-forged manacles which is most agonizing, as we see in Blake's poem called *Urizen* (Plate III), where the faculty of man's reason is in chains, his light-giving divinity bound down to earth. The manacles on his wrists and ankles are made by reason; Urizen does not recognize that he has chained himself, that he is his own prisoner. He also does not know, perhaps Blake had not then discovered, that Urizen has the keys to his own chains. The weeping man in this design has shut his eyes to the world, to the nature and cause of his imprisonment, to the source of his freedom.

In these same years, Blake's astonishingly fertile genius invented a method of colour-printing which is still not well understood, by means of which he produced a number of magnificent designs. These too show even the greatest men with their heads bowed to earth, as in the splendid design of 'Newton' displaying his astronomical theories on the floor of the sea. He is an awesome figure, but he has confined himself to the merely earthly; he is dead to the spiritual world. As Blake wrote later,

May God us keep
From Single vision & Newtons Sleep.

[p. 1566]

Newton's action with the compasses, circumscribing matter, is echoed in one of Blake's greatest designs, the frontispiece to his poem called *Europe*, the Ancient of Days (p. 24), in which a mighty, bearded god leans out of the sun to separate the light from the darkness, the land from the sea. Here is a god who believes in the divinity of light, who is the very principle of light. But as Blake wrote elsewhere:

God Appears & God is Light
To those poor Souls who dwell in Night
But does a Human Form Display
To those who Dwell in Realms of day

[p. 1315]

However stupendous that act of creation may seem, bringing order into existence by the forked light from God's fingers, it is the gesture

Pl. 3 Urizen enchained in Blake's *First Book of Urizen* (1794), pl. 22 (Copy B, with a variant order of the plates), from the colour-printed original in the Pierpont Morgan Library (New York). The helpless misery of the Job-like prophet is self-inflicted but (in 1794) inescapable.

of a mistaken god—for in Blake even God is subject to error. In his great colour-print of 'Elohim Creating Adam', the heavy bronze wings of Elohim and his expression of despair are echoed in the agony of Adam wrapped in the worm of mortality. This is not a joyful creation nor one enacted for Adam's benefit, and both creator and creature are in agony.

Blake's vision of these years, however magnificent, is one of torment and despair. Man's ills are clearly seen, but no escape from them is visible. Much of Blake's best known poetry comes from these twenty years, but they are years which Blake found dark and tormented.

At the end of his twenty years of bondage, Blake broke free. In an ecstatic letter of October 1804, Blake wrote to his friend William Hayley:

now! O Glory! and O Delight! I have entirely reduced that spectrous Fiend to his station, whose annoyance has been the ruin of my labours for the last passed twenty years of my life. . . . Nebuchadnezzar had seven times passed over him, I have had twenty . . . I was a slave bound in a mill among beasts and devils . . . [*but now*] my feet and my wife's feet are free from fetters. . . . Suddenly . . . I was again enlightened with the light I enjoyed in my youth, and which has for exactly twenty years been closed from me as by a door and window-shutters. . . . Dear Sir, excuse my enthusiasm or rather madness, for I am really drunk with intellectual vision whenever I take a pencil or graver into my hand, even as I used to be in my youth, and as I have not been for twenty dark, but very profitable years. [pp. 1613, 1614]

And after 1804, Blake's designs and his poems are works of joy and of aspiration, and the figures in his designs look outward and upward. When his young brother Robert had been desperately ill in 1787, Blake had sat up with him for three days and nights, and, when at last Robert died, Blake saw his 'released spirit ascend heavenward through the matter-of-fact ceiling, "clapping its hands for joy"' (*BR*, 32). In his *Four Zoas*, Blake wrote a passage which seems to echo this incident in his own life: the redeemed Urizen 'rose up from his couch On wings of tenfold joy clapping his hands' (p. 1267). After 1804 much of Blake's poetry and painting celebrates this reunion with the spirit, clapping its hands for joy.

The poetry of the dark years had been full of terrible questions: 'Why cannot the ear be closed to its own destruction?' 'Can wisdom be put in a silver rod? Or Love in a golden bowl?' 'Can delight Chain'd in night The virgins of youth and morning bear?' 'Did he who made the Lamb make thee?' (pp. 72, 62, 175, 186) After 1804 Blake had learned that it is the questions which are terrible, not the answers. As he told

George Cumberland in 1827, 'God keep me from the Divinity of Yes & No too[,] The Yea Nay Creeping Jesus' (p. 1667).

Blake's theme is now reconciliation and forgiveness. The old covenant of slavery to the law is destroyed, as in his design of Christ rending the Decalogue, with his arms raised before him. Now God is seen in everything, and 'Everything that lives is holy' (pp. 99, 116, 143, 1126, 1364). Everything leads to vision. In his 'Vision of the Last Judgment', Blake wrote:

I assert for My Self that I do not behold the outward Creation . . . it is as the Dirt upon my feet, No part of Me. 'What' it will be Questiond 'When the Sun rises do you not See a round disk of fire somewhat like a Guinea?' O no no, I see an Innumerable company of the Heavenly host crying 'Holy Holy Holy is the Lord God Almighty!' . . . I look thro . . . [*my eye*] & not with it. [p. 1027]

Many of Blake's most characteristic designs are illustrations not of actions but of metaphors, not of men's deeds but of their visions. His design of 'Ezekiel's Vision' shows one of the men whom Ezekiel saw by Chebar's flood, going forth from a mighty God, beings with four faces who are called Zoas or Living Creatures in the Greek text and who are the central beings, indeed the entire universe, of Blake's long epics, particularly in *The Four Zoas*. Ezekiel's Living Creatures are marching forward through heaven in glory, not bound down to earth in tears, as in the vision of Urizen ten years before.

Yet more apt is the design of 'Jacob's Vision' (Plate IV) with the stairway curving beautifully from the sleeping visionary through the stars to heaven. The design of 1793 to his little book *For Children* had shown a man vainly trying to raise a ladder from the earth to the moon (p. 654), to indicate the futility of longings for material things. In this design of Jacob's ladder, the connection of man to heaven is complete in imagination, and the angels are already ascending the stairway to heaven. It only remains for Jacob and all men who see it to follow the ladder in imagination to heaven.

The same lifting towards the skies may also be seen in the designs which Blake made even for such a dark and earth-bound a poem as Blair's *Grave*. The design for his vignette dedication 'To the Queen' shows Christ floating upward with two keys to release mankind from the gates of death and hell:

The Grave is Heaven's golden Gate,
And rich and poor around it wait[1]

[1] p. 819; the design is reproduced in *BR*, at p. 184.

Pl. 4 Jacob's dream of the stairway to heaven (*c.* 1805), from the original watercolour in the Department of Prints and Drawings of the British Museum (London). The scene reveals a renewed two-way intercourse with heaven.

Christ here bears the keys, but they are also in the hands of each of us. As Blake wrote in his 'Everlasting Gospel' about 1818:

> Mutual Forgiveness of each Vice
> Such are the Gates of Paradise.
>
> [p. 645; cf. p. 1055]

As the world offered less and less to Blake in gold and glory, he came to treasure its imaginative beauties more and more. Once when he was 'a poor old man', 'dressed in . . . shabby clothes', 'a very beautiful' little girl was presented to him at a fashionable party. She felt sorry and perhaps embarrassed for him, but Blake 'looked at her very kindly for a long while without speaking, and then stroking her head and long ringlets said, "May God make this world to you, my child, as beautiful as it has been to me."' [*BR*, 274–5]

During his last years he lived in a 'squalid' two-room walk-up flat off the Strand (p. 315), where he was visited by his young disciples. The rooms were narrow and dark, but 'Blake often spoke of the beauty of the Thames, as seen from the window, the river looking "like a bar of gold"' (*BR*, 566), and once he pointed down into the narrow courtyard between the buildings where children were playing and said to Samuel Palmer, 'That is heaven' (*BR*, 566 n. 4). Heaven lay around him everywhere, and he gathered to himself its bars of poets' gold, though what he called The God of This World had forgotten him. The God of This World, or Satan, had been defeated by Christ's offer of self-sacrifice to the agonized God the Father, as in Blake's watercolour for *Paradise Regained*.

In his last years, Blake lived more and more like a man from Paradise, like a man who was sustained by food and drink other than that of this world. In a letter of 1802 he had written:

> We eat little[,] we drink less[;]
> This Earth breeds not our happiness[.]
>
> [p. 1565]

Once, when Catherine Blake was asked where Blake was, she replied that she could not tell: '[*You see*,] I have very little of Mr. Blake's company; he is always in Paradise' (*BR*, 221). His young disciples were awestruck by him and believed that he was '"*a new kind of man*, wholly original, and in all things"' (*BR*, 294). When George Richmond met him as a boy of sixteen and was allowed to walk home with him, he felt, he said, 'as if he were walking with the Prophet Isaiah' (*BR*, p. 293).

John Giles told Edward Calvert rapturously that Blake 'had seen God, Sir, and had talked with angels', and Samuel Palmer used to 'kiss Blake's bell-handle before venturing to pull it' (*BR*, 294, 292).

But though the young disciples felt him to be enormously above them in artistic capacity and in spiritual power, he effortlessly brought himself down to their level. Once young Samuel Palmer told Blake that for two whole weeks he had

felt deserted by the power of invention. To his astonishment Blake turned to his wife suddenly and said: 'It is just so with us, is it not, for weeks together, when the visions forsake us? What do we do then, Kate?'

'We kneel down and pray, Mr. Blake.' [*BR*, 293–4]

Blake knew the answer to the riddle of the Sphinx, 'What art thou, Œdipus?' and he could have answered with Swellfoot the Tyrant, 'Only a man, my Lord!' But Blake knew more than Œdipus or the Sphinx, for he knew the answer to the greater question, 'What are the gods who make eternal holiday beyond the Mountains of the Moon?', for the answer is the same: 'Only a man, my Lord!' Blake had dis-covered the divinity within himself, as when he wrote:

Thou art a Man[.] God is no more[!]
Thine own Humanity learn to Adore

[p. 1065]

When he was asked by Crabb Robinson about the Divinity of Jesus Christ, he replied: '"*He is the only God*[."] But then he added—["]And so am I and so are you"' (*BR*, p. 310).

The greatest poets and philosophers have said that we bear within us the seeds of divinity, but very few of them have lived as Blake did, as if it were true. When Serjeant Yorke led his men across the bullet-swept bridge at Belleau Wood saying 'Come on, men, do you want to live for-ever?', Blake could have replied, 'We cannot help it.' He told Crabb Robinson, 'We are all coexistent with God—Members of the Divine body—We are all partakers of the divine nature' (*BR*, 310). He said he could not 'consider death as any thing but a removing from one room to another' (*BR*, 337), and in a letter he wrote: 'I verily believe . . . [*that*] Every Death is an improvement in the State of the Departed' (p. 1652).

His joy lay in his art, and nothing else mattered. He told Crabb Robinson with glistening eyes that a spirit had said to him, 'Blake, be an artist & nothing else. In this there is felicity' (*BR*, 311). In his last years, his letters speak regularly of 'another desparate Shivering Fit' and of 'a Species of Delerium & Pain too much for Thought', but they often concluded: 'I can draw as well aBed as Up & perhaps better' or the drawing for 'Dante goes on the better which is all I care about' (pp. 1657, 1660, 1652–3, 1657). In April 1827 he wrote to his old and faithful friend George Cumberland: 'I have been very near the Gates of Death & have returned very weak & an Old Man feeble & tottering, but not in Spirit & Life not in The Real Man The Imagination which Liveth for Ever. In that I am stronger & stronger as this Foolish Body decays.' (p. 1667)

Four months after the date of this letter, his generous young patron John Linnell visited him and wrote in his Diary, 'Friday [*August*] 10 [*1827*] . . . Mʳ Blak*e* Not expected to live' (*BR*, 341), but Blake was still hard at work. 'One of the very last shillings spent was in sending out for a pencil' (*BR*, 341). Allan Cunningham wrote:

three days before his death, he sat bolstered up in bed, and tinted . . . [*his great engraving of 'The Ancient of Days'*] with his choicest colours and in his happiest style. He touched and retouched it—held it at arm's length, and then threw it from him, exclaiming, 'There! that will do! I cannot mend it.' He saw his wife in tears—she felt this was to be the last of his works—'Stay, Kate (cried Blake) keep just as you are—I will draw your portrait—for you have ever been an angel to me'—she obeyed, and the dying artist made a fine likeness. [*BR*, 502; cf. pp. 527–8]

Three days later,

On the day of his death, August 12th, 1827, he composed and uttered songs to his Maker so sweetly to the ear of his Catherine, that when she stood to hear him, he, looking upon her most affectionately, said, 'My beloved they are not mine—no—they are not mine.' [*BR*, 475]

His young friend Frederick Tatham wrote that after drawing for an hour,

*H*e then threw that down . . . & began to sing Hallelujahs & songs of joy & Triumph which Mʳˢ Blake described as being truly sublime in music & in Verse. *H*e sang loudly & with true extatic energy and seemed too happy that he had finished his course, that he had ran his race, & that he was shortly to arrive at his Goal, to receive the prize of his high & eternal calling. . . . His bursts of gladness made the room peel again [*and again*]. [*BR*, 528]

Blake died quietly that evening, 'without any visible pain. His wife, who sat watching him, did not perceive when he ceased breathing' (*BR*, 502). His disciple George Richmond wrote to Samuel Palmer:

Lest you should not have heard of the Death of Mr Blake I have written this to inform you—He died on Sunday Night at 6 Oclock in a most glorious manner[.] He said He was going to that Country he had all His life wished to see & expressed Himself Happy hoping for Salvation through Jesus Christ— Just before he died His Countenance became fair—His eyes brighten'd and He burst out in Singing of the things he Saw in Heaven[.] In truth He Died like a Saint as a person who was standing by Him Observed—[*BR*, 346–7]

We do not know what songs Blake sang in his last hours, but they may have been like his great lyric called 'Jerusalem':

> Bring me my Bow of burning Gold
> Bring me my Arrows of desire:
> Bring me my Spear: O clouds unfold:
> Bring me my Chariot of Fire!

> I will not cease from Mental Fight
> Nor shall my Sword sleep in my hand:
> Till we have built Jerusalem,
> In Englands green & pleasant Land.

> [p. 381]

For Blake, the immortal spirit of imagination had been loosed from its prison and freed to

> Seek . . . after that sweet golden clime
> Where the travellers journey is don*e*:

> Where the Youth pined away with desire,
> And the pale Virgin shrouded in snow:
> Arise from their graves and aspire
> Where my Sun-flower wishes to go.

> [p. 187]

There can be few biographers more fortunate than William Blake's. It is not merely that Blake created poems and paintings of enduring fascination and power, nor that his works are now lodged in homes of such wonderful beauty as the Bodleian Library and the Fitzwilliam Museum and the Huntington Library. It is not merely that the fra- ternity of Blake scholars and Blake lovers is a congenial and rewarding one. Much of this is true of the works of other scholars.

What makes Blake so very unusual as a man, and perhaps unique among poets and painters, is that the attractions of his personality are in some ways as strong as, and almost independent of, the beauties of his poems and paintings. Many are attracted to the man who know little of his poetry and his art. This is of course not for what he did, for

Blake was a man not of action but of mind. No envious governments cursed or coveted his powers, no beautiful women begged for babies by him, no publishers or patrons clamoured at his door. He might have said with more truth than Byron did, 'I have not loved the world, nor the world me'.[1] The world did not love him, it is true, but he does not lack for lovers.

This curious love-affair with Blake began almost unnoticed during his last years, among his young disciples, and it became visible in the first accounts of him which were published after his death in 1827. Men such as Blake's childhood friend John Thomas Smith in 1828 and the sculptor Allan Cunningham in 1830 found his ways bizarre and his verse obscure. Smith, for instance, wrote: 'As for his later poetry, if it may be so called, attached to his plates, . . . it was not always wholly uninterest-ing' (*BR*, 457–8). But all agree in such terms as 'extraordinary', 'original', and 'genius'. Crabb Robinson wrote in 1810 that he was 'a man in whom all the elements of greatness are unquestionably to be found' (*BR*, 455), and Allan Cunningham said that he was 'a man of genius, some of whose works are worthy of any age or nation' (*BR*, 499).

To the advanced spirits of the Nineteenth Century, Blake came to seem a kind of model of the artist as superman, heroically sacrificing himself for the beauty or urgency of his message to mankind. It is no coincidence that Carlyle was developing such ideas just as Blake was being rediscovered thirty years after his death or that Blake's first important biographer Alexander Gilchrist was both an admirer and a friend of Carlyle. Gilchrist's biography in 1863 helped to hold up Blake the man as a model to poets and other authors such as Swin-burne, Rossetti, Yeats, Alan Ginsberg, and Joyce Cary.

Beyond the poetry and the paintings were Blake's gnomic sayings which were entrancing. 'I walked last night to the end of my garden and touched the sky with my stick.' 'Eternity is in love with the pro-ductions of time.' 'Exuberance is beauty.' (pp. 81, 84.)

The gnomic verses are even more wonderful:

> He has observed the Golden Rule
> Till hes become the Golden Fool
>
> [p. 941]

And

> He who bends to himself a joy
> Does the winged life destroy

[1] *Child Harold*, Canto III (1816), stanza 113.

> But he who kisses the joy as it flies
> Lives in Eternitys sun rise
>
> [p. 968]

And, best of all,

> a Tear is an Intellectual Thing
> And a Sigh is the Sword of an Angel King
> And the bitter groan of the Martyrs woe
> Is an Arrow from the Almighties Bow
>
> [p. 1311; cf. p. 930]

What is most impressive in his life is the devotion of himself, the sacrifice of his worldly self, to art, to imagination, to Christ—for in Blake they are the same thing. Blake told Crabb Robinson: 'I shᵈ be sorry if I had any earthly fame[,] for whatever natural glory a man has is so much detracted from his spiritual glory[.] I wish to do nothing for profit. I wish to live for art—I want nothing whatʳ[.] I am quite happy—' (*BR*, 311–12). And in what is perhaps his last engraved poem, the epilogue to his *Gates of Paradise*, he bid a defiance 'To the Accuser Who is The God of This World' which may serve in a sense as the motto of his life:

> Truly My Satan thou art but a Dunce
> And dost not know the Garment from the Man[.]
> Every Harlot was a Virgin once
> Nor canst thou ever change Kate into Nan[.]
>
> Tho thou art Worshipd by the Names Divine
> Of Jesus & Jehovah thou art still
> The Son of Morn in weary Nights decline[,]
> The lost Travellers Dream under the Hill[.]
>
> [p. 661]

IMPORTANT DATES IN BLAKE'S LIFE

Family and Milieu

1752 Oct. 15	Marriage of Catherine Harmitage to James Blake at **St George's, Hanover Square, London**
1753 July 10	Birth of James Blake, probably at **28 Broad Street, Golden Square**
July 15	and baptized at the family church, **St James, Piccadilly**
1755 May 12	Birth of John Blake, baptized 1 June at **St James, Piccadilly** (died young)

The Visionary Apprentice

1757 Nov. 28	Birth of WILLIAM BLAKE, baptized Dec. 11, **St James, Piccadilly**
1760 March 20	Birth of John Blake, baptized March, **St James, Piccadilly**
1762 April 25	Birth of Catherine Sophia Boucher, baptized on May 16, **St Mary's, Battersea**
1762 June 19	Birth of Richard Blake, baptized July 11 at **St James, Piccadilly** (died young)
1764 Jan. 7	Birth of Catherine Elizabeth Blake, baptized Jan. 28 at **St James, Piccadilly**
1767 Aug. 4	Birth of Robert Blake, but he was not baptized in the family church of St James, Piccadilly
1771 Aug. 4	Apprenticeship of WILLIAM BLAKE as an engraver to James Basire, **Stationers' Hall, London**
1772–9	Blake presumably lived at James Basire's residence at **31 Great Queen Street, Lincoln's Inn Fields, London**

From Artisan to Artist

1779 Oct. 8	Blake admitted as a student at the Royal Academy, **Somerset House, Strand**
1780 May	Exhibited 'Death of Earl Goodwin' at the Royal Academy, **Somerset House, London**
1780 June 6	Involuntarily participated in the Lord George Gordon 'No Popery' riots. **Newgate Prison** burned
1780? Sept.?	Arrested with Stothard and others while on a sketching trip, **River Medway**
1782 Aug. 18	Married to Catherine Butcher (or Boucher) of Battersea, at **St Mary's, Battersea**
1782–3	Engraved 8 plates after Stothard for *The Novelist's Magazine*
1782–4	The Blakes moved to lodgings in **23 Green Street, Soho**
1782–4	Patronized by Harriet Mathew and her genteel salon, **Rathbone Place**, where Blake sang his poems to his own tunes
1783	Engraved 9 plates after Stothard for [Ritson] *English Songs*
1783	*Poetical Sketches* printed at the expense of A. S. Mathew and John Flaxman with a Preface by Mathew
1784 May	Exhibited 'A Breach in a City' and 'War' at the Royal Academy, **Somerset House**
1784 July 4	Blake's father (James Blake) died and was buried in the Dissenter's burying ground, **Bunhill Fields**
1784	Engraved 5 plates after Stothard for *The Wit's Magazine* (Harrison, 1784)
1784?	Wrote his satiric *Island in the Moon*
1784–5	The Blakes moved with James Parker into **27 Broad Street**, where they had a print-shop
1785 April	Blake exhibited 'The Bard from Gray' and three 'Joseph' drawings at the Royal Academy, **Somerset House**

1785–90	The Blakes moved to a house near his birthplace, **28 Poland Street**
1787 Feb. 11	Blake's favourite brother Robert died in his arms at **28 Poland Street** and was buried near his father in **Bunhill Fields**
1788?	Etched *There is No Natural Religion* and *All Religions are One*
1789 April 13	The Blakes signed the manifesto of the Swedenborgian New Jerusalem Church
1789	Published *Songs of Innocence* and *The Book of Thel*
1789?	Wrote and Illustrated *Tiriel*
1790–1800	The Blakes moved to a row house across the River, **13 Hercules Buildings, Lambeth**, where he composed the Lambeth Books
1790–3?	Etched *The Marriage of Heaven and Hell*
1791	Designed and engraved 6 plates for Mary Wollstonecraft's *Original Stories from Real Life* (Johnson, 1791) and engraved 10 plates for Darwin's *Botanic Garden* (Johnson, 1791).
1791	*The French Revolution* Book I printed for Johnson but not published
1792 Sept. 9	Blake's mother Catherine died and was buried near her husband and son at **Bunhill Fields**
1792–3	Engraved 16 or more plates for his friend J. G. Stedman's *Expedition to . . . Surinam* (Johnson, 1796)
1793	Published *Visions of the Daughters of Albion*, *For Children: The Gates of Paradise*, and *America*
1793	Engraved 12 plates for Gay's *Fables* (Stockdale, 1793)
1794	Published *Songs of Experience*, *Europe*, and *The First Book of Urizen*
1794–5	Engraved 8 plates for his friend George Cumberland's *Thoughts on Outline* (Wilson, 1796)
1795	Published *The Song of Los*, *The Book of Los*, and *The Book of Ahania*

1795?	Made his great series of colour prints
1796–7	Engraved 43 of his own designs for Young's *Night Thoughts* (Richard Edwards, 1797) in folio
1796–1807?	Wrote and illustrated his *Vala* or *The Four Zoas*
1797–8	Made 116 designs from Gray's poems for John Flaxman
1799–1809	Made scores of large designs from the Bible for his friend Thomas Butts
1800	Engraved 10 plates for Salzmann's *Gymnastics for Youth* (Johnson, 1800)
1800 May	Exhibited 'The Loaves and Fishes' at the Royal Academy

Patronage and Dependence

1800–3	The Blakes moved to the seaside to work under the patronage of William Hayley at **Felpham, Sussex**
1800–3	Painted 18 Heads of the Poets for Hayley's Library, **Felpham**
1801, 1815	Made two sets of designs (8 each) for *Comus*
1802	Engraved 14 of his own designs for Hayley's *Designs to A Series of Ballads* (Blake, 1802)
1802–4	Engraved 6 of his own designs for Hayley's *Life . . . of William Cowper* (Johnson, 1803–4)
1803	Engraved 6 plates after Maria Flaxman for Hayley's *Triumphs of Temper* (Cadell & Davies, 1803)
1803 Aug. 12	Blake ejected a soldier named Scofield from his **Felpham** cottage garden
1803 Aug. 15	Private Scofield laid a formal Complaint that Blake had committed sedition
1803–21	The Blakes moved back to London to a flat near his birthplace, **17 South Molton Street**
1803 Oct. 4	A True Bill was found against Blake at his trial at the Quarter Sessions, **Petworth, Sussex**
1804 Jan. 11	Blake was acquitted of sedition at his trial at the **Guildhall, Chichester**
1804–20	Composed, etched, and published *Milton* and *Jerusalem*

1804 Oct.?	Blake was suddenly 'enlightened' after 20 years of darkness
1805	Engraved 5 plates after his own designs for Hayley's *Ballads* (Phillips, 1805) and 3 after Flaxman for *The Iliad* (Longman, 1805)
1805 Nov.	Commission for etching Blake's designs for Blair's *Grave* transferred abruptly from Blake to Schiavonetti
1805–6	Made his great series of designs from Job for Butts

Independence and Obscurity

1805–10?	Tutored Tommy Butts at £26. 5s. 0d. per annum
1806	Account of Blake in Malkin's *A Father's Memoirs of his Child* with a plate after Blake
1807 or later	Transcribed his Ballads or Pickering Manuscript
1807, 1808	Made two sets of designs (12 in each) for *Paradise Lost*
1808 May	Exhibited 'Jacob's Dream' and 'Christ in the Sepulchre' at the Royal Academy
1808 July	Blake's 8 designs etched by Schiavonetti for Blair's *Grave* published by R. H. Cromek
1808 Aug. 7, Nov.	Savage reviews of Blake's *Grave* designs by Robert Hunt in *The Examiner* and in the *Antijacobin Review*
1809–10	Exhibition of his own pictures in his brother's house, **28 Broad Street**, accompanied by his *Descriptive Catalogue* (1809)
1809 Sept. 17	Savage review of his exhibition and *Descriptive Catalogue* by Robert Hunt in *The Examiner*
1808, *c.* 1815	Made two sets of designs (6 in each) for Milton's 'On the Morning of Christ's Nativity'
1810	Published his 'Canterbury Pilgrims' plate and wrote his 'Vision of the Last Judgment'
1811?	Wrote his 'Public Address'
1811	Account of Blake by H. C. Robinson in *Vaterländisches Museum*
1812	Showed 'Sir Jeffrey Chaucer and Twenty-seven Pilgrims', the Spiritual Forms of Pitt and Nelson, and

1827 Aug. 12	Blake died and was buried near his parents and brothers at **Bunhill Fields**; there were obituaries in the *Literary Gazette*, *Monthly Magazine*, *Gentleman's Magazine*, *New Monthly Magazine*, *Annual Biography and Obituary*, and *Annual Register*

A Fading Shadow

1827–8	Catherine Blake lived as a housekeeper with the John Linnells at **Cirencester Place**
1828	Life of Blake in J. T. Smith, *Nollekens and His Times*
1828–31	Catherine Blake lived with Frederick Tathams at **20 Lisson Grove**
1830	Life of Blake in Allan Cunningham, *Lives of. . . British Painters . . .*
1830 March	Long essays on Blake appeared in the *London University Magazine* and *Fraser's Magazine*
1831	Catherine Blake lived by herself at **17 Charlton Street**
1831–3	Tatham quarrelled with Linnell about the ownership of Blake's Dante designs
1831 Oct. 18	Catherine Blake died and was buried on the 20th at **Bunhill Fields**
1832?	Frederick Tatham finished his manuscript 'Life of Blake'
1852	Crabb Robinson revised his MS 'Reminiscences' of Blake
1863	Publication of Alexander Gilchrist, *Life of William Blake, 'Pictor Ignotus'*, with a separate volume of poems and designs.

BLAKE RECORDS SUPPLEMENT

As an apprentice, Blake spent many happy hours copying designs in Westminster Abbey, and years later his young disciple Samuel Palmer *1779* asked him how he would like to paint on glass, for the great west window, his 'Sons of God shouting for Joy', from his designs in the *Job*. 'He said, after a pause, "I could do it!" kindling at the thought.'[1] An essay of 1834 commented:

The taste and study of Mr. Stothard, led him to look for objects in which grace and simplicity are found to unite, and in the same pursuit, and on the same objects, we find the late justly admired Flaxman, as well as the eccentric Blake, fix their attention, and derive their invention; namely, the ancient monuments in Westminster Abbey. Many of which are in the purest style of Art, and must have been to these artists a mine of pictorial wealth. The versatility of Mr. Stothard's powers, enabled him to take a wider range, both in subject and manner, than either Flaxman or Blake.[2]

The radical publisher Joseph Johnson had been employing Blake's graver in a desultory way since Blake finished his apprenticeship, but in 1783 Blake had commissions for ten plates from Johnson. One of these was for a frontispiece after Dunker for Thomas Henry's *Memoirs of Albert de Haller*, the text of which was being printed at Warrington near Manchester, while the plates were evidently to be printed in London. Not for the last time, Blake seems to have been late in finishing his plate, for Henry wrote to Johnson from Manchester on 13 April 1783:

Pray hasten the head of Haller—The Book is finished, and very neat; and the *13* Season is advancing rapidly. The heads might come in Clark's parcel, or in *April* Newton's. The one deals with Mr. Bow, the other with Rivington—[3] *1783*

Such complaints doubtless did Blake no good with the publisher, and it was not until 1788 that Blake began engraving for Johnson again.

---

[1] *BR*, 14. According to *The Richmond Papers*, ed. A. M. W. Stirling (1926), p. 378, in the 1890s Sir William Blake Richmond 'frankly copied Blake's noble figure' of 'The Sons of God Shouting for Joy' in the mosaics for the vault of St Paul's Cathedral.
[2] Anon., 'On the Genius of Stothard, and the Character of His Works', *Arnold's Magazine of the Fine Arts*, NS iii (April 1834), 536.
[3] Quoted from a reproduction of the MS in Bodley, generously pointed out to me by Professor Gerald P. Tyson.

William Blake grew up in the Parish of St James, Piccadilly, one of the most prosperous and enlightened parishes in England, and its institutions of Workhouse, Infirmary, School, and Burying Ground were very near the house where he lived in Broad Street, Golden Square. One of the most enlightened acts of the Parish, beginning in the 1760s, was to send the small children of the workhouse to wet nurses and temporary foster mothers in the country parish of Wimbledon, on account of the appalling mortality rate of babies brought up in the city workhouses—often 50 per cent to 100 per cent *per annum*, even in St James Parish.[1] 'They remain at Wimbledon till six or seven Years of Age'[2] but then return to the Parish Workhouse in Poland Street, where 'Examples of Vice and Profligacy being continually before their Eyes, very little Good could be expected to arise to the Children.'[3] Therefore in September 1782 a separate 'Parish School of Industry' was opened for them in King Street, Golden Square, to train children seven to fourteen years old to be housemaids and apprentices.

William Blake's father James began to supply haberdashery to the School almost as soon as it was in operation. Previously, in the period 18 July 1777 to 17 December 1779 (and perhaps earlier), before the School was established, Mrs Limm, the Midwife to the Workhouse, was reimbursed for disbursements for Haberdashery. Almost certainly she was merely the purchaser of the goods, not their supplier. The Minutes of the Governors and Directors of the Poor for 1780–July 1782 are missing, but then 'Mr Blake Haberdasher' appears in the very first accounts thereafter and continued steadily, without a break, for almost two years (see Table 1).

On 25 June; 9, 23 July; 20 August; 3, 17, 31 September; 29 October; and 12 November 1784, there is no sum entered for Haberdashery; on 6 August Messrs Jones & Co, Haberdashers, had a bill for 16s. for the School, and on 14 October there was another for the huge sum of £7. 17s. 7d. for the Workhouse, and then no more.

James Blake [Senior], the poet's father, supplied Haberdashery to the School of Industry and the Workhouse for almost two years, from August 1782 or earlier until June 1784. By then, however, his health must have been failing, and he died probably in June and was buried on 4 July 1784. His eldest son, also named James, took over the family

---

[1] *Abstract of the Annual Registers of the Parish Poor . . . [for] 1783* (1784), and *Sketch of the State of the Children of the Poor in the Year 1756, and of the Present State and Management of all the Poor in the Parish of Saint James, Westminster* (1797), p. 1.

[2] *Sketch of . . . the Poor, in the Parish of Saint James* (1797), pp. 3–5.   [3] Ibid., pp. 5–6.

business in Broad Street, Golden Square, but evidently he did not know much about his father's dealings with the Governors and Directors of the Poor of St James, Westminster—or at any rate the Blake firm was replaced sporadically in supplying Haberdashery to the Parish by Messrs Jones & Co, Haberdashers, in two accountings in August and October 1784.

By the spring of 1785, James Blake [Junior] was anxious to recover the lost business with the Workhouse and the School of Industry, and he knew that at the April meeting annually the twenty-one Directors and Governors of the Poor were chosen and that they in turn chose their servants, such as the Matron of the Workhouse and the Messenger of the Committee, among whose duties was 'apprehending the reported Fathers of Bastard Children'.[1] They also chose their suppliers for the rest of the year[2] such as the butcher, baker, chandler, milkman, and vendors of greens and butter. James Blake therefore wrote to them, and his letter was recorded in their Minutes for the meeting at 4:00 P.M. on 1 April 1785:

A Letter from M.r Blake was deliv.d to the Board & read[;] Copy th[*ere*]of is as follows

Gent.n

As at this Se[*a*]son of the year you appoint your several Trades persons permit me to offer myself to serve you with Articles of Haberdashery for I flatter myself I am able to supply the Infirmary & School of Industry with every Article upon as low terms as any house in London & being an Inhabitant of this P[*ari*]sh & my family for many years[3] hope a preference may be given me for which should I succeed shall make it my study to deliver for the use of the same such Articles as will bear the strictest Examination. Sh.d any be found not agreable or otherwise not suiting shall be happy to provide such as will every way answer the use intended or exchange the Articles if not approved—

I remain Gent.n for Mother & Self

Broad S.t Golden Sq[*ua*]re: Your very hble Serv.t

Ja.s Blake

Resolved that the Consideration thereof be referred to the next Board.

1 April 1785

---

[1] D1872, p. 48.

[2] According to the *Rules . . . of the Poor of the Parish of St James* (1768), 10, 'all Tradesmen who serve the poor, [shall] be appointed once a Year, or oftener, as Occasions shall require'. Occasionally the Governors and Directors became dissatisfied with the quality or price of the goods supplied, and they summoned the merchant to explain himself or even advertised for a new supplier.

[3] James Blake (Junior) was born at 28 Broad Street, Golden Square, on 10 July 1753, his father had lived in the Parish at least from 1744, and his mother at least from 1748 (see *BR*, 2, 551).

TABLE I. *Sums Paid to* 'M.ʳ Blake Haberdasher'[a]

Date of Meeting	'For the Workhouse'	'For the Schoolhouse'	Total
9 Aug 1782			£1. 6. 3
23 Aug 1782			£2. 3. 2
6 Sept 1782			£1. 2. 5
20 Sept 1782			£1. 8. 6
4 Oct 1782			£1. 3. 8
18 Oct 1782			£1.14. 3
1 Nov 1782			£1.19. 0
15 Nov 1782			£1. 9.10
29 Nov 1782	£1.16. 2	11. 9	[£2. 7.11]
13 Dec 1782	£2. 8. 2	10. 0	[£2.18. 2]
27 Dec 1782	£1.18. 4	14. 6	[£2.12.10]
10 Jan 1783	£1. 6.10	3. 1	[£1. 9.11]
24 Jan 1783	£1. 8. 6	12. 1	[£2. 0. 7]
7 Feb 1783	£1. 4.11	6. 7	[£1.11. 6]
21 Feb 1783	£1.12.10	16. 9	[£2. 9. 7]
7 March 1783[b]	[£1. 9. 2]	[7. 9]	[£1.16.11]
21 March 1783[b]	£1.11.10	6. 9	[£1.18. 7]
4 April 1783[b]	£1. 7. 4	16. 1	[£2. 3. 5]
18 April 1783[b]	£1.18. 5	12. 0	[£2.11. 2]
2 May 1783[b]	£1. 2. 2	7. 3	[£1. 9. 5]
16 May 1783[b]	£1. 7. 8	11. 0	[£1.19. 5]
30 May 1783[b]	£1. 3. 2	9.10	[£1.13. 0]
27 June 1783	£2.11. 3	5.11	[£2.17. 2]
11 July 1783	£1. 0.10	11.10	[£1.12. 8]
25 July 1783	£1. 2. 8	13. 4	[£1.16. 0]
8 Aug 1783	£1. 0. 3	13. 1	[£1.13. 4]
22 Aug 1783	£1. 2. 7	7.11	[£1.10. 6]
5 Sept 1783	£1.12. 4	10. 7	[£2. 2.11]
19 Sept 1783	12. 9	10. 9	[£1. 3. 6]
3 Oct 1783	£1. 4. 8	19. 9	[£2. 4. 5]
17 Oct 1783	£1.11. 1	14.10	[£2. 5.11]
31 Oct 1783	£1. 0. 3	£1. 2. 5	[£2. 2. 8]
14 Nov 1783	£1. 3. 3	17. 9	[£2. 1. 0]
28 Nov 1783	£1. 4. 7	14. 3	[£1.18.10]
12 Dec 1783	19. 1	£1.14. 6	[£2.13. 7]
26 Dec 1783	£1.19. 3	£1. 1. 4	[£3. 0. 7]
9 Jan 1784	19. 4	14. 2	[£1.13. 6]

Date of Meeting	'For the Workhouse'	'For the Schoolhouse'	Total
23 Jan 1784	£1. 1. 7	£1. 5. 9	[£2. 7. 4]
6 Feb 1784	£1. 5. 6	£1. 1. 2	[£2. 6. 8]
20 Feb 1784	£1. 7. 2	£1. 2.10	[£2.10. 0]
5 March 1784	15. 1	£1. 7.11	[£2. 3. 0]
19 March 1784	£1.10. 6	£2.16. 5	[£4. 6. 1]
2 April 1784	15. 8	— —	[15. 8]
16 April 1784	£1.10.11	— —	[£1.10.11]
30 April 1784	£1. 4. 7	— —	[£1. 4. 7]
14 May 1784			£1. 3. 8
28 May 1784	£1. 4. 1	— —	[£1. 4. 1]
11 June 1784	£1.13. 6	— —	[£1.13. 6]
49 fortnights or 1 year, 10 months, 3 days	£1.19. 2 per fortnight	15. 5 per fortnight	£95. 9.10

---

[a] Minutes of the Governors and Directors of the Poor D1870.

The Minutes of the Meetings of the Governors and Directors of the Poor of the Parish of St James, Westminster, are in the Archives Department of Westminster City Libraries, Buckingham Palace Road, London; the volume with pressmark D1869 covers 11 July 1777–17 Dec. 1779; D1870 begins 2 Aug. 1782 (NB The Minutes for Dec. 1779–July 1782 are missing); D1871 begins 19 Nov. 1784; and D1872 begins 9 March 1789. The Minutes are written in fair, clerkly hands and are, of course, in chronological order.

The Committee met weekly, and at alternate meetings the accounts were itemized under 'Provisions', i.e. food, and 'Other Bills', and they are always referred to the Treasurer for verification and authorized to be paid at the subsequent meeting. (This was more frequent than was called for in the *Rules, Orders, and Regulations, Made by the Governors and Directors of the Poor of the Parish of St James, within the Liberty of Westminster* [1768], 9: 'all Bills [*shall*] be paid once a Month'.)

'Neither is there any Article bought for the Poor entered into Stock until the same has been duly examined and compared with the Samples. And there are Tables for every Article consumed, which are compared every Fortnight with the Bills, both by the Committee and Board, and also the Abstracts thereof, so that no Waste or Embezzlement can be made, but it must be known every Fortnight.' (*Sketch of . . . the Poor, in the Parish of Saint James* [1797], 20.)

The bills are for the fortnight which ended six days before the meeting at which they are first considered, so there was always at least a fortnight between the presentation of a bill and its payment. A good many clothes are ordered, but there is no indication of from whom.

For March 1789 the bills are no longer itemized, and only a lump sum is given 'For the Schoolhouse' and 'For the Workhouse'.

In some accounts there is no distinction between Workhouse and Schoolhouse, in others there are separate entries for each. In the Blake periods, when there are separate Schoolhouse Committee Minutes, the totals run from £33. 16s. 4d. to £65. 8s. 10d., averaging £42. 17s. 6d., of which James Blake's share of 10s. 6d. per fortnight is 1.1 per

[*See p. 6 for n. a cont. and n. b*]

The fact that James Blake was writing 'for Mother & Self' suggests that they were managing the shop together—had he merely wished to evoke sympathy, he surely would have referred explicitly to her recently widowed state. She may have helped to manage the shop until her death in 1792. The reference to supplies for 'the Infirmary & School of Industry' suggests that the Haberdashery supplied was chiefly for the Infirmary in the Workhouse and for the School. Some confirmation of this hypothesis may be seen in the fact that previously, in 1777–9, the haberdashery for the Workhouse had been supplied by the Workhouse midwife.

A few other letters were received at the same meeting from merchants, one referring to 'your Advertizement' for bread,[1] and several, like that of James Hartley, [?Knife] Grinder of 39 Broad Street, Golden Square, ask as James Blake did for special consideration as a parish resident. James Blake's letter seems to imply that his competitors Jones & Co were *not* residents of the parish.

The immediate decision of the Committee about James Blake's letter was the usual one, to refer the matter to the next meeting of the Board. However, there is no mention of Blake at the next meeting, and indeed no Haberdasher is named as appointed to supply the poor at the April meetings of 1783–9, though a Hosier (Mr Humphreys) and a Linen Draper (Messrs Evans & Williams) in allied trades were so

cent. The totals for combined School and Workhouse expenses for a fortnight ranged from £130. 8s. 1d. to £250. 14s. 10d. during James Blake's period, averaging £182, of which James Blake's share of £1. 19s. 1d. was also about 1.1 per cent.

Occasionally other documents are interspersed among the Minutes of the weekly meetings of the Governors and Directors of the Poor, such as letters to or from the Committee and, very occasionally, Minutes of the subordinate Committee for the Schoolhouse. There are references to other reports, etc., which one would like to see in connection with James Blake, such as the regular 'Minutes of the Committee of the Parish School of Industry' (D1871, p. 96), and 'books of Cloathing' (D1871, p. 99), the 'book of Recommendations' (D1871, p. 99), and the 'Book of Orders' (D1871, p. 99), which one might expect to find either among the Westminster City Libraries Archive or in the Greater London Record Office, to which records of schools were supposed to be transferred, but they are not known to the indices or officers of either institution.

The references to the Blake family firm in the Westminster Public Library archives were discovered by Dr Stanley Gardner, who cites them in his book *Blake's INNOCENCE and EXPERIENCE Retraced* (1986) which he kindly showed me in draft.

   ᵇ There are separate Schoolhouse Committee Minutes and accounts a few days after the meeting of the Governors and Directors of the Poor, on 10, 25 March; 8, 22 Apr.; 6, 20 May; 3, 17 June 1783, giving the same figures for Mʳ Blake Haberdasher.

   ¹ D1871, p. 76. Present at the meeting which received James Blake's letter were William Jones, Robert Johnson, Cornelius Neep, Sefferin Nelson, John Butler, Henry Daws, and William Johnson, the last two as Overseers of the Poor.

named repeatedly. However, James Blake's application was clearly approved in principle, for in subsequent accounts are recorded bills for James Blake & Co (or Mr Blake) Haberdasher (see Table 2).

TABLE 2. *Sums Paid to* 'Mr Blake Haberdasher'

Date of Meeting	'For the Schoolhouse'
15 April 1785	£11. 3. 6
29 April 1785	£ 1.10. 6
13, 27 May; 10, 24 June 1785	—
8 July 1785	£ 5. 2. 1

These are much larger sums than had previously been recorded for haberdashery in the fortnightly School accounts, and presumably James Blake was building up the supplies depleted since his father's death. The total of £17. 16s. 1d. for the seven fortnightly accounts from 1 April to 8 July 1785 average a full £2. 10s. 0d. per fortnight, a good deal more than his father had received (10s. 6d.) when he was supplying haberdashery to the School regularly.

However, no further reference to the Blake family Haberdashery Shop in Broad Street, Golden Square, has been found in these records.

The commercial standards of the Governors and Directors of the Poor in the Parish of St James were admirably high, and they scrupulously framed their rules and practice to avoid the possibility of persistent theft and embezzlement from the School and Workhouse and even of conflict of interest among their own members. The Governors 'are prohibited from having any Benefit in any Contract or in the Service of Goods, Materials, Provisions, Necessaries for the Poor'.[1]

---

[1] *Sketch of... the Poor, in the Parish of Saint James* (1797), 3. 'Holy Thursday' in *Songs of Innocence* (1789) with its 'children walking two & two in red & blue & green' probably does not refer to the Parish School, for, according to [William Combe] *Microcosm of London*, III (1809), 242, the children in the St James School of Industry do not wear livery, but the 'Babes reduced to misery, Fed with cold and usurous hand' of 'Holy Thursday' from *Songs of Experience* (1794) may in part be a protest against the introduction of the factory system into the Parish School about 1786. Blake's intimacy with the Parish may be seen in his letter of 7 June 1825 in which he laments the death of Gerrard Andrewes, who had been rector of St James, Piccadilly, many years earlier.

Almost certainly, therefore, William Blake was not thinking of his own parish when he wrote in *America* (1793) pl. 13 that 'pity is become a trade, and generosity a science, That men get rich by . . .'. Blake's own parish of St James was apparently proof against such charges. His indignation was reserved for the politics not of the parish but of the nation.

On 23 May 1785, an anonymous review of the 'Exhibition of the Royal Academy (Concluded)' in the *Daily Universal Register* remarked *23* severely: '607. Gray's Bard, W. Blake, appears like some lunatic, just *May* escaped from the incurable cell of Bedlam; in respect of his other *1785* works, we assure this designer, that grace does not consist in the sprawling of legs and arms.'

By 1787 Blake was experimenting vigorously with the materials of his professions. Not only did he invent his unique method of Illumin-*1787* ated Printing, but he was also adapting the techniques and tools of painting as well. Gilchrist had been told that Blake

> ground and mixed his water-colours himself on a piece of statuary marble, after a method of his own, with common carpenter's glue diluted, which he had found out, as the early Italians had done before him, to be a good binder. Joseph, the sacred carpenter, had appeared in vision and revealed *that* secret to him.[1]

And J. T. Smith added that:

> Blake's modes of preparing his ground, and laying them over his panels for painting, mixing his colours, and manner of working, were those which he considered to have been practised by the earliest fresco-painters . . . His ground was a mixture of whiting and carpenter's glue, which he passed over several times in thin coatings: his colours he ground himself, and also united them with the same sort of glue, but in a much weaker state.[2]

The details of 'Blake's modes of preparing his ground' are given by Samuel Palmer in a letter of 29 October 1866:

> I add Mr. Blake's receipt. Glue as a vehicle was recommended to him by St. Joseph in a dream or vision, he said. . . .
> Blake's White.
> Get the best whitening—powder it.
> Mix thoroughly with water to the consistency of cream.
> Strain through double muslin. Spread it out upon backs of plates, white tiles are better, kept warm over basins of water until it is pretty stiff.

---

[1] Alexander Gilchrist, *The Life of William Blake* (1863), pp. 69–70; (1942), 60, 61 (*BR*, 33).
[2] J. T. Smith, *Nollekens and his Times* (1828), quoted in *BR*, 472. Smith notes that Blake heated his colours in preparing them.

Have ready the best carpenters' or cabinet makers' glues made in a very clean glue pot, and mix it warm with the colour:—the art lies in adding just the right portion of glue. The TEST is, that when dry upon the thumb nail or on an earthenware palette it should have so much *and no more* glue as will defend it from being scratched off with the finger nail.

This, and the cleanliness of the materials are the only difficulties.[1]

Palmer's son said that 'Blake gave my father the recipe' for Palmer's 'pure white grounds',[2] and Palmer valued it so much that in October 1828 he recommended to George Richmond 'Mrs. Blake's white, which is brighter, and sticks faster than chalk; and it seems such a quick way of getting a showy, but really good effect'.[3] Palmer took seriously Blake's account of learning the method from St Joseph: 'Don't think I am laughing: I am not yet shrunk to such inspissated idiotcy as grins at every thing beyond its own tether.'[4]

In the latter part of the 1780s, Blake was becoming more popular with the publishers. He was commissioned by the successful printseller, John Raphael Smith, to engrave two plates of 'The Industrious Cottager' and 'The Idle Laundress' (12 May 1788) after the very popu- *1788* lar and dissolute pig and poultry painter George Morland, and Morland's biographer J. Hassell remarked in 1806 that 'Few of Morland's works have had a better sale' than these two engraved by 'Blake' and sold at 6s. each.[5] But the success of the prints was clearly attributed largely to the artist rather than the engraver, for Blake engraved no more plates after Morland.

Blake joined the Swedenborgian New Jerusalem Church in April 1789 and, according to Crabb Robinson (*BR*, 440 and n. 6), was later invited to join the congregation of Joseph Proud, who became a Swedenborgian minister in 1790 and opened a church in Hatton Garden on 30 July 1797.

[1] *The Parting Light: Selected Writings of Samuel Palmer*, ed. Mark Abley (1985), pp. 213–14, quoting from the MS in Bodley. Palmer's letter was sent to Henry Wentworth Ackland with some 'cakes of White'. Palmer remarks of Blake's recipe, 'I have tried Russian isinglass which has less color, but does not work so pleasantly as the glue' and he sends directions 'to show how you may get a Better article with less trouble'.

The 'White hard Varnish' which Mrs Blake suggests as a preservative for Lord Egremont's picture of The Faerie Queene in her letters of 1 and 4 Aug. 1829 is probably a standard commercial product rather than either Palmer's 'Blake's White' or the 'very thin transparent wash of glue-water [*which Smith said Blake* would pass] over the whole of the parts he had worked upon' (*BR*, 472).

[2] A. H. Palmer, *The Life and Letters of Samuel Palmer* (1892), p. 51.

[3] *The Letters of Samuel Palmer*, ed. R. Lister (1974), p. 38.

[4] *The Parting Light* (1985), p. 214.

[5] J. Hassell, *Memoirs of the Life of the Late George Morland, with Critical and Descriptive*

'Dr. Garth Wilkinson tells us that Charles A. Tulk averred that Blake told him that he wrote it ["The Divine Image"] in the New Jerusalem Church, Hatton Garden.'[1] The place cannot be right, for 'The Divine Image' was published in 1789 in *Songs of Innocence*, and the Swedenborgians did not establish their Hatton Garden Church until much later. Further, the poem was almost certainly written before the New Church was founded at all. We can only guess, therefore, whether Blake did write a poem in a New Jerusalem Church.

In the context of Tatham's claim (*BR*, 41 fn.) that Blake 'had a most consummate knowledge of all the great writers in all languages', note that, in a letter of 1[?] September 1862, Samuel Palmer wrote: 'W.B. *was* mad about languages'.[2]

During the early 1790s, Johnson was employing Blake on more and more important engraving work. In the summer of 1791 he apparently asked Blake's advice about Erasmus Darwin's plan to have the Wedgwood replica of the Portland Vase copied for Darwin's *Botanic Garden*. On Saturday 9 July Darwin wrote to Josiah Wedgwood:

Dear Sir,

Mr. Johnson's engraver now wishes much to see Bartolozzi's plates of the vase, & will engrave them again if necessary—I told Johnson in my own name, *not in yours*, that I thought the outlines too hard, & in some places not agreeable. Now if you could be so kind as to send Bartolozzi's prints to Mr Johnson St. Paul's Churchyard,—or let him know if He can have them at your house in Greek Street—as he said he can not anywhere procure them. He promises to take great care of them, the name of the engraver I don't know, but Johnson said He is capable of doing anything well. . . .[3]

9 July 1791

A fortnight later Johnson wrote to Darwin, giving the engraver's name and explaining the copyright difficulties (*BR*, 43–4).

In the catalogue of the *Exhibition of Pictures*, Painted for Bowyer's Magnificent Edition of the History of England, at the Historic Gallery, Pall Mall ([?May] 1793), 'W. BLAKE' was still listed (p. 26) among the nineteen engravers for the undertaking.

?May 1793

Observations on the Whole of His Works Hitherto before the Public (1806), pp. 78, 170–1. The two plates were later offered in *A Catalogue of Prints Published by J. R. Smith* (*c*. 1800) and still later had the imprints altered to that of H[annah] Macklin (the widow of the great publisher Thomas Macklin), 1 Jan 1803.

[1] J. Spilling, 'Blake, Artist and Poet', *New Church Magazine*, vi (1887), 254.
[2] *Letters of Samuel Palmer*, ed. R. Lister (1974), vol. ii, p. 669.
[3] G. Keynes, *Blake Studies* (1971), p. 60, quotes the letter from the 'Wedgwood papers now deposited at Keele University', but neither the Keele librarian nor the curator of the Wedgwood Museum (where the letter was previously kept) can trace the manuscript.

On 6 December 1795, Blake sent George Cumberland directions for 'laying on the Wax' on a copperplate to be etched, evidently in connection with Cumberland's *Thoughts on Outline* (1796), for which they were both etching plates after Cumberland's designs. It may have been at the same time that Cumberland wrote in his Commonplate Book (GEB), fo. 75ʳ:

Blakes Instructions to Print Copper Plates

Warm the Plate a little and then fill it with Ink by dabbing it all over two or three times.—then wipe off the superfluous In*k*, till the surface is clean—then with the palm of the hand *beneath the little finger* rubbed over with a little of the Ink & smoothed with whiting by rubbing it on a Ball of it. Wipe the surface of the Plate till it shines all over—then roll it through the Press with 3 blankets above the Plate, and pastboards beneath it next the Plank—Paper may be used instead of Pastboard.

On 16 March 1796 Nancy Flaxman wrote:

apropos of Young [a friend of ours *del*] ˄One of the Edwards˄ has inserted the letter press Close cut of youngs [Night Th *del*] into large Margins Making a folio Size[;] this [he *del*] ˄a friend of ours˄ is ornament^g with most beautifully [*sic*] designs in water colours[;] the man who does it, is himself a Native Poet [& an Artist *del*] ˄& sings his woodnotes˄,[1] [unfettered by any rule *del*] whose genius soars above all rule[.] twill be a ˄very˄ lilly of the Valley [a *del*] or [Mountain daisy[2] *del*] ˄the meadows queen˄[.] Twill be in short[?] the choicest ˄wild˄ flower in Linneas System[.] tell me in your next the name of it—I never read the [Author *del*] ˄Bard˄ in Question & have him not in my collection, but [I *del*] ˄soon˄ will [both read & possess (.) ˄I have some hopes it will be publishd˄ eer I am much older for *del*] from what little I have seen [they *del*] ˄his writings˄ seem like the orient Pearls at random strung—[3]

16 March 1796

Gilchrist had repeated the story of Thomas Butts calling on the Blakes and finding them 'reciting passages from *Paradise Lost*, in character [*i.e., in a state of nature*], and the garden of Hercules Buildings had to represent the Garden of Eden: a little to the scandal of wondering neighbours, on more than one occasion.' (*BR*, 54.) The story

---

[1] Cf. Milton, *L'Allegro*, ll. 133–4: '*sweetest Shakspeare* fancies childe, / Warble[*s*] his native Wood-notes wild . . .'

[2] In his dedicatory poem 'To M.ʳˢ Ann Flaxman' with his Gray designs, Blake wrote of 'A little Flower . . . in a lonely Vale' transplanted by 'One standing in the Porches of the Sun' to 'a Mountain brow', in metaphors curiously reminiscent of this letter.

[3] British Library, Add. MSS 39,780, fo. 212, the letter is a draft, and the recipient is unidentified.

evoked the incredulity of Blake's friends on more than one occasion.
Linnell wrote indignantly to Adam White on 17 May 1866:

> I wish you wd. let Blake rest in his grave & not seek to make a handle of
> him for big talk[;] surely enough has been said about him in the life lately
> published to which nothing can be added except a denial of some slander-
> ous assertions respecting his sanity, the story of his acting Adam & Eve
> which I believe to be a malicious invention, other things injurious to his
> reputation as an Artist I was in time to hinder from publication, had I known
> of the Adam & Eve story in time I wd. certainly have remonstrated, had it
> been true I must certainly have heard of it before as Blake told me every-
> thing about himself.[1]

In 1864 Samuel Palmer wrote of Gilchrist's *Life*: 'Mr. Butt's visit to
"Adam and Eve" had grown in the memory, I think. I do not believe it:
it is unlike Blake.'[2]

In a letter of 2 March 1880 to Mrs Gilchrist, Linnell calls the Adam
and Eve story an '[unmitigated falsehood *del*] invention'.[3]

According to Thomas Dodd's manuscript account of Cumberland,
1796 'Mr Cumberland's inventions in outline as far as his hand hath been
concerned in them is [*sic*] not in unison with his ideas— ... However
some few of the accompanying pieces are etch'd by *W. Blake*, which
are decidedly more correct than those produced by the author.'[4]

An announcement for Blake's new publication appeared in *The
Monthly Magazine*, ii (Nov. 1796), 807, as

> *November* A splendid edition of YOUNGS NIGHT THOUGHTS, in large quarto, enriched
> *1796* with 150 etchings upon the borders, and frontispiece of each book, from
> original designs by BLAKE, is in forwardness. The price of the work to sub-
> scribers is FIVE GUINEAS; to non-subscribers SIX GUINEAS

Later statements omit the references to the frontispieces (by which is
probably meant title-pages) and the price to non-subscribers.

---

[1] The letter is transcribed thus far in the Sotheby catalogue of 21 July 1959, lot 521,
sold to J. Schwartz for £7 with Gilchrist's *Life*. For a similar comment by Linnell, see
BR, 257 n. 1.

[2] *Letters of Samuel Palmer*, ed. R. Lister (1974), vol. ii, p. 691.

[3] See *Blake*, xi (1978), 259, quoting a letter in the Huntington.

[4] British Library, Add. MSS 33,398, fo. 257; Thomas Dodd did not die until 1850, but
he had been old enough to see William Wynn Ryland (to whom Blake's father wanted to
apprentice him) hanged in 1783 (Add. MSS 33,404, fo. 104). In an index of engravers of
perhaps the same date (*c.*1835), Dodd entered 'Blake D? [*of England, flourished*]. 1790',
omitting the city, medium (e.g. burin), date of death, and age at death (Eng MS 1115,
John Rylands Library, University of Manchester).

About half Blake's plates for Young's *Night Thoughts* were finished and dated by 27 June 1796, and apparently the publisher believed that the rest would be completed and the book ready for publication six months later, for it was announced in *The Monthly Epitome and Catalogue of New Publications* for January 1797:

Young's Night Thoughts, with Etchings and Engravings, in Four Parts, Atlas sized 4to. to Subscribers 51.5s. to Non-subscribers 61.6s. (Part I. in a few days.) *January*
Edwards, Bond-street.[1]   *1797*

(Notice that William Blake's name is not mentioned.) However, the last plates were not dated until 1 June 1797, when the work may not have been published until November.

As a result of the small payment he received for his *Night Thoughts* work and the subsequent failure of the edition, Blake was in special need of commissions at this time. One evidently came from Dr James Curry, a young physician struggling to establish himself in Kettering, near Northampton. Curry wrote to Ozias Humphry on 15 August 1797 thanking him for a 'kind invitation':

To you who know the pleasure I have in seeing works of Art, and conversing with Artists, I need scarcely say how much I should be gratified could I avail myself of it . . . in spending some time along with you [*but I must decline. I admire*] . . . Mr Daniel's Views[2] . . . & I have had the pleasure of gratifying a *15* great number of ladies & gentlemen with a sight of them. Should he think of *August* publishing any more, I beg to be a subscriber. . . . *1797*
    As poor Blake will not be out of need of money, I shall beg you to pay him for me, and to take the trouble when you return to town of having a box made for the prints, & sending them by the Kettering Coach from the White Hart S! John Street Clerkenwell.—[3]

The 'prints' may be a set of the Large or Small Book of Designs similar to the ones Blake had created for Humphry, probably the previous year (see 19 Feb. 1796).[4] The fact that Blake was in 'need of money' so

---

[1] *The Monthly Epitome and Catalogue of New Publications*, i (Jan. 1797), 79. The journal was published by W. Clarke of New Bond Street, Richard Edwards's neighbour. This is one of three known contemporary periodical notices of Edwards's *Night Thoughts*; no review is known.

[2] *Oriental Scenery*: Twenty-Four Views in Hindoostan, Taken in the Year 1793; Drawn by Thomas Daniell, and Engraved by Himself and William Daniell (London, 'August 1797').

[3] Quoted from the MS with the extensive Humphry MSS in the Royal Academy Library, vol. iv, no. 44. Some more context is given in 'Dr. James Curry as a Patron of Blake', *Notes and Queries*, ccxxv (1980), 71–3.

[4] No Blake work is listed in the Sotheby sale on 27 March 1820 and following days of the Medical and Miscellaneous Library of the late James Curry, M.D., F.A.S. &c one of

soon after the completion of the *Night Thoughts* indicates something of the modesty of his payments for it. We may hope that Curry 'had the pleasure of gratifying a great number of ladies & gentlemen with a sight of them', as well as of Daniell's *Oriental Scenery.*

Young's *Night Thoughts* was probably published in November, for under November 6th Richard Edwards's brother James billed William Roscoe for 'Young's N. Tho.^ts N.º 1 /£^s_{1/1} & Sub. 1/1/.−[£]2.2—'.[1]

In early November 1797 Nancy Flaxman wrote in the draft of a letter to 'My Good Friend' 'Signora B—' that her previous epistle, which never arrived, probably

November 1797 contain'd to the best of my Remembrance an Account of some designs made by a friend of ours for your favorite Bard—Young[.] Blake is the artists name, '*Native Poet* he['] &c one who has sung his wood notes wild—of a Strong & Singular Imagination[;]—he has treated his Poet most Poetically—Flaxman has employ'd him to Illuminate the works of Grey for my library—[2]

According to George Cumberland, the critics of his friend Horne Tooke's philological *Diversions of Purleigh*, Part I (1786), complained of the frontispiece of Mercury by William Sharp 'that it was impossible to say whether he was taking off or putting on his Sandals and winged appendages'.[3] He therefore made a drawing 'shewing that he was pulling them off' and sent it to Tooke with a motto from Shakespeare on 19 February 1798:

19 February 1978 If you approve them, both the Motto and the drawing will be honoured by appearing, as you propose, with your second volume—in which case I shall take the liberty to recommend that neglected man of genius, and true son of Freedom Mr Blake, as your engraver, both on account of the pleasure I know he will have in executing a work with your portrait in it, and the general moderation of his charges[.]

However, the new editions of 1798, 1805, and 1829 (including the new

the physicians of Guy's Hospital . . . Removed from his Residence in Grafton Street, Bond Street.

[1] James Edwards letter to William Roscoe 2 Jan. 1798 (Roscoe MS No. 1415 in Liverpool Public Library, seen on xerox).
[2] British Library Add. MSS 39,790, fos. 3–4, undated (watermark 1795) and unaddressed; the letter says she has seen the Hares on their return from France and Germany—and the Hares reached London by 1 Nov. and stayed there until 4 Nov. 1797 (J. C. A. Hare, *Memorials of a Quiet Life* [1872], pp. 127–9). This letter is the chief evidence for dating Blake's 116 watercolours for Gray commissioned by John Flaxman for Nancy.
[3] Cumberland's note is on his 'Copy' of his letter to Tooke (quoted below) in his MS 'Anecdotes of, and Letters from, John Horne Tooke' (GEB).

Part II) had the same design newly engraved by Sharp (dated 1 January 1798) and omitted Cumberland's motto.

Richard Edwards went out of business almost as soon as his work was published, and its publication was recorded in *The Monthly Magazine*, V (June 1798), 455 as

> Young's Night Thoughts, decorated with appropriate Designs, by Mr. Blake,
> Part I. 1l. 1s.   Robson.

June 1798

Apparently the stock had been acquired by James Edwards's some-time partner and long-time friend James Robson, but the ownership has not been traced further.

On 17 August 1798 Fuseli wrote to his Liverpool patron William Roscoe:

> I include Mr. H.[*aughton'*]s proof which, if my recollection do not impose on me, might have done more justice to my drawing—it is done with more freedom than taste, and with more assurance than penetration or Amore; the drapery especially, which ought to be much deeper to give delicacy & relief to the naked part. I have not the drawing by me and therefore it would be idle to touch it. it wants much more finishing to front Your work with propriety[1]—or to be intitled to the pompous Fecit under it. Let him look at the Anubis [*engraved by Blake*] in the first part of the Botanic Garden,[2] and he will have a Clue.[3]

17 August 1798

In the spring of 1801, Blake was apparently kept busy making miniatures for Hayley. On Tuesday 19 May, Hayley wrote to his old friend George Romney who was failing and had recently returned to his devoted wife in the north country after an absence of almost forty years:

> I am much pleased to hear you say, that you have a most dutiful & affectionate Wife, & in proportion as she promotes the Happiness of your Life, I shall be truly glad to shew her every Mark of friendly regard—as a proof of my Sincerity, I beg you will allow me to send her as a present, copies (by the good enthusiastic Blake, whom I have taught, with the aid of Meyers' & yr portraits to paint miniature with considerable success) of *the two infinitely best Resemblances* of *yrself*, that I am so happy as to possess—one, you may recollect, is in Water Colours, with a Hat on—this He will copy exactly,—the Head from the large unfinished sketch He shall reduce to the same Size as its Companion—....[4]

19 May 1801

[1] L. Tansillo, *The Nurse*, tr. William Roscoe (1798).
[2] In Erasmus Darwin, *The Botanic Garden*, Part I: The Economy of Vegetation (1791), at p. 127, is Fuseli's 'Fertilization of Egypt' showing the god Anubis engraved by Blake.
[3] Quoted from a xerox of the MS among the Roscoe MS (No. 1654) in Liverpool City Libraries.
[4] Quoted from a photocopy of the MS with the Osborn Collection in Yale.

Blake was the cause of exuberant spirits at the same time in Germany. Jean Paul Richter in Meinigen wrote on Friday 20 November 1801 to Erbprinz Emil August von Gotha (Hereditory Prince of Gotha) about a gift of whose donor he pretended to be ignorant:

> Vorgestern erhielt ich ein Geschenk, das mich zu einer Bitte nöthigt, deren Erfüllung das zweite ist. Youngs Nachtgedanken, die ich mit meinen eigenen vermehrte, um vergeblich zu errathen, welcher reichen Hand in der Wolke ich die Gabe verdanke. Wenn sie, wie ich vermuthen kan, die Youngische Verklärung durch Blake—hier der englische Titel [The Complaint, and the Consolation; or Night Thoughts, by Edward Young, London 1797]—vielleicht gesehen: so finden Sie meinen Wunsch zu danken gewis gerecht und den Weg dazu verzeihlich.—Die metall[*ische*] und künst[*erische*] Kostbarkeit—die Liebe gegen meine litterarischen Wasserschöslinge—seine schöne Schmeichelei meines Geschmacks—und der Ort der Aufgabe auf die Post (es ist Gotha, wie ich höre) lassen mich errathen, dass Sie gewis diesen Geber näher kennen als ich. Darf ich an Sie, da Sie seine Nachsicht vielleicht nicht ganz misbilligen, die Bitte wagen, Ihrem Freunde meinen Dank zu übergeben und so der chargé d'affaires meinem Herzens zu werden? Sie werden diese Kühnheit mit meinem Vertrauen und mit meiner Sehnsucht entschuldigen und ich verlasse mich auf die Fürsprache Irhes gleichges[*inten*] Freundes.[1]

20 November 1801

This letter may be translated:

The day before yesterday I received a gift, which makes it necessary for me to ask a second favour of you. [*It is*] Young's *Night Thoughts*, to which I add my own, when trying in vain to guess the munificent hand in the cloud to which I am indebted for this gift. If you, as I surmise, have perhaps seen the Young illuminated by Blake—here [*is*] the English title [*The Complaint, and The Consolation*; or Night Thoughts, by Edward Young, London, 1797],—you will doubtless think my wish to express my thanks is just and the way to it pardonable. The metallic and artistic value—the love of my literary water-sprouts,—its delicate flattery of my taste,—and the place where it was posted (it is Gotha, as I hear) leads me to guess that you know the donor better than I do. May I ask you, although your indulgence is perhaps not immoderate, to deliver my thanks to your friend and so become the chargé d'affaires of my heart? You will excuse this boldness with my confidence and my yearning, and I abandon myself to the mediation of your like-minded friend.

In a letter probably of the same day, though dated 'M[*einigen*] d. 21. Nov. 1801', Richter wrote to Christian Ott somewhat more explicitly:

[1] *Jean Pauls sämmtliche Werke, Historisch-kritische Ausgabe, Dritte Abteilung: Briefe*, ed. Eduard Berend [Berlin, 1960], vol. iv, p. 117 (also given in *Die Briefe Jean Pauls*, ed. Eduard Berend [Munchen, 1926], vol. iv, p. 321). The two Richter letters were pointed out and translated by D. W. Dörrbecker in *Blake*, xi (1977), 124–5.

Vorgestern abends fand ich von der Post eine Folio-Kapsel, und darin eine englische Folio-Ausgabe von Young mit 20 oder 25 herlichen phantastischen Kupferstichen von Blake, englisch prächtig vergoldet und Saffian [*und*] Atlas und alles wieder in schwarzer L[*eder*] Hülse; eine ächte Gold[*kette*] geendigt *20.?* mit einer grossen Perle dient stat der Zwerg=Zettel die du in Bücher legst. *November* Anonym kams, ist aber vom gothaischen Erbprinzen. Ich taxier' es 15 *1801* Guineen. Die Kette bin ich gesonnen abzulösen und meiner Frau an den Hals zu henken. Es ist vielleicht nicht zweimal in Deutschland, was mir sehr bei dem Verkaufen einmal helfen kan.—[1]

The day before yesterday in the evening I received from the post office a folio-box and in it a folio-size English edition of Young with 20 or 25 [*should be 43*] magnificent fantastic copper engravings by Blake, [*bound in the*] English [*style*] in morroco and satin, splendidly gilt, and all again in a black l[*eather*] case; a real gold [*chain*] ending with a huge pearl serves in place of the dwarf paper-markers that one puts in books. It came anonymously, but it is from the Heir of the Prince of Gotha. I value it at 15 guineas. The chain I am inclined to remove and hang round my wife's neck. Perhaps there is not a second [*copy of the book*] in Germany, [*a fact*] which may help me a good deal in selling it.

Richter had recently been married. Three years later he referred to the book in print.

Beginning in February 1802 there are references to Blake in letters to Hayley from his enthusiastic young friend Edward Garrard Marsh,[2] then an undergraduate at Wadham College, Oxford.[2] Marsh's parents apparently lived in the neighbourhood of Hayley's residence at Felpham, Sussex, for in a letter of 23 May 1804 Marsh gives a message to deliver 'If you see my father', and on 19 March 1805 he refers to a joint letter from Hayley and his mother. He writes of reading Sussex newspapers, he refers in a letter of 23 November 1803 to Hay's history of 'our city' (Chichester), and he mentions visits to Chichester and Felpham. His first letter to Hayley, written on his eighteenth birthday, 8 February 1801, refers to the time 'when I last had the pleasure of

---

[1] *Jean Pauls sämmtliche Werke* (1960), vol. iv, pp. 118–19.
[2] All Marsh's letters (save that of 6 Nov. 1802 in *BR*, 111) are quoted from the black morocco volume of 64 letters of 1801–14 from E. G. Marsh to William Hayley which were offered by 'a lady' at Sotheby's, 6 Dec. 1984, lot 87, and 22 July 1985, lot 74, withdrawn each time, and sold privately to my friend Professorf Robert N. Essick, by whose permission they are given here. (Thirty-seven of the letters had appeared in Hayley's sale at Sotheby's, 20–2 May 1878, lot 219.) Professor Essick gives much of the context of the letters in 'Blake, Hayley, and Edward Garrard Marsh: "An Insect of Parnassus"', which he generously showed me in typescript in May 1986 and which is printed in *Explorations*, i (1987), 58–84. The 1984 catalogue says, without citing evidence, that 'Marsh met Blake at Felpham in September 1801', which may be true.

seeing you at Mrs Poole's' at Lavant, near Felpham, and on 22 June 1803 he says he hopes to be at Chichester in a fortnight. He wrote with adolescent confidence to Hayley, and on 3 December 1804 he said, 'you set me[1] at my ease, perhaps, more than any other man could do'. Like Hayley he was a prolific poet, most of his letters to Hayley contain poetry, and some contain nothing else, and Blake, who clearly knew and liked the impulsive young student, seems to be referring to him when he writes on 27 January 1804 of 'the Bard of Oxford'.

Marsh's first reference to Blake is intriguing. About Monday 8 February (his nineteenth birthday) Marsh wrote about a composition of his: 'It was written for the most part, while I was walking homeward from the land of inspiration, or (to use the words of the poetical sculptor) "from Felpham, mild village"'.[2] 'The land of inspiration' sounds Blake-like enough itself, and the words 'from Felpham, mild village' were probably used in conversation by Blake. They do not occur in his surviving writings, but he does, however, mention 'mild Felpham' (*Milton* [1804–?8], pl. 39, l. 13)—as well as mild Lambeth and 'Chichester, lovely mild' (*Jerusalem* [1804–?20], pl. 41, l. 11; pl. 40, l. 50); clearly 'mild' was a favourite word with Blake. Of course Hayley may have quoted Blake in a letter to Marsh, but it seems more probable that Marsh had heard Blake use the phrase, and his repetition of it here suggests an intimacy between the two men which we might otherwise find surprising. Blake clearly expressed his most characteristic ideas with particular freedom to young men like Marsh.

8 February 1802 (margin)

On 21 February 1802 Marsh wrote to Hayley about Blake as a musician in tantalizingly vague terms. He thanked Hayley for the sonnet and hymn, and continued:

The hymn which inspired our friend, whom I have some idea I mistitled in my last a poetical sculptor instead of a poetical engraver,[3] was quite—But if I run on in this strain, I shall find the letter ended, before I have said one half of the things I wish to say . . . I long to hear Mr Blake's devotional air, though (I fear) I should have been very aukward in the attempt to give notes to his music. His ingenuity will however (I doubt not) discover some method of preserving his

21 February 1802 (margin)

---

[1] The word 'me' is torn off.

[2] This leaf is pasted between the leaves of Marsh's letter of 21 March 1802, and it is cited with that letter in the Sotheby sale catalogue of Marsh's letters to Hayley, 6 Dec. 1984, lot 87, but it is clearly a separate epistle, and it is postmarked 9 Feb. 1802.

[3] Marsh's phrase for Blake, 'poetical sculptor', is not a mistitle, as Hayley apparently reassured him, for engravers signed their plates with 'sc' or 'sculpsit', e.g., 'Blake sc', and later letters by Marsh use the same term.

compositions upon paper, though he is not very well versed in bars and crotchets . . .

Marsh's reference to Blake's 'devotional air' and 'his music' is exceedingly tantalizing. No poem by Blake which is obviously a 'devotional air' is known,[1] though he may have been writing about this time the great 'Jerusalem' lyric for *Milton* (1804–?8) pl. 2, which begins

> And did those feet in ancient tim*e*
> Walk upon Englands mountains green

which is often sung today as a hymn. J. T. Smith 'heard him read and sing several of his poems' at the literary salons in 1784 of Mrs Mathew, 'a great encourager of musical composers'; 'He was listened to by the company with profound silence, and allowed by most of the visitors to possess original and extraordinary merit.'[2] Elsewhere J. T. Smith remarks that Blake wrote 'many' songs, and 'These he would occasionally sing to his friends; and though according to his confession, he was entirely unacquainted with the science of music, his ear was so good, that his tunes were sometimes most singularly beautiful, and were noted down by musical professors.'[3] But, as Allan Cunningham remarked, 'Of his music there are no specimens—he wanted the art of noting it down— if it equalled many of his drawings, and some of his songs, we have lost melodies of real value.'[4] And according to Gilchrist, even in his old age, 'He himself still sang, in a voice tremulous with age, sometimes old ballads, sometimes his own songs, to melodies of his own.'[5]

Since Marsh speaks of Blake's 'air' rather than his poem, it is at least imaginable that Blake had set to music a poem by Hayley or someone else, though the later reference to 'his [*Blake's*] compositions' makes it seem more likely that both words and music were Blake's. But no music by Blake is yet known, and even the words to which Marsh refers cannot be identified except by the most distant conjecture.

In his letter to 'My dear friend' Hayley of Sunday 21 March, E. G. Marsh concluded 'With kind remembrances to Mr Blake, with thanks for all your instructions . . .

21 March 1802

---

[1] For the context, see especially Martha Winburn England & John Sparrow, *Hymns Unbidden*: Donne, Herbert, Blake, Emily Dickinson, and the Hymnographers (1966), 44–112.

[2] J. T. Smith, *A Book for a Rainy Day* (1845), pp. 81–3—see *BR*, 26. A number of poems in *Poetical Sketches* are called simply 'Song'.

[3] J. T. Smith, *Nollekens and his Times* (1828)—see *BR*, 457.

[4] Allan Cunningham, 'William Blake', in his *Lives of the Most Eminent British Painters, Sculptors, and Architects* (1830)—see *BR*, 482.

[5] Gilchrist (1942), pp. 295–7; (1863), pp. 293–4—see *BR*, 305.

In a letter to Hayley of Tuesday 19 April 1802 partly about the death
19 of his father, Flaxman concluded: 'Nancy unites in love to You—&
April kind remembrance to M.ʳ & M.ʳˢ Blake.'¹
1802
E. G. Marsh, Hayley's undergraduate friend, wrote to Hayley on
Sunday 9 May about the German poet Klopstock, about whose poetry
9 Hayley was exceedingly enthusiastic: 'I may perhaps expect to hear
May you read it [*i.e. translate it at sight*], as the good M.ʳ Blake has heard you
1802 read French authors ...' Blake apparently found these sessions
trying—he writes of

> Remembering the verses that Hayley sung
> When my heart knockd against the root of my tongue[.]²

The practice for Blake's French and German, however, may have
been appreciated as an end in itself, for Blake was enthusiastic about
learning languages—'He would declare that he learnt French, suf-
ficient to read it, in a few weeks.'³ Blake quotes French in his annotations to Reynolds of about 1808, and we cannot be confident that he
knew much French before 1802. Hayley taught Blake Greek and Latin,
and Blake was very pleased with the rapid progress he made with the
languages. He may have been thinking of E. G. Marsh, perhaps the
only Oxford undergraduate he had known, and a frequent translator
from the Greek in his letters to Hayley, when he wrote to his brother
on 30 January 1803: 'I read Greek as fluently as an Oxford scholar.'
Marsh concludes this letter

with the sincerest wish, that happiness and peace may everywhere attend you;
that your Blake may speedily recover his sick wife; and that you may both,
amidst the multiplicity of more important business, and amidst the crowd of
more deserving friends, occasionally bestow a kind thought
    on your devoted friend
        Edward Garard Marsh

Apparently Catherine Blake was ill of a fever, and next week Hayley
reported that Blake had succumbed to the same malady.
The plates of the first Hayley Ballad were (?post-)dated 1 June 1802,
and they were apparently published by this date, for they were noticed

¹ Quoted from reproduction of the MS in the Pierpont Morgan Library.
² Letter of 22 Nov 1802. Cp. 'When Klopstock England defied Uprose William Blake
in his pride'—from the bog house in Lambeth (*Notebook*, p. 5). Blake painted a portrait
of Klopstock for Hayley's library in 1800 (*BR*, 69), and on 26–7 April 1802 Hayley wrote
in his diary that he 'read Klopstock into English to Blake'.
³ Gilchrist (1942), p. 15; (1863), p. 167—see *BR*, 290 n. 2.

on 2 June in an anonymous column which appeared regularly in *The Sussex Chronicle & Chichester Advertiser*:

We have had the pleasure of perusing yesterday, the first Number of Mr. Hayley's new publication, under the plain title of Ballads, to the Engravings of Mr. Blake. These moral Poems will add a sprig to the Poetic crown of the Author, and will give Rank to our County and City for producing that which in its Poetry, Typography, and skill of the *Burin*, will claim competition with some of the proudest efforts of the Metropolis—Could the benevolence of the Author's mind receive additional lustre, it would arise from the reasons for the undertaking detailed in the Preface, viz. its being intended both as relaxation and remuneration to the Engraver and Typographer, for the weighty call on their assiduity, in proceeding upon the splendid life of Cowper (also by Mr. Hayley) now advancing towards publication.[1]

2 June 1802

On Sunday 20 June E. G. Marsh wrote both about Hayley's Elephant ballad and about another work,

my version of the Rhodian . . . Should it happen in any degree to please you, I cannot but flatter myself, that your friendly artist will be glad to see this small portion of his [*Rhodius's*] work translated by even my hand. I wish him success on his elephant, which from its rider [*?Blake*] might (I think) be called the Apollonian elephant,[2] and hope to contribute my little assistance to the payment of the next turnpike on his tour. . . . I long to listen to your goat, your elephant, and your stag, and shall be glad to be a fellow=listener with your expe[rt?] friend.

20 June 1802

The Elephant's turnpike tour is fairly clearly a reference to subscriptions for Hayley's ballad with Blake's engravings for it which Marsh had found, or hoped to find, though he does not mention such subscriptions again. Marsh's 'version of the Rhodian' is his translation of *The Argonautica* of Apollonius Rhodius (295–215 BC). It had been frequently printed and translated (e.g. by Edward Burnaby Greene [1780], by Francis Fawkes [1780, 1794], and by W. Preston [1803]), and first editions of the translations by Greene and Fawkes were in the sale of Hayley's library by R. H. Evans on 13–27 February 1821.

Perhaps Blake had been studying Greek with Hayley using *The Argonautica* as a text. Gilchrist remarks, perhaps with merely rhetorical casualness, 'He [*Blake*] did not look out for the works of the purest

---

[1] Anon., 'Sussex and Adjacencies. Chichester', *Sussex Chronicle & Chichester Advertiser*, no. 22 (2 June 1802), 172. The *Ballads* and *The Sussex Chronicle* were both printed by Seagrave, but no other notice of the former seems to have appeared in the latter.

[2] There is no reference to elephants in Apollonius of Rhodes, *The Voyage of Argo: The Argonautica*, tr. E. V. Rieu (1983).

ages, but the purest work of every age and country—Athens or Rhodes, *Tuscany or Britain* . . .'[1] Perhaps we may come to identify a design of Blake with *The Argonautica* of Apollonius Rhodius.

Only two other Ballads reviews are known; one of them does not mention Blake (see *BR*, 109 n. 2), and the other spends almost half its few words in silently quoting from Hayley's Preface:

It appears by the Preface to this work, . . . that Mr. [']Blake has devoted himself with indefatigable spirit to engrave the plates intended to decorate the['] work [*Hayley's life of Cowper*]. [']To amuse the artist in his patient labour, and to furnish his fancy with a few slight subjects for an inventive pencil that might afford some variety to his incessant application, without too far inter-rupting his['] most [']serious business,['] Mr. Hayley proposed to furnish him with a series of ballads for a few vacant moments' employment, to be

August published periodically, and to be [']completed in fifteen numbers[']. Two of
1802 these are now before us. The subjects, the gratitude of an elephant, and the heroism of a mother in rescuing her child from the fangs [*sic*] of an eagle. The artist has executed his share of the undertaking much to his credit; and from Mr. Hayley's pen, though carelessly employed, the Public will not be dis-appointed in their expectations of elegant, chaste, and pathetic composi-tions. . . .[2]

This at least was encouraging if laconic.

E. G. Marsh, in his letter to Hayley of Tuesday 11 January, praised
11 Hayley's life of Cowper and concluded with a 'Postscript—Mr Blake is
January (I hope) proceeding vigorously in the triumphs of temper, the ballads,
1803 and the little quintettoes of Cowper's hares–'. Hayley's *Triumphs of Temper* was published with six plates by Blake after Maria Flaxman in 1803, and Blake's own design of Cowper's tame hares, Puss, Tiney, and Bess, appeared in the second volume of Hayley's *Cowper* in 1802, but Marsh's references to 'the ballads' seems to indicate that he did not know that Blake's work on them had been temporarily suspended.

Hayley had apparently expressed to Marsh, as he had to Lady Hesketh on 20 December 1802, Blake's idea that 'all the Demons, who tormented our dear Cowper when living, are now labouring to impede

---

[1] Gilchrist (1942), pp. 301–2; (1863), pp. 302–3—see *BR*, 282–3.
[2] Anon., '*Designs to a Series of Ballads written by William Hayley, Esq. and founded on Anec-dotes relating to Animals, drawn, engraved, and published, by William Blake. With the Ballads annexed by the Author's permission. Two Numbers.* 4to. Printed at Chichester.' *European Magazine*, xlii (Aug. 1802), 125–6. It seems likely that Blake sent few if any copies of the fourth Number of his *Designs* to his London publisher R. H. Evans, for in Evans's *Cata-logue of a Useful, Curious, and Valuable Collection of Books, for the Year 1804*, lot 1001 was 'Hayleys Ballads, 3 Numbers', without price.

the publication of his Life', and on Thursday 3 February Marsh replied:

Your twins [*the first two volumes of Hayley's life of Cowper*] are ordered, as two cherubs, to adorn the library of Magdalen College: and I am sorry to hear, that they are not yet ready to take their station in that valuable repository. Blake's idea diverted me. But though I wish even a double portion of Cowper's spirit both to his biographer and his engraver, I hope they will have no concern with his dæmons.

3 February 1803

On Tuesday 9 February 1803 the ageing Sussex novelist and poet Charlotte Smith wrote pathetically to Hayley's friend Samuel Rose soliciting assistance with her vexed legal and financial difficulties, and continuing:

My present purpose is, to enquire, whether there is not an ingenious Engraver, who executed certain plates for a small work of Mr Hayley's relating to Animals—I know not what it is as I have never seen it. Now I am going to tell a story all about myself. I have a little Girl of five years old, the daughter of my second Son, sent over to my care from India—She is *not* what is usually call'd an *half-cast*, her Mother being a Georgian Woman & her darkness (for perhaps you saw her little face when you calld on Charlotte) she derives from her father who is I understand *quite black*. Of this little creature, I am become passionately fond, & fancy that she has a very uncommon understanding—& I have written some little pieces of poetry to exercise *her* memory: while they may peradventure replenish my pocket & finish my Parnassian tour in the respectable character of an affectionate Grandmother. I am advised to add plates to those namby pambyisms, and print them on my own account. The subjects are entirely from natural history, & some of the drawing I should make myself if I had not the Rhumatism so dreadfully as often to lose the use of my hands—I imagine however the drawings w^d not be *very* expensive—& if Mr Hayley could, to use a French phrase, indicate to me, an artist not above engaging in such a work, I should consider myself under a great obligation to him—tho I fear to be troublesome, unless you will prefer my request[.]¹

9 February 1803

---

¹ Quoted from a xerox of the MS in McMaster University Library, generously pointed out to me by Professor James King. In a letter in the same collection of 9 September 1802 she confesses: 'I hardly dare boast the advantage of knowing you personally Sir, . . . but had Mr Rose been only a character respectable for professional talents, I had not ventured it' (soliciting his kindness). She writes to Rose, a comparative stranger, rather than to Hayley, her former patron and intimate friend, because, as she says in the 1803 letter, 'I am afraid of addressing myself to Mr Hayley, now on any subject whatever'; 'I cannot help considering myself as singularly unfortunate, & doubting whether there is not something in my destiny, which changes the nature of all those with whom I happen to be concern'd.'

The work to which she refers is probably her *Conversations Introducing Poetry* (1804), which introduces children to natural history through poems on, for example, 'The Lady Bird' and 'The Snail'; however, there is no plate in this work or in her *Natural History of Birds, Intended Chiefly for Young Persons* (1807). She clearly knew little of Blake or of his *Designs to A Series of Ballads* (1802), but she had doubtless heard of the book at least from some of her old Sussex friends. I do not know whether the proposal was every conveyed to Hayley, Blake, or her publisher.

In a letter 'To the Editor of the Monthly Magazine' defending his views of 'appropriate form and ornament' expressed in his *Thoughts on Outline* (1796), George Cumberland refers in passing to 'a mind full of images, (such as the fruitful one of our own Blake)'.[1] He also speaks of 'the object I have at heart, the recovery of the fine arts', reminding one that Blake had written on 16 August 1799: 'the purpose for which alone I live . . . is in conjunction with such men as my friend Cumberland to renew the lost Art of the Greeks'.

1 March 1803

In his perturbation at the accusation of sedition by a soldier who had been demoted for drunkenness, Blake may have inscribed a drinking-vessel called a rummer with an unfinished angel, 'THOU HOLDER OF IMMORAL DRINK / I GIVE THEE PURPOSE NOW I THINK', and 'BLAKE IN ANGUISH FELPHAM AUGUST 1803'.[2] The attribution to Blake is somewhat uncertain.

A manuscript True Bill against Blake was returned at the October Quarter Sessions:

THE SAID WILLIAM BLAKE late of the Parish of ffelpham in the County of Sussex Designer and Engraver came here in Court in his proper person and desired to hear the Indictment of Record against him Read why he on the twelfth Day of August in the fforty third year of the Reign of our Sovereign Lord George the Third of the United Kingdom of Great Britain and Ireland now King with fforce and Arms at the Parish of ffelpham aforesaid in the County aforesaid in and upon one John Scholfield in the Peace of God and of our said Lord the King then and there being Did make an Assault and him the said John Scholfield then and there Did beat wound and ill treat, so that his life was greatly despaired of and other wrongs to the said John Scholfield then and there did, to the great Damage of the said John Scholfield and against the Peace of our said Lord the King his

4 October 1803

[1] *Monthly Magazine*, xv (1 March 1803), 102.

[2] In 1983–5 the vessel was on sale by Pickering & Chatto in London, who concluded hopefully in their Catalogue 651 (1983), Item 1 that '*forgery can . . . be eliminated as a possibility*'; see 'The Felpham Rummer: A New Angel and "Immoral Drink" Attributed to William Blake', *Blake*, xviii (1985), 94–9.

Plea not Guilty Crown and Dignity, And having heard the same Read says and pleads that he is thereof not Guilty and for his Trial puts himself upon the County and William Ellis Gentleman Clerk of the Peace for the said County who for our Sovereign Lord the King in this behalf prosecute &c doth so likewise therefore the Sheriff of the said County is Commanded &c to cause to Come a Jury &c To try &c

*Recogn.*ˢ AND the said William Blake Acknd.   *100!*

to prosecute AND William Hayley of ffelpham aforesaid Esquire and Joseph *50!* Seagrave of Chichester in the said County Printer . . . . Acknᵈ   *each*

UPON CONDITION for the said William Blake to appear at the next Sessions and try his Traverse with Effect &c Then &c Otherwise &c   // .—[1]

If Blake had pleaded Guilty to the Indictment (a rare occurrence in eighteenth-century rural courts), the case would have been tried immediately. When the accused pleads Not Guilty, however, 'the officer of the court asks the party whether he be ready to try then, or will traverse [put off the trial] to the next sessions',[2] as was normal. Blake clearly denied his guilt and chose to be tried for sedition and assault at the next Quarter Sessions in January 1804, so the Bill was marked 'Travᵈ'

And in the summary of the proceedings in the Minute Book was recorded:

Wᵐ Blakes Indᵗ for Seditⁿ   Indᵗˢ travᵈ
Dᵒ for an assault

. . .

Wᵐ Blake's 2 Travˢ tried—[3]

Purged of redundancies, 'said' and 'to wit', what Blake was alleged to have said was:

The English know within themselves that Buonaparte could take possession of England in an hour's time, and then it would be put to every Englishman's choice for either fight for the French or have his throat cut. I think that I am as strong a man as most, and it shall be throat cut for throat cut, and the strongest man will be the conqueror. You will not fight against the French. Damn the King and Country and all his subjects. I have told this before to greater people than you. Damn the King and his Country; his subjects and all you soldiers are sold for slaves.

In his letter of 23 November 1803 Edward Marsh refers again (as he

---

[1] East Sussex Record Office.
[2] Richard Burn, *The Justice of the Peace, and Parish Officer*, revised by George Chetwynd (1825), vol. v, p. 541.
[3] East Sussex Record Office QM/EW 16 (Minute Book).

had on 1 February 1803) to the 'dæmons' of the press which were impeding the publication of Hayley's life of Cowper:

> I hope your literary pursuits are carrying on with great alacrity. As far as you are concerned there can indeed be no doubt of it. But since you have devils for your coadjutors, I cannot answer for your progress. I trust however the printer's devils will not be blue ones, and that if you must go on slowly, you will at least be allowed to proceed in good humor; and perhaps too when I guess, that ten sheets of the third volume are already completed, I may not violently exceed the mark.

23 November 1803

The primary references here are to 'printer's devils' or apprentices (so called doubtless because of the ink with which they covered themselves and the trouble they caused by carelessness) and to 'blue devils', what Keats in the 'Ode on Melancholy' called 'the melancholy fit'. But it may also allude to Blake, for Blake wrote on 22 November 1802 of encounters with 'Golden Demons', and his friend Thomas Butts had expressed to Blake in a letter of September 1800 his difficulty in 'discerning whether your Angels are black white or grey' and concluding that Blake is probably under 'the protection of the blackguard'. Blake then may be one of the 'devils' Marsh had in mind as Hayley's 'coadjutors' in his life of Cowper.

Marsh had come to Felpham on 1 September 1803,[1] and must then have learned a great deal about Blake's fracas with the soldier and his consequent trial for sedition before the Grand Jury impending on 4 October. He must have learned subsequently that the jury returned a true bill against Blake and that he was to stand his trial for sedition in Chichester in January 1804. He was clearly sympathetic to Blake, and in the same letter of 23 November he wondered whether the prosecution might have to be dropped if Private Schofield, Blake's accuser, were shipped overseas on military duty. 'Is Blake's accuser ordered out of England; or are we to expect a specimen of Mr Rose's eloquence in the winter? Have you any farther news concerning the living Romney, the poet?'[2] This is the first indication that Hayley's friend the barrister Samuel Rose might defend Blake at the ensuing Quarter

23 November 1803

---

[1] Autobiographical *Memoirs of the Life and Writings of William Hayley*, ed. John Johnson (1823), vol. ii, p. 44; another visit is recorded in early 1806 (vol. ii, p. 58).

[2] In the same letter, Marsh speaks of the 'pleasure' which Hayley's manuscript 'life of Alphonso' (Hayley's dead son) had given him and of 'one night in the turret [*Hayley's house at Felpham*], after we had read part of it together', when Marsh 'etched' some lines on it (which he quotes). I presume that 'etched' means merely 'wrote' rather than cut with acid, as on 'The Felpham Rummer'. Marsh's story of Hayley's unpublished MS suggests the strength of his intimacy with Hayley.

Sessions in January 1804, a possibility which must have originated with Hayley, since Blake would scarcely have been able to afford such a defence attorney. 'The living Romney, the poet' must refer to Blake (Romney had died in 1802), and, considering Hayley's love and admiration for Romney, it implies that Marsh assumed that Hayley held Blake in similarly high regard.

In his letter to Hayley of Wednesday 28 December 1803, Marsh wrote anxiously: 'I shall hope for an account from you of Mʳ Blake and *28* his advocate' Samuel Rose at Blake's trial for sedition at Chichester *December* on 11 January. *1803*

There is no indication that Hayley replied to Marsh's request, but Blake continued to feel a fondness for the young man. After his trial at Chichester, he wrote to Hayley on 27 January 1804:

God Bless & preserve you and . . . my much admired & respected Edward the Bard of Oxford whose verses still sound upon my Ear like the distant approach of things mighty & magnificent[,] like the sound of harps which I hear before the Suns rising[,] like the remembrance of Felphams waves & of the Glorious & far beaming Turret, like the Village of Lavant[,] blessed & blessing[.]

This estimate of Marsh seems to be repeated in *Jerusalem* (1804–?20), pl. 46, ll. 7–9:

> Oxford, immortal Bard! with eloquence
> Divine, he wept over Albion: speaking the words of God
> In mild perswasion: bringing leaves of the Tree of life.

The emphasis seems to be upon Marsh's 'musical voice',[1] 'like the sound of Harps' as Blake said in his letter, rather than upon Marsh's own verse, whose quality in these letters and elsewhere is rarely better than indifferent. The 'verses [*which*] still sound upon my Ear like the distant approach of things mighty & magnificent' are evidently 'the words of God', literally 'eloquence Divine'.

On 4 January 1804 Prince Hoare had complained that he had been 'disappointed of a . . . proof of Mʳ Blake's Etching' (*BR*, 139). Hoare was expecting rapid work, for the engraving for his *Academic Correspondence* had apparently been commissioned only ten days earlier (see 25 Dec. 1803). In fact, the plate must have been completed within a few days of Hoare's letter, for the book was announced on 16 January, and in a review of 1 February S. Q. complained in *The*

---

[1] Hayley, *Memoirs*, ed. John Johnson (1823), vol. ii, p. 44.

1 Literary Journal: 'Surely . . . the Royal Academy of England might have offered an engraving worthy of the subject and of the country.'[1]

As a last formality of Blake's acquittal, Hayley, Seagrave, and Blake were discharged from their recognizances, since they had appeared at the trials:

Sussex / s[*essions*]s / Epiphany Sessions at Chichester on Tuesday the 10.ᵗʰ Day of Janry 1804—
. . .

In Co.! last Sess W.ᵐ Blake of Felpham Com Sussacku 100.! W.ᵐ Hayley of the
same place Esq & Joseph Seagrave of Chiches-
ter Com praed printerucku 50.! ea. Cond[*iti*]on
Disch.ᵈ   for s.ᵈ W.ᵐ Blake to app.ʳ at the Sess & try his
traverse with effect for Sedition
D.º The s.ᵈ W.ᵐ Blake ackn 100.! & the s.ᵈ W.ᵐ Hayl[*e*]y & Joseph Seagrave
ackn 50.! ea. Cond.ᵈ for s.ᵈ W.ᵐ Blake to app.ʳ at
the next Sess & try his traverse with effect for
an Assault on John Scholfield—
William Blake of Felpham Com Suss [*in, Sussex County*] Designer &
Engraver ackn 100.!
Disch.ᵈ William Hayl[*e*]y of the same place Esq.ʳᵉ Joseph Seagrave of the
City of Chichester Printer ackn 50.ˡ ea Condn for s.ᵈ W.ᵐ Blake to
app.ʳ & answer to the above——[2]

Blake's vehemence became proverbial among his disciples, and on 29 January 1862 Samuel Palmer wrote to William Linnell: 'Mr Blake would have said "That is a lie".'[3] On 1[?] September 1862 he wrote to Anne Gilchrist, 'I never saw a *perfect* embodiment of Mr C[*arlyle*]'s *idea* of a *man in earnest* but in the person of Blake'.[4]

During 1804 Jean Paul Richter published his *Vorschule der Aesthetik* with a paragraph on the representation of the human figure deriving in part from the lavish gift of the *Night Thoughts* with Blake's engravings which he had received in November 1801:

Ausser der äussern Bewegung giebt es noch eine höhere Malerin der Gestalt, die innere Bewegung. Unsere Phantasie malt nichts leichter nach

---

[1] S. Q., '*Academic Correspondence* . . .', *Literary Journal*, iii (1 Feb. 1804), 94–5; see *BR*, 33.
[2] Quoted from a reproduction of QZ/EW 9 (Recognizance Book) in the East Sussex Record Office.
[3] *The Letters of Samuel Palmer*, ed. R. Lister (1974), vol. ii, p. 637.
[4] Ibid. vol. ii, p. 668.

als eine zweite. In einer Folio=Ausgabe von Youngs Nachtgedanken mit phantastischen Randzeichnungen von Blake ist z. B. auf dem Blatte, wo Träume gezeichnet werden,[1] die Gestalt für mich fürchterlich, die *1804* gekrümmt und schaudernd in ein Gebüsch starrt; den ihr Sehen wird mir Gesicht. Um also unserm Geiste eine schöne Gestalt zu zeigen— —; zeigt ihm nur einen, der sie sieht; aber um wieder sein Sehen zu zeigen, müsst ihr irgend einen Körpertheil, und wär' es ein blaues Auge, ja ein weisses grosses Augenlied, mitbringen; denn ist alles gethan.[2]

This has been translated:

Besides external motion there is a still higher paintress of the figure: internal motion. We imagine nothing more easily than another's imaginings. In a folio edition of Young's *Night Thoughts* with fantastic marginal designs by Blake on the page where dreams are described, there is a figure terrifying to me, which stares, bent over and shuddering, into a bush; its seeing becomes vision for me. In order to show a beautiful figure to our minds, simply show somewone who sees it; but to show his perception, you must accompany it with some part of the body, a blue eye or even a great white eyelid, and it will be there.

Charlotte Smith wrote to Mrs Rose on 10 September that she hesitated to send Hayley a set of her *Conversations Introducing Poetry* (1804) with poems about animals for children: 'Before I would ven- *10* ture to send him my little book, I wrote[*?*] to know if it would be *September* acceptable for notwithstanding he has begun a Poetical Buffon him- *1804* self, to assist his worthy friend Mr Blake, I was afraid mine, would be deam'd *too puerile*[*?*]—'[3] She clearly found Blake's pretensions as comic as Hayley's.

On 27 November 1805 Blake wrote to Hayley about how

Mr Cromek the Engraver came to me desiring ... me to Produce him Illustrations of The Grave A Poem by Robert Blair, in consequence of this I produced about twenty designs which pleasd so well that he with the same liberality ... has now set me to Engrave them. He means to Publish them by Subscription with the Poem as you will see in the Prospectus which he

---

[1] Edward Young, *Night Thoughts* (1797), p. 4 bottom left.

[2] Jean Paul [Friedrich Richter], *Vorschule der Aesthetik, nebst einigen Vorlesungen in Leipsiz über die Parteien der Zeit* (Hamburg, bei Friedrich Perthes, 1804), vol. ii, pp. 476–7. Paragraph 73. The work was repeatedly reprinted (1813, vol. ii, pp. 628–9; 1815; in *Jean Pauls sämmtliche Werke*, 1827, vol. xlii, p. 167; 1836; 1868–79; 1897; 1908; 1923; 1935; 1937; and 1963) and translated into French (1862), Spanish (1884), Japanese (1953–62), and English (by Margaret R. Hale, 1973). In the Zweite, verbesserte und vermehrte Auflage (1813) and subsequent editions, this passage became Paragraph 79 in XIV Programme and very small changes were made in the text. 'gibt ... welche gekrümmt ... zeigen:— —'. The translation is by D. W. Dörrbecker in *Blake*, xi (1977), 125.

[3] Quoted from a reproduction of the MS in McMaster University Library.

sends you in the same Pacquet with the Letter . . . You will be pleased to see that the Royal Academy have Sanctioned the Style of work.

The Prospectus of 'Nov. 1805' which Blake expected Cromek to enclose was clearly the one which described 'FIFTEEN PRINTS FROM DESIGNS INVENTED AND TO BE ENGRAVED BY *WILLIAM BLAKE*'. The number of designs to be published has been cut down from the 'twenty' Blake described to Hayley to 'FIFTEEN PRINTS',[1] but otherwise the Prospectus corresponds closely with Blake's letter. (See pp. 31–3.)

By the end of the month Flaxman knew at least the gist of the Prospectus, for he wrote to Hayley on Sunday December 1st:

Blake is going on gallantly with his drawings from the Grave, which are patronized by a formidable list of R.A's and other distinguished persons—I mentioned before that he has good employment besides, but still I very much fear his abstracted habits are so much at variance with the usual modes of human life, that he will not derive all the advantage to be wished from the present favourable appearances[.][2]

When he received the commission from Cromek, Blake probably began etching vigorously, and evidently by the time of the 'Nov. 1805' Prospectus he had finished 'a Specimen of the Stile of Engraving' which the Prospectus announced could 'be seen at the Proprietor's, Mr. CROMEK'. This specimen must be the only plate of the series which Blake is known to have completed, the rugged 'Death's Door'.[3] This plate is certainly not in a popular style, and Flaxman may have been thinking of it when he wrote on 12 November 1805 that Blake is 'in a way to do well' as an engraver 'if he will only condescend to give that attention to his worldly concerns which every one does that prefers living to Starving'. The sight of Blake's engraving must have

---

[1] John Knowles, *The Life and Writings of Henry Fuseli, Esq. M.A. R.A.* (1831), vol. i, pp. 290–3, was apparently referring to this first Prospectus (as no other contemporary does) when he wrote that 'Mr. Blake, who was not only a celebrated engraver, but known also for his original designs, distributed this year (1805) a prospectus for publishing an edition of the poem of "The Grave" of William [*i.e. Robert*] Blair, to be illustrated with fifteen plates designed and engraved by himself.' The other actions Knowles attributes to Blake—submission of the drawings to the Royal Academicians for praise and solicitation of Fuseli's encomium—should rather probably be attributed to Cromek.

NB The new matter here (not in *Blake Records* [1969]) is this Nov. 1805 Prospectus; the rest, largely from 'Blake and Cromek: The Wheat and the Tares', *Modern Philology*, lxxi (1974), 367–72, is to provide context—and to correct the 1969 version.

[2] British Library Add. MSS 39,780, fo. 92.

[3] Well reproduced in G. Keynes, *Engravings by William Blake: The Separate Plates* (Dublin, 1956), pl. 25.

PROSPECTUS

OF A NEW AND ELEGANT EDITION OF

BLAIR'S GRAVE,

ILLUSTRATED WITH

FIFTEEN PRINTS

FROM DESIGNS INVENTED AND TO BE ENGRAVED

BY

WILLIAM BLAKE;

WITH A PREFACE

CONTAINING AN EXPLANATION OF THE ARTIST'S VIEW IN THE DESIGNS,

AND

A CRITIQUE ON THE POEM.

The Work has been honoured with the Subscriptions and Patronage of the following Gentlemen:

BENJAMIN WEST, ESQ. PRESIDENT OF THE ROYAL ACADEMY.

SIR WILLIAM BEECHEY, R. A.	JAMES NORTHCOTE, ESQ. R. A.
RICHARD COSWAY, ESQ. R. A.	JOHN OPIE, ESQ. Pr. in Painting.
HENRY FUSELI, ESQ. R. A.	THOMAS STOTHARD, ESQ. R. A.
JOHN FLAXMAN, ESQ. R. A.	MARTIN ARCHER SHEE, ESQ. R. A.
THOMAS LAWRENCE, ESQ. R. A.	HENRY THOMSON, ESQ. R. A. and
JOSEPH NOLLEKENS, ESQ. R. A.	HENRY TRESHAM, ESQ. R. A.

THOMAS HOPE, ESQ. and WILLIAM LOCKE, Jun. ESQ.

The Preface will be contributed by BENJAMIN HEATH MALKIN, Esq. M. A. F. S. A.

THE Proprietor of the present Work, diffident of his own Judgment in general, and more particularly so in a Case, where private Friendship and personal Interests might be suspected of undue Influence, was afraid to venture on ushering this Prospectus into the World, merely on his own Opinion. That he might know how far he was warranted in calling the Attention of the Connoisseurs to what he himself imagined to be a high and original Effort of Genius, he submitted the Series of Drawings to Mr. WEST, and Mr. FUSELI, whose Character and Authority in the highest Department of the Art are unquestionable. The latter Gentleman has favoured the Proprietor with some Observations from his elegant and classical Pen, with Permission to make them public: they are decisive in their Testimony, and as they preclude the Possibility of any additional Remarks, they are here subjoined in the Author's own Words.

" The Moral Series here submitted to the Public, from its Object and Method of Execution, has a
" double Claim on general Attention.

" In an Age of equal Refinement and Corruption of Manners, when Systems of Education and Seduc-
" tion go hand in hand; when Religion itself compounds with Fashion; when in the Pursuit of present
" Enjoyment, all Consideration of Futurity vanishes, and the real Object of Life is lost—in such an Age,
" every Exertion confers a Benefit on Society which tends to impress Man with his Destiny, to hold the
" Mirror up to Life, less indeed to discriminate its Characters, than those Situations which shew what all
" are born for, what all ought to act for, and what all must inevitably come to.

" The Importance of this Object has been so well understood at every Period of Time, from the earliest
" and most innocent, to the latest and most depraved, that Reason and Fancy have exhausted their Stores
" of Argument and Imagery, to impress it on the Mind: animate and inanimate Nature, the Seasons, the
" Forest and the Field, the Bee and Ant, the Larva, Chrysalis and Moth, have lent their real or supposed
" Analogies with the Origin, Pursuits, and End, of the Human Race, so often to emblematic Purposes,
" that Instruction is become stale, and Attention callous. The Serpent with its Tail in its Mouth, from a
" Type of Eternity, is become an Infant's Bauble; even the nobler Idea of Hercules pausing between
" Virtue and Vice, or the varied Imagery of Death leading his Patients to the Grave, owe their Effect
" upon us more to technic Excellence than allegoric Utility.

" Aware of this, but conscious that Affectation of Originality and trite Repetition would equally impede
" his Success, the Author of the Moral Series before us, has endeavoured to wake Sensibility by touching
" our Sympathies with nearer, less ambiguous, and more familiar Objects, than what Mythology, Gothic
" Superstition, or Symbols as far-fetched as inadequate could supply. His Invention has been chiefly
" employed to spread a familiar and domestic Atmosphere round the most Important of all Subjects, to
" connect the visible and the invisible World, without provoking Probability, and to lead the Eye from the
" milder Light of Time to the Radiations of Eternity.

" Such is the Plan and the Moral Part of the Author's Invention; the technic Part, and the Execution of
" the Artist, though to be examined by other Principles, and addressed to a narrower Circle, equally
" claim Approbation, sometimes excite our Wonder, and not seldom our Fears, when we see him play
" on the very Verge of legitimate Invention; but Wildness so picturesque in itself, so often redeemed by
" Taste, Simplicity, and Elegance, what Child of Fancy, what Artist would wish to discharge? The
" Groups and single Figures on their own Basis, abstracted from the general Composition, and considered
" without Attention to the Plan, frequently exhibit those genuine and unaffected Attitudes, those simple
" Graces which Nature and the Heart alone can dictate, and only an Eye inspired by both, discover.
" Every Class of Artists, in every Stage of their Progress or Attainments, from the Student to the finished
" Master, and from the Contriver of Ornament, to the Painter of History, will find here Materials of Art
" and Hints of Improvement!"

The Work will be printed by T. BENSLEY, in Imperial Quarto.

The Price to SUBSCRIBERS will be TWO GUINEAS; one Guinea to be paid at the Time of subscribing,
and the Remainder on Delivery of the Work.

SUBSCRIPTIONS are received by J. JOHNSON, St. Paul's Church Yard; T. PAYNE, Mews' Gate;
J. WHITE, Fleet Street; LONGMAN, HURST, REES, and ORME, Paternoster Row; CADELL and DAVIES,
Strand; and W. MILLER, Albemarle Street.

The original Drawings, and a Specimen of the Stile of Engraving, may be seen at the Proprietor's,
Mr. CROMEK, No. 23, Warren Street, Fitzroy Square, London; where also the Names of SUBSCRIBERS
will be received.

LONDON, NOV. 1805.

T. Bensley, Printer,
Bolt Court, Fleet Street, London.

THE SUBJECTS PROPOSED TO BE ENGRAVED.

1. *The good old Man dying.*
2. *The strong and wicked Man dying.*
3. *Christ descending into the Grave, with the Keys of Death and Hell.*
4. *The Widow embracing her Husband's Grave.*
5. *The Valley of Death.*
6. *Death's Door.*
7. *The Counsellor, King, Warrior, Mother, and Child, in the Tomb.*
8. *The Soul suspended over the Body, unwilling to part with Life.*
9. *The Meeting of a Family in Heaven.*
10. *Friendship.*
11. *Death pursuing the Soul through the Avenues of Life.*
12. *The Soul exploring the Caverns of Death.*
13. *The Re-union of the Soul with the Body at the last Day.*
14. *The last Judgment.*
15. *A characteristic Frontispiece.*

T. Bensley, Printer,
Bolt Court, Fleet Street, London.

been a shock to the commercial hopes of Cromek, who evidently told Thomas Stothard that Blake 'had etched one of the subjects but so indifferently and so carelessly ... that he employed Schiavonetti to engrave them' instead.[1]

Perhaps Cromek had not actually seen Blake's specimen engraving when the first Prospectus was composed; or perhaps he saw it and tried vainly to persuade Blake to re-engrave it in a more popular style. At any rate, Cromek evidently changed his mind very rapidly,[2] for almost immediately he arranged for a different engraver to make the

[1] R. T. Stothard ('Stothard and Blake', *Athenaeum*, 19 Dec. 1863, p. 838) reporting what his father had said. The spelling of the engraver's name in the *Athenaeum* was 'Schrovenetti'.

[2] In the copy of the first prospectus offered at Sotheby's, 23 July 1985, lot 550, sent 'With Mr Cromek's respects' to 'Mr Tomkinson / Dean Street / Soho' (perhaps intended for John Townley), Cromek deleted the words 'AND TO BE ENGRAVED', and beneath 'BY *WILLIAM BLAKE*' he added in his own hand 'and to be engraved by I. Schiavonetti'. He also added at the end that the price to non-subscribers would be £3. 3s. od. (The next prospectus, also of Nov. 1805, merely says that 'The Price will be considerably advanced to Non-Subscribers'.)

plates and issued another Prospectus in 'Nov. 1805' contradicting the first one (see the accompanying facsimile).

The evidence of the rapidity of the change is strong: the first Prospectus must have been issued about the end of November, for Blake had evidently not yet seen its account of 'FIFTEEN PRINTS' when he wrote, on 27 November that he was to 'Engrave' 'about twenty Designs' for Blair's *Grave*; further, the second Prospectus, like the first, is also dated 'Nov. 1805', and indeed most of it seems to have been printed from standing type.[1] The change of engravers from Blake to Schiavonetti seems to have been made in the last few days of November 1805 and to be recorded in the two prospectuses dated 'Nov. 1805'.

The differences between the two prospectuses are comparatively small but very striking. The first speaks of 'FIFTEEN PRINTS' and the second of 'TWELVE ... ENGRAVINGS'; the first says they are 'TO BE ENGRAVED BY *WILLIAM BLAKE*' and the second that there will be 'VERY SPIRITED ENGRAVINGS BY *LOUIS SCHIA-VONETTI*'; the first gives only the 'Price to Subscribers' and the second adds that 'The Price will be considerably advanced to Non-Subscribers'; the first speaks of 'Original Drawings, and a Specimen of the Stile of Engraving [*which*] may be seen at the Proprietor's, Mr. Cromek', but the second speaks only of 'specimens', obscuring the distinction between designs and engravings—presumably because Schiavonetti's engravings were not yet ready in November 1805 (the earliest date on surviving proofs, that on 'Death's Door', is 1 February 1806); the first identifies the designs and the second does not.

Of the fifteen designs listed in the first Prospectus, numbers 1–3, 5–9, 12–14 were etched by Schiavonetti. Number 4, 'The Widow embracing her Husband's Grave', was described by Flaxman in his letter of 18 October 1805 as one of 'the most Striking', but it had evidently been abandoned by November 1805; it is now in the collection of Mr Paul Mellon and was reproduced, *inter alia*, in *Blake Records* (1969, pl. xviii). Number 10, 'Friendship', is not known from other references and is difficult to identify from this vague title. Number 11, 'Death pursuing the Soul through the Avenues of Life', is in the

---

[1] The type seems to be identical in most of the two prospectuses except for double rules in the first Prospectus and single rules in the second, the different divisions between page 1 and page 2, and the lines at the end where words were added or altered. Note particularly that the comma at the bottom of the first page 1 ('Remarks,') is similarly defective in both prospectuses and that the 'N' of 'Nov. 1805' in the imprint is damaged at the top left corner in both.

PROSPECTUS

OF

A NEW AND ELEGANT EDITION

OF

BLAIR'S GRAVE,

ILLUSTRATED WITH

TWELVE VERY SPIRITED ENGRAVINGS

BY

LOUIS SCHIAVONETTI,

FROM DESIGNS INVENTED

BY

WILLIAM BLAKE;

WITH A PREFACE

CONTAINING AN EXPLANATION OF THE ARTIST'S VIEW IN THE DESIGNS,

AND

A CRITIQUE ON THE POEM.

The Work has been honoured with the Subscriptions and Patronage of the following Gentlemen:

BENJAMIN WEST, ESQ. PRESIDENT OF THE ROYAL ACADEMY.

SIR WILLIAM BEECHEY, R.A.	JAMES NORTHCOTE, ESQ. R.A.
RICHARD COSWAY, ESQ, R.A.	JOHN OPIE, ESQ. Pr. in Painting.
HENRY FUSELI, ESQ. R.A.	THOMAS STOTHARD, ESQ. R.A.
JOHN FLAXMAN, ESQ. R.A.	MARTIN ARCHER SHEE, ESQ. R.A.
THOMAS LAWRENCE, ESQ. R.A.	HENRY THOMSON, ESQ. R.A. and
JOSEPH NOLLEKENS, ESQ. R.A.	HENRY TRESHAM, ESQ. R.A.

THOMAS HOPE, ESQ. and WILLIAM LOCKE, Jun. ESQ.

The Preface will be contributed by BENJAMIN HEATH MALKIN, Esq. M.A. F.S.A.

THE Proprietor of the present Work, diffident of his own Judgment in general, and more particularly so in a Case, where private Friendship and personal Interests might be suspected of undue Influence, was afraid to venture on ushering this Prospectus into the World, merely on his own Opinion. That he might know how far he was warranted in calling the Attention of the Connoisseurs to what he himself imagined to be a high and original Effort of Genius, he submitted the Series of Drawings to Mr. WEST, and Mr. FUSELI, whose Character and Authority in the highest Department of the Art are unquestionable. The latter Gentleman has favoured the Proprietor with some Observations from his elegant and classical Pen, with Permission to make them public: they are decisive in their Testimony, and as they preclude the Possibility of any additional Remarks, they are here subjoined in the Author's own Words.

"The Moral Series here submitted to the Public, from its Object and Method of Execution, has a "double Claim on general Attention.

"In an Age of equal Refinement and Corruption of Manners, when Systems of Education and Seduc- "tion go hand in hand; when Religion itself compounds with Fashion; when in the Pursuit of present "Enjoyment, all Consideration of Futurity vanishes, and the real Object of Life is lost—in such an Age, "every Exertion confers a Benefit on Society which tends to impress Man with his Destiny, to hold the "Mirror up to Life, less indeed to discriminate its Characters, than those Situations which shew what all "are born for, what all ought to act for, and what all must inevitably come to.

"The Importance of this Object has been so well understood at every Period of Time, from the earliest "and most innocent, to the latest and most depraved, that Reason and Fancy have exhausted their Stores "of Argument and Imagery, to impress it on the Mind: animate and inanimate Nature, the Seasons, the "Forest and the Field, the Bee and Ant, the Larva, Chrysalis and Moth, have lent their real or supposed "Analogies with the Origin, Pursuits, and End, of the Human Race, so often emblematic Purposes, "that Instruction is become stale, and Attention callous. The Serpent with its Tail in its Mouth, from a "Type of Eternity, is become an Infant's Bauble; even the nobler Idea of Hercules pausing between "Virtue and Vice, or the varied Imagery of Death leading his Patients to the Grave, owe their Effect "upon us more to technic Excellence than allegoric Utility.

"Aware of this, but conscious that Affectation of Originality and trite Repetition would equally impede "his Success, the Author of the Moral Series before us, has endeavoured to wake Sensibility by touching "our Sympathies with nearer, less ambiguous, and less ludicrous Imagery, than what Mythology, Gothic "Superstition, or Symbols as far-fetched as inadequate could supply. His Invention has been chiefly "employed to spread a familiar and domestic Atmosphere round the most Important of all Subjects, to "connect the visible and the invisible World, without provoking Probability, and to lead the Eye from the "milder Light of Time to the Radiations of Eternity.

"Such is the Plan and the Moral Part of the Author's Invention; the technic Part, and the Execution of "the Artist, though to be examined by other Principles, and addressed to a narrower Circle, equally "claim Approbation, sometimes excite our Wonder, and not seldom our Fears, when we see him play "on the very Verge of legitimate Invention; but Wildness so picturesque in itself, so often redeemed by "Taste, Simplicity, and Elegance, what Child of Fancy, what Artist would wish to discharge? The "Groups and single Figures on their own Basis, abstracted from the general Composition, and considered "without Attention to the Plan, frequently exhibit those genuine and unaffected Attitudes, those simple "Graces which Nature and the Heart alone can dictate, and only an Eye inspired by both, discover. "Every Class of Artists, in every Stage of their Progress or Attainments, from the Student to the finished "Master, and from the Contriver of Ornament, to the Painter of History, will find here Materials of Art "and Hints of Improvement!"

———————————

The Work will be printed by T. BENSLEY, in Imperial Quarto.

The Price to SUBSCRIBERS will be TWO GUINEAS; one Guinea to be paid at the Time of subscribing, and the Remainder on Delivery of the Work.—The Price will be considerably advanced to NON-SUBSCRIBERS.

SUBSCRIPTIONS are received by J. JOHNSON, St. Paul's Church Yard; T. PAYNE, Mews' Gate; J. WHITE, Fleet Street; LONGMAN, HURST, REES, and ORME, Paternoster Row; CADELL and DAVIES, Strand; W. MILLER, Albemarle Street; and Mr. CROMEK, No. 23, Warren Street, Fitzroy Square, where Specimens may be seen.

LONDON, NOV. 1805.

T. Bensley, Printer,
Bolt-court, Fleet-street, London.

1

---

[1] British Library Add. MSS 33,397, fo. 144, among the papers of Robert Dodd. All the booksellers named here also appeared on the 1808 title-page, with the addition of Murray, and Constable and Co.

collection of Professor Robert Essick.[1] Number 15, 'A Characteristic Frontispiece', cannot be identified with confidence; the published frontispiece was a portrait of Blake after Thomas Phillips, but this number 15 may well refer to the design eventually used for the engraved title page, the only published design which does not appear by name in the first Prospectus.

The designs were all referred to by title in four places: (1) the first Prospectus; (2) another Prospectus published with Cromek's edition of *Reliques of Robert Burns* (December 1808);[2] (3) the description 'Of the Designs' in the 1808 *Grave*; and (4) the engraved titles on the 1808 plates. (See Table 3, pp. 38–9.)

A note at the head of the description 'Of the Designs' in the 1808 *Grave* states: 'By the arrangement here made, the regular progression of Man, from his first descent into the Vale of Death, to the last admission into Life eternal, is exhibited. These Designs, detached from the Work they embellish, form of themselves a most interesting Poem.' Much emphasis has occasionally been put on the significance of this order.[3] However, the designs were arranged in at least five different ways, and Blake is likely to have had at least as much to do with the first order as with the last (see Table 4, p. 40).

This variety suggests that we need to be cautious in drawing conclusions about Blake's intentions as to the order in which his designs were to be arranged. Considering that the number of designs was cut from forty to twenty to fifteen to twelve, that Blake may scarcely have been consulted about some of these cuts, and that the integrity of the series and the relationship of design to design must have been altered by each cut, it is difficult to draw confident conclusions about Blake's original intention as to the order and relationship of the designs. Indeed, there is little evidence to indicate that Blake had control over the number, order, titles, or engraving of his designs after October 1805.

We do not know when or how Blake learned that the promised— indeed advertised—commission to engrave the plates had been given

---

[1] Robert Essick, 'A Preliminary Design for Blair's *Grave*', *Blake Studies*, iv (1972), 9–13.

[2] The manuscript of the Burns book was almost complete in November 1807 (see below). Probably the Prospectus printed there was composed before Blair's *Grave* was published in the summer of 1808.

[3] Foster Damon prepared an edition of *Blake's Grave: A Prophetic Book Being William Blake's Illustrations for Robert Blair's 'The Grave', Arranged as Blake Directed* (Providence, Rhode Island, 1963).

TABLE 3. *Titles of Blake's designs for Blair's* Grave

Design No. and Title	Referred to in First Prospectus 1805 (1)	1807 *Manchester Gazette* ad (2)	Prospectus in *Reliques* 1808 (3)	1808 *Grave* order (4)	1808 Titles (5)
1(a) The Skeleton Re-animated [on the sound of the Archangel's Trumpet *added in 4*]			X	X	
1(b) A Skeleton discovering the first symptoms of animation		X			
2(a) Christ Descending into the Grave [with the Keys of Death and Hell *added in 2, 5*]	X	X			X
2(b) The descent of Christ into the Grave			X	X	
3(a) The meeting of a Family in Heaven	X	X			X
3(b) The Family Meeting in Heaven			X	X	
4 The Counsellor, King, Warrior, Mother, & Child [in the Tomb *added in 1–3, 5*]	X	X	X	X	X
5(a) The strong and wicked Man dying	X	X	X	X	
5(b) Death of the Strong Wicked Man					X
6(a) The Soul suspended over the Body, unwilling to part with Life	X	X			

	C1	C2	C3	C4
6(b) The Soul reluctantly parting with the Body			×	
6(c) The Soul hovering over the Body [reluctantly parting with Life *added in 5*]	×	×		
7(a) The Valley of Death [*also the title on proofs*]	×		×	×
7(b) The descent of Man into the Vale of Death	×	×	×	
8(a) The Last Judgment	×	×	×	×
8(b) The Day of Judgment	×		×	
9(a) The Soul exploring the Caverns of Death	×	×	×	
9(b) The Soul exploring the recesses of the Grave	×	×	×	
10(a) The good old Man dying	×	×	×	
10(b) The Death of The Good Old Man	×	×	×	
11 Death's Door	×	×	×	
12(a) The Re-union of the Soul with the Body [at the last Day *added in 1*]	×	×	×	
12(b) The Reunion of the Soul & [the] Body	×	×	×	

T ABLE 4. *Five arrangements of Blake's designs by number*

First Prospectus Nov. 1805	Prospectus in *Reliques* 1808	1807 Manchester *Gazette* advt.	1808 *Grave* 'Of the Designs'	1808 Titles
15?	9	10	2	1
3	1	5	7	2
9	11	2	11	3
7	8	7	5	4
2	4	11	10	5
8	6	4	6	6
5	2	6	9	7
14	12	3	4	8
12	7	1	1	9
1	5	9	12	19
6	3	12	3	11
13	10	8	8	12

to Schiavonetti. Perhaps he learned it from the second Prospectus of November 1805. Blake had accepted the comparatively trifling sum of '20 guineas' (as Cromek said in his letter of May 1807) for the 'twenty Designs' (according to Blake's letter of the 27 November 1805), presumably because he expected to make much more in engraving the 'twenty' or 'FIFTEEN PRINTS'—Schiavonetti later asked £63 for just one plate and may have had over £500 for etching thirteen of them.

It is little wonder then that Blake, crippled for the moment in both pocket and pride, reacted with violence. His Notebook erupted with little pustules of irritated verse:

> A petty sneaking Knave I knew
> O M^r Cr—how do ye do[?]
>
> Cr—loves artists as he loves his Meat
> He loves the Art but tis the Art to Cheat[.][1]

On 20 March 1806 Charlotte Smith wrote to Samuel Rose's widow Sarah that she had no intention 'of *attacking* M^r H[*ayley*]', her erstwhile patron and intimate friend;

Now Heaven forfend! . . . I said [*to you*] I wished he could recall his two last publications, 'the triumphs of Music & The ballads'[1] . . . tho I have sufferd

[1] *Notebook*, p. 29.

myself in writing confidentially to you, to smile at our friend; at his odd weekly[?] tittups[?] to a female critic,[2] (whose remarks certainly have not profitted him much;) & at his strange tho benevolent fancy of writing such very sad doggrell, for the purpose of serving a Man, who might be anything *20* rather than an engraver; Yet I never went *beyond* such a laugh between our- *March* selves . . . Years have pass'd since we have met . . .[3] *1806*

And on 25 April 1806 she wrote again to Sarah Rose of her regret for the loss of Hayley's friendship; but then

I lose a great part of the regret I might otherwise feel in recollecting, that a mind so indiscriminating, who is now seized with a rage for a crooked figure-maker[4] & now for an engraver of Ballad pictures (the young Mans tradgedy; & the jolly Sailers Farewell to his true love Sally—I dont mean the Hayleyan collection of pretty ballads)—Such a mind, can never be really attached; [*n*]or is the attachment it can feel worth having—Who the present most aimable *being 25* is, I do not know; I mean as an entremêt, for Miss Poole is like a French *April* family's constant, Soup a bouillé—a standing dish . . .[5] *1806*

Mrs Smith seems to scorn Flaxman and Blake not so much as artists but as rivals for Hayley's affection, and her petulant bitterness seems almost that of a neglected lover.

[1] She had probably not seen either the *Designs for A Series of Ballads* (1802) or the *Ballads* (1805)—certainly she had not seen the former by 9 Feb. 1803—and probably wrote from hearsay.

[2] This 'female critic' is plainly Anna Seward who formed an extraordinarily public mutual admiration society with Hayley. A poem beginning

'"Tickle me," said Mr. Hayley,
"Tickle me, Miss Seward, do . . ."'

'was circulated (and attributed to Blake) in the first decade of the present [*nineteenth*] century', according to W. M. Tartt in Anon., '"Pictor Ignotus;" A Biography [*by Gilchrist*]', *New Monthly Magazine*, cxxx (1864), 312, 316, reprinted without the verses in Tartt's *Essays on Some Modern Works* (1876), 200, 207 (see *BR*, 626–7). However, the poem apparently first appeared in the newspaper called *The World* on 15 Feb. 1790 (long before Blake had met Hayley) with the attribution to an anonymous author of '*St. John's* [*College*], *Cambridge*', was reprinted in *The Poetry of the World*, iii (1791), 184, and in the review thereof in *The Analytical Review*, ix (1791), 444–7. (On 24 Dec. 1793 Joseph Farington reported that George 'Steevens is supposed to be the author' of these lines [*Diary*, ed. K. Garlick & A. MacIntyre, vol. i (1978), p. 107], but this is unlikely, for Steevens was at *King's* College many years before [1753–56].) From the statement in *Blake Records* (1969) that 'Blake almost certainly did not write these lines' the word 'almost' may now be deleted.

[3] Quoted from the MS in the Huntington Library; the passage was first given in A. D. McKillop, 'Charlotte Smith's Letters', *Huntington Library Quarterly*, xv (1952), 237–55.

[4] Flaxman was apparently slightly hunchbacked.

[5] Quoted from the MS in the Huntington Library; the parentheses are both over dashes, there is a superfluous closing parenthesis after 'Sally)', and the contents of the parentheses are meaningless to me, unless they presume that Blake was a professional engraver of ballads, of which these are hypothetical examples.

Apparently one of the first steps in Cromek's public campaign to woo the public on behalf of his edition of Blair's *Grave* with Blake's designs was to place substantially identical advertisements in Aris's *Birmingham Gazette* and in the *Birmingham Commercial Herald* for 28 July 1806. The one in the former, based on the November 1805 flyers though omitting a good deal and adding the paragraph about Messrs Knott & Lloyd, was a

PROSPECTUS OF

A NEW and elegant Edition of BLAIR's GRAVE, illustrated with twelve very
28 spirited Engravings by LOUIS SCHIAVONETTI, from Designs invented by
July WILLIAM BLAKE.
1806
    The Work will be printed by T. Bensley, Fleet-street, London, in Imperial Quarto.

The Price to Subscribers will be two Guineas; one Guinea to be paid at the Time of subscribing, and the Remainder on Delivery of the Work. The Price will be considerably advanced to Non-subscribers.

Messrs. Knott and Lloyd, Birmingham, will give the Address of the Proprietor of the Work, who will shew the original Drawings and Specimens of the Style of Engraving.

The Work has been honoured with the Subscriptions and Patronage of the following Gentlemen:

BENJAMIN WEST, Esq. President of the Royal Academy.

Sir William Beechey, R.A.	James Northcote, Esq. R.A.
Richard Cosway, Esq. R.A.	J. Opie, Esq. Pr. in Painting.
Henry Fuseli, Esq. R.A.	Thomas Stothard, Esq. R.A.
John Flaxman, Esq. R.A.	Martin Archer Shee, Esq. R.A.
Thomas Lawrence, Esq. R.A.	Henry Thomson, Esq., R.A.
Joseph Nollekens, Esq. R.A.	Henry Tresham, Esq. R.A.

Thomas Hope, Esq. and William Locke, jun. Esq.[1]

Notice that the drawings and specimen engravings were to be shown in Birmingham and that the advertisement was presumably placed before Cromek had arrived in Birmingham and established an address at which he could show the designs and plates. Presumably similar advertisements were placed in other commercial cities where Cromek exhibited the designs and solicited subscriptions in the next year or so.

---

[1] The advertisement in the *Birmingham Commercial Herald* was identical except in lineation, punctuation, capitals, the omission of 'Fleet-street, London' (after 'Bensley') and 'Birmingham' (after 'Lloyd'), and readings of 'show' for 'shew' and 'engravings' for 'engraving' (paragraph 4).

All these new Blair advertisements in newspapers were generously pointed out to me by my friend Dr Dennis Read, the biographer of Cromek.

The puffs too were substantially identical in the two newspapers, indicating clearly that they represented not the aesthetic judgement of the editor but the interested cupidity of the speculator:

FINE ARTS.—We have never experienced greater satisfaction than in announcing to our readers, that there are now in this town, for the inspection of the lovers of the fine arts, some most beautiful designs, intended to illustrate a new and elegant edition of Blair's Grave. At a period when the labours of the pencil are almost wholly directed to the production of portraits, they who dare to soar in the sublimer regions of fancy, surely claim the patronage of men of taste and discernment; and the specimens here alluded to, may, with the strictest adherence to truth, be ranked amongst the most vigorous and classical productions of the present age.—*See advert. in this page*.[1]

28 July 1806

The superlative 'satisfaction' felt by the author, his certainty that the designs rank 'amongst the most vigorous and classical productions of the present age', and his 'strictest adherence to truth' may all strike us somewhat differently when we observe that the two puffs in the different newspapers on the same day are substantially identical— and written by Cromek.

Blake was persuaded that Cromek or Stothard stole his idea for a large design representing the procession of Chaucer's Canterbury Pilgrims, but Stothard's innocence of the charge is indicated in a circumstantial though anonymous account almost twenty years later:

Mr. Cromek gave the commission for painting the subject of the Canterbury Pilgrims. There had been no previous conversation on the subject, though it must long have occupied the thoughts of the projector, for, on the matter being first mentioned to Mr. Stothard, and before he gave answer to the proposal, he took from his folio a sketch of the subject, shewing that it had been long contemplated and only wanted the sanction of a commission to set him to work. . . .

One more circumstance may be related, connected with the painting of the Pilgrims, during the time it was in the hands of the engravers I. and P. Schiavonetti. Mr. Blake, of eccentric memory, whose designs to illustrate Blair's Grave, and other works of great genius and talent were well known, undertook to produce an engraving of the Canterbury Pilgrims, from a design of his own, in one year from a certain date, and he accomplished the task. But it was, as might have been expected, eccentric and extraordinary—

---

[1] Quoted from Aris's *Birmingham Gazette*; the *Birmingham Commercial Herald* differs in capitalization and in the substitution of '*Vide advert.*' after 'Blair's Grave' for the last sentence.

a curiosity in Art, and might in its character and execution have passed for a performance or work of Art, contemporary with the times of Chaucer.[1]

The account admits Blake's rivalry with Stothard but scarcely conceives his claim to priority.

The penultimate reference to Blake in the correspondence of Hayley's young friend E. G. Marsh is in a letter of Tuesday 14 October 1806 in which Marsh writes of his visits to Blenheim Palace and Warwick Castle, 'This mighty ruin':

> I wonder, whether M[r] Spilsbury [*the painter*] has ever seen Warwick castle, because there is a painting of two lions there, which pleased me, who know *14* nothing at all about the matter, except as far as M[r] Blake's sentiment goes, that *October* every Englishman ought to be a judge of painting, beyond anything of the kind *1806* I had ever seen. I saw also a vast collection of Raphaels and Reubenses and Vandykes without having an idea, which was which. Only I was vastly delighted with a queen of Naples.

Marsh may have heard Blake say 'that every Englishman ought to be a judge of painting' when they were both at Felpham in September 1803, and Blake certainly expressed the opinion later. For instance, in his 'Public Address' of about 1810 he wrote:

> It has been said of late years The English Public have no Taste for Painting[.] This is a Fals[*e*]hood[.] The English are as Good Judges of Painting as of Poetry & they prove it in their Contempt for Great Collections of all the Rubbish of the Continent brought here by Ignorant Picture dealers[;] an Englishman may well say 'I am no Judge of Painting' when he is shewn these Smears & Dawbs at an immense Price & told that such is the Art of Painting[.] I say the English Public are true Encouragers of Great Art while they discharge & look with contempt on False Art[.] [p. 1051]

Marsh was clearly much struck by the gnomic qualities of Blake's conversation.

[1] Anon., 'On the Genius of Stothard, and the Character of His Works', *Arnold's Magazine of the Fine Arts*, NS iii (March 1834), 436, 440. The anonymous author's information is very good, for in his prospectus called 'Blake's Chaucer: The Canterbury Pilgrims' (1809)—and apparently nowhere else—Blake 'engages to deliver' an engraving 'similar to' those of Durer, Lucas van Leyden, H. S. Beham, and Heinrich Aldegrever (all *c*. 1500) 'in One Year from September next', and its imprint is 8 October 1810. Only one copy of this prospectus is known (now in the BMPR), and no contemporary owner of a copy has been identified.

In March Hoppner had shown Stothard's 'Canterbury Pilgrims' to the Prince of Wales, who permitted Cromek to dedicate the print to him, according to an article dated 21 March 1807 from an unidentified source found in the Whitley Papers (BMPR) by S. M. Bennett, 'Thomas Stothard, R.A.' California (Los Angeles) Ph.D. (1977), p. 226.

In the spring of 1807 Blake went to the home of the Royal Academician Thomas Phillips at 8 George Street, Hanover Square, to have his portrait painted. When it was finished, Phillips wrote in his 'List of Portraits': 'Apl. 4 [*1807*] Blake the Artist'.[1]

4 April 1807

Despite Cromek's actions of November 1805, which seem from surviving evidence to have been pretty high-handed, Blake continued to take a keen interest in Blair's *Grave* and to suggest improvements in it. Evidence of this continuing interest may be seen in an important letter of April 1807 from Cromek to the Sheffield poet James Montgomery, which is given at length here because it displays Cromek's character so vividly:

Dear Sir,

I was much pleased the other Day to observe in a Letter you wrote to my Friend M.r Hopwood[2] that you very kindly inquired after me & my speculations. The little Cabinet Picture [*by Stothard*] of Chaucer's Designs is indeed, the most extraordinary production of the Age & perhaps it contains a greater combination of excellencies than any one Painting of *any* Age. You must know that I give myself great Credit for thinking of such a glorious Subject—it is true that it was sufficiently obvious—but, it is equally true that what is obvious is [not *del*] often overlooked.[3] I assure you it would give me much happiness to

---

[1] The 'Size' is given as 'k[*it*]. c[*at*]' and the 'Nᵒ' in the comprehensive list of his works is '246'. This information appears in 'Tho.º Phillips / 1795 / – / Catalogue of his Works' 'Copied from T. Phillips's original note-book. 1 23.ʳᵈ Sep.ʳ 1899' now in the National Portrait Gallery, London. I do not know where Phillips's original notebook is. The date of the portrait in this list is supposed to indicate 'When Painted', but apparently the entries are cumulative, for under 4 April 1807 are also three other portraits, and the previous date is 27 Dec. 1806. There are other portraits of 'M.r Blake' (No. 62, 25 Nov. 1797, ¾ size) and of 'W.m Blake Esq.' (No. 855, 2 July 1843, k.c.), the second one certainly and the first one probably not representing the poet.

In his account of Sir Thomas Lawrence's rise to fame in his *Lives*, vol. vi (1833), p. 193, Cunningham wrote: 'Phillips, too, had shown such poetic feeling in his portrait of Blake, as raised him high among his brethren.'

[2] This is probably one of a family of engravers named Hopwood, either James (?1752–1819) or one of his sons, James (*fl.* 1800–50) and William (1784–1853).

[3] The vexed history of the origin of Stothard's design was thus given by John Linnell: 'Cromec according to Blake employed or engaged him to finish [*NB*] the frescoes as he called it of the Canterbury Pilgrims for him for 20 Guineas with the understanding that the remuneration for the whole would be made adequate by the price to be paid to Blake for the Engraving which [Blake *del*] stipulated he should execute, but ... Cromec secretly negotiated with Bromley to engrave this subject from Blakes Drawing which he tried to obtain from Blake without paying more than the 20Gs but Blake who had some good reason to suspect Cromec refused to let him have it & Blake supposed that Cromek then went to Stothard and commissioned him to paint his Canterbury pilgrims of the size & character that it had been arranged by Blake to engrave his Drawing ... Stothard[*'s*] account of the affair ... [*was that*] when Cromec went to him to commission him to paint the subject having been disappointed in the trick he attempted with

shew this work of Art to *you*—I do think you would relish its humour exceedingly; it is the shy covert humour of Addison=the humour of refined, legitimate Comedy—you first smile, & *then* laugh.—

[The *del*] One half of Blake's Work is completed.¹ I shall not be able to publish it 'till the next Winter—² That 'wild & wonderful genius' is still in Fairy Land; still believing that what has been called *Delusion* is the only *Reality*! What has been called Fancy & Imagination the Eternal World! & that this World is the only Cheat, Imagination the *only Truth*! I intend to set off to Edinburgh in about a Month, &, if possible will make Sheffield in my way—I will then entertain you with the perusal of some of his Noble though extravagant Flights.³

17–20   I have enclosed a Prospectus of my new Work=⁴ Do give me *laud & praise*
April for its Composition. Lo, the advantages of humble Talent! too humble even to
1807 be noticed by the Edinburgh Review. To be serious, I congratulate you on the conduct of the Reviewers=⁵ I say *congratulate* you; for your Friends will now rally around you & protect your Poetical as much as (if there were an occasion) they would your Moral Character. If these *hired* Miscreants have done you an injury it is only with those who have neither Heads nor Hearts. A Reviewer is as incapable of destroying a love & relish of Poetry as he is of destroying the Poetic Character itself=The origin of one & of the other is equally Divine.

Blake he of course said nothing to Stothard about Blakes design though he must have suggested the size and treatment as they are so much alike' (see *BR*, 464). Thus Blake, at least, thought that *he* was the originator of the 'glorious Subject' for which Cromek gave himself such 'great Credit'.

¹ Evidently this means that Louis Schiavonetti had finished half his etchings (three proofs of which are dated 1 February and 1 June 1806) after Blake's twelve designs for Blair's *Grave*, which had been sold to Cromek in September 1805 (see *BR*, 166–7).
² Blair's *Grave* with Schiavonetti's etchings of Blake's designs was evidently published in the summer of 1808 (see *BR*, 190–5). Montgomery received a subscription copy, but, finding that 'several of the plates were hardly of such a nature as to render the book proper to lie on a parlour table for general inspection', he sold it shortly thereafter (*BR*, 194). Years later, Charles Lamb contributed 'The Chimney Sweeper' from *Songs of Innocence* to a charitable compilation by Montgomery called *The Chimney-Sweeper's Friend* (1824).
³ Cromek is not known to have owned any printed or manuscript works by Blake, so we can only guess that it was the *Poetical Sketches* (1783) or letters from Blake which he was going to show to Montgomery (see *BR*, 191).
⁴ This 'Prospectus of my new Work' might be either that of November 1805 for Blake's designs illustrating Blair's *Grave*, or, rather more probably, that of February 1807 for Bromley's engraving of Stothard's painting of 'The Procession of Chaucer's Pilgrims to Canterbury' (a copy is in the British Museum Print Room pressmark 1890 e 2). His puffing did not escape scatheless, for a reviewer in the *Antijacobin Review*, xxxi (Nov. 1808), accused Cromek of dispensing 'quackery' in his 'Advertisement' to *The Grave* (see *BR*, 201).
⁵ The third edition of James Montgomery's *The Wanderer of Switzerland, and Other Poems* (1806) had been impatiently reviewed [by Jeffrey] in the *Edinburgh Review*, ix (Jan. 1807), 347–54; this 'sickly affectation of delicacy and fine feeling' is 'a feeble outrage on the public' (p. 347).

I am certain—and it is the opinion of M.ʳ Roscoe[1] & M.ʳ Blake as well as myself—that your volume will *command* the applause & admiration of all good Men, & of all Lovers of the Higher kinds of Poetry; and indeed the suffrage of this sort of Men is the only Reputation worth cultivating and enjoying. For, what is Fame? Being talked of by Ignorance? No! Milton says it is the approbation of 'Fit audience tho' few'.[2] These few of all Ages being secured all the rest follow. Besides my dear Sir, would it not be *unreasonable* to have received such a gift as you have from the inspirer of all good gifts & to expect to enjoy it without a drawback! The value of genius is considerably enhanced by its rarity—it is by no means a common thing—No Age every [*sic*] produced many great Minds & few Ages have produced any—As there can be but few Men of Genius so, I grant, to be one of them, is to be, as far as relates to this World, unhappy, unfortunate; the Mock & scorn of Men; always in strife & contention against the World & the World against him; but, as far as relates to another World, to be one of these is to be Blessed! He is a Pilgrim & stranger upon Earth, travelling into a far distant Land, led by Hope & sometimes by Despair but—surrounded by Angels & protected by y.ᵉ immediate Divine presence he is the light of the World. therefore Reverence thyself, O Man of Genius!—

There exists in this Country a vast, formidable Party with the Edinburgh Reviewers at their Head who contemn, & to the utmost of their power spread abroad their contempt for *Poets & Poetry*, & of all the Works of Fancy & Imagination[,] denying & blaspheming every power of the Mind except reasoning & thence[?] demonstrating their Design is to depress true Art & Science & to set up false Art & science in their stead—The false art & the true Art are the Tares & Wheat—the encouragement which Men of Genius receive from Men of the World is the same encouragement as the Wheat receives from the Tares: they *must* grow together 'till the time of Harvest—It was so with Cowper's Works; it will be so with yours—For do you not remember when that eminent Bard first published, the Reviewers treated him with the most marked Contempt saying, that for any thing they knew M.ʳ Cowper might be a very good sort of a Country Gentleman & a very honest Man—but they advised him to lay down his Pen & never to reassume it, for certainly, he had not the remotest pretensions to Poetry!![3] In despite of these *Toothless* Mumblers of Reputation Cowper's *Soul*

[1] William Roscoe (1753–1831), a Liverpool merchant and patron of Fuseli, subscribed to the *Grave* designs, after Cromek called on him with an introductory letter from Fuseli dated 16 July 1806 (*BR*, 179).

[2] This phrase from *Paradise Lost* was used as the motto for Blake's advertisement of his 'Exhibition of Paintings in Fresco' (1809).

[3] The *Critical Review*, liii (April 1782), 289, said that Cowper's *Poems* (1782) were 'coarse, vulgar, and unpoetical, no better than a dull sermon'. Similarly, the *Antijacobin Review*, xxxi (Nov. 1808), 234 concluded that Blake's 'dedication' to *The Grave* was 'abortive'; 'Whatever license we may allow him as a painter, to tolerate him as a poet would be insufferable' (*BR*, 208).

of Poetry soared far, very far above mortal Ken, and the Muse of Montgomery will fly to an immeasurable height even with the Weight of an Edinburgh Reviewer at her Tail.*

I have just finished an engraved Portrait of the late benevolent Dr Currie of Liverpool[1]—I wish I knew how to send you a Print of it.

Do you ever see My Friend Chantrey?[2] If you do ask when I am to see him in Town—

Have the goodness to make my best Respects to the Ladies I had the pleasure of seeing with you at Sheffield, & accept my very good and kind Wish yourself—

I am Dear Sir

Your most ob! hble Serv!

R. H. Cromek

London

64, Newman Street

April 17.th 1807.

Since I wrote the above Blake's Drawings for 'The Grave' have been presented to the Queen & Princess at Windsor—I received a Letter from Miss Planta,[3] stating Her Majesty's wish that Mr Blake would dedicate the Work to Her[4]—This circumstance has so much pleased Blake that he has already

* Pray pardon this Boyish-Kite-ish allusion–

---

[1] The portrait of 'James Currie, M.D. F.R.S.', 'Engraved by R. H. Cromek' and 'respectfully Inscribed by Permission to Wm Roscoe', was 'Published March 2.nd 1807, by R. H. Cromek, 64 Newman Street, Oxford Street, Price 10.6.' (A copy is in the British Museum Print Room.)

[2] The sculptor Sir Francis Legatt Chantrey (1781–1841) grew up near Sheffield and often returned on professional visits.

[3] Perhaps she was Margaret Planta, English teacher to the Royal Nursery until 1812 (as I am informed by Mr Robert Mackworthy Young, librarian, Windsor Castle). The correspondence concerning permission to dedicate Blake's *Grave* designs to the queen does not survive in the Royal Archives. The copy of *The Grave* for which the queen subscribed (according to the 1808 subscription list) does not appear in the royal collections or in the British Library, and it was not listed in the catalogue of the queen's anonymous posthumous sale at Christie's, 19 June 1819 ff.

[4] Ozias Humphry's letter to 'D[ea]r William' of 15 June 1806 was associated with William Blake (*BR*, 178–9) chiefly because of the alleged identification of what it calls 'your Copy of my Statement' which 'I shall without hesitation submit . . . to the Queen & all the Royal Family' with the dedication of Blake's designs to Blair's *Grave* 'To the Queen'. However, we now know from this April 1807 letter that this dedication was submitted to the Queen by Cromek, not by Humphry, apparently soon after Blake's poem and design for it were made, in April 1807, not in June 1806. It seems likely, therefore, that this letter from Ozias Humphry to Dear William of 15 June 1806 has nothing to do with William Blake.

In March, Hoppner had presented Stothard's 'Canterbury Pilgrims' painting to the prince of Wales, who permitted Cromek to dedicate the print to him (according to an article dated 21 March 1807 from an unidentified source found in the Whitley Papers produced a *Design* for the Dedication[1] & a poetic Address to the queen marked with his usual Characteristics—Sublimity, Simplicity, Elegance and Pathos, his wildness *of course*. I shall transcribe the Lines=I have only to request that you will not suffer them to be copied—

To The Queen.

The Door of Death is made of Gold
That Mortal Eyes cannot behold;
But when the Mortal Eyes are clos'd,
And cold, and pale, the Limbs repos'd,
The Soul awakes, and wond'ring, sees
In her mild Hand the golden Keys:
The Grave is Heavn's golden Gate,
And rich, and poor, around it wait;
O Shepherdess of England's Fold
Behold this Gate of Pearl and Gold.

To dedicate to England's Queen
The Visions that my Soul has seen,
And by [their *del*] Her kind permission, bring
What I have borne on solemn Wing
From the vast Regions of The Grave,
Before Her Throne my Wings I wave,
Bowing before my Sovereign's Feet[:]
'The Grave produc'd these Blossoms sweet'
'In mild repose from Earthly strife',
'The Blossoms of Eternal Life'.[2]
Your Majesty's devoted Subject and Servant

William Blake

Poor Opie was Buried toDay—[3] I understand he died worth 10,000£[.] M.ʳˢ Opie produced 400£ last Year by her Writings![4]

(BMPR) by S. M. Bennett, 'Thomas Stothard, R.A.' (California (Los Angeles) Ph.D., 1977), p. 226).

[1] This design (now in the British Museum Print Room) is reproduced, *inter alia*, in *BR* at p. 184.
[2] Except for minor variants of punctuation, capitalization, and spelling, the poem was published in the same form in Blair's *Grave* (1808), omitting the prose subscription. De Quincey quoted Blake's dedication to *The Grave* in his anonymous 'Sketches of Life and Manners, from the Autobiography of an English Opium-Eater', *Tait's Edinburgh Magazine*, vii (March 1840), 166.
[3] John Opie (born 1761), R.A., died on 9 April 1807, and at one o'clock 'on the 20th instant his remains were removed from his late residence, to St. Paul's Cathedral' with great pomp and buried near Sir Joshua Reynolds (*Gentleman's Magazine*, lxxvii, no. 1 [April 1807], 387).
[4] Joseph Farington had heard by April 11 that 'Opie died worth property to the

This letter presents important new information of several kinds. For one thing, it allows us to establish the date of composition of Blake's water-colour vignette and his dedication for Blair's *Grave* between 17 and 20 April 1807.[1] It indicates as well that no substantive changes in the poem were made between its rapid transmission to Cromek in mid-April 1807 and its publication in the summer of 1808.

For another thing, it suggests a connection between Blake and James Montgomery and Blake's admiration for Montgomery as a 'Man of Genius', of which we should not otherwise have known. Cromek's letter implies an easy and personal contact between the two men.

More important, the letter suggests a breadth of intellectual sympathy between Cromek and Blake not elsewhere apparent. The admiration which Cromek expressed for Blake's extraordinary powers is remarkably acute, even though balanced by a tolerant amusement at Blake's lack of worldliness. Cromek's recognition of Blake's 'wonderful genius' expressing itself in 'Noble . . . Flights' marked by 'his usual Characteristics—Sublimity, Simplicity, Elegance and Pathos'—this recognition is very remarkable for 1807 and demonstrates that Cromek's taste and judgement were valuable and independent, however subservient they might be at times to his worldly motives. This emphasis upon the purely aesthetic is a useful reminder of what may have drawn Blake to a man who seems in many of his dealings to have been characterized primarily by a low cunning.

Much of the tone and language of Cromek's letter is strikingly Blakean. Not only is Cromek intimately aware of small details of Cowper's life, as Blake would have been from helping Hayley with his biography of Cowper, but the distinction he draws through Cowper's example between contemporary notoriety and eternal fame is one close to Blake's heart, and, one might have thought, far from the ambitions of a worldly publisher. When he quotes Blake as asserting

amount of £12000' and that 'The last year she [*his widow (1769–1853), the novelist*] recd. £400', presumably for her *Simple Tales* (1806).

The Cromek letter, in Sheffield Public Library, transcribed here from a photocopy by permission of the City Librarian, was pointed out to me by Dr Robert Woof and published with much of the context given here in *Modern Philology*, lxxi (1974), 372–7.

Montgomery was involved in Cromek's edition of *The Grave*, for Cromek quoted eight lines of verse by Montgomery on the verso of the typeset title-page of the book.

[1] The only other contemporary manuscript of the poem which has been traced is in an unknown hand, also without substantive variants, in the Flaxman Collection in the British Library (Add. MSS 39,788, fo. 89). On the date of Blake's dedication to *The Grave*, *BR* (178) guessed inaccurately.

that 'Fancy & Imagination [*are*] the Eternal World! & that this World is the only Cheat', Cromek is anticipating what Blake wrote only a few years later, that 'Visionary Fancy or Imagination is ... the Eternal nature', and that 'this world of Dross is beneath my Notice'.[1]

Yet more strikingly, when he is offering comfort to Montgomery for the attacks of the *Edinburgh Review*, Cromek might almost be speaking in Blake's voice. The poet as 'a Pilgrim & stranger upon Earth', 'in strife & contention against the World', a man particularly 'Blessed! . . . & protected by yͤ immediate Divine presence', is a peculiarly Blakean idea: 'One Power alone makes a Poet—Imagination The Divine Vision.'[2] This literal identification of the poet and the prophet was very unusual in 1807.

Similarly Blakean is Cromek's attack upon those who show 'their contempt of *Poets & Poetry*, . . . blaspheming every power of the Mind except reasoning & thus demonstrating their Design is to depress true Art & Science & to set up false Art & Science in their stead'. Blake denounced 'those who pretend to despise the labours of Art & Science, which alone are the labours of the Gospel'.[3] And the apocalyptic reference to 'the time of Harvest', when the Wheat will be winnowed from the Tares (from Matthew 13: 26–30), seems astonishing in the worldly Cromek, though it is the very heart of Blake's poems of the time, such as *Milton* (1804–?8), which concludes with 'the Great Harvest & Vintage of the Nations'. In Blake, too, the end of the world comes about through art: 'The Last Judgment is an Overwhelming of Bad Art & Science.'[4]

It is thus plain from this letter that Cromek and Blake spoke the same language, that Blake expressed his unworldly ideas openly, and that his ideas were echoed more literally by R. H. Cromek than by almost any other man of his generation. The grounds for sympathy between the two men are surely plain.

Between 17 and 20 April, 'Blake's Drawings for "The Grave"' were presented to the Queen, permission was given to dedicate the edition to her, and Blake 'produced a *Design* for the Dedication' and the

---

[1] 'Vision of the Last Judgment' (1810), part c (*Notebook*, p. 69); Public Address (*c.* 1811), part uu (*Notebook*, p. 20).

[2] Annotation (1826) to Wordsworth, *Poems* (1825), p. 1.

[3] *Jerusalem* (1804–?20), pl. 77; cf. *Descriptive Catalogue* (1809), Paragraph 51, and letter of 11 Dec. 1805.

[4] 'Vision of the Last Judgment' (1810), part x (*Notebook*, p. 94). In chap. 8 of his *Island in the Moon* (?1784), Blake quoted from an untitled poem by Chidiock Tichborne: 'My crop of corn is but a field of tares' (Henry Wotton, *Reliquae Wottonianae* [1685], 395–6).

dedicatory poem. Blake sent the drawing as well as the poem to Cromek, accompanied by a letter requesting four guineas for what Cromek called 'the *sketched vignette*, ded^n to the Queen' (i.e. it was not a finished or whole page drawing). The amicable relationship between Blake and Cromek implied by Cromek's letter was abruptly terminated by a letter which Cromek wrote to Blake a few weeks later, probably early in '*May*, 1807':

I rec^d, not with^t great surprise, your letter, demanding 4 guineas for the *sketched vignette*, ded^n to the Queen. I have returned the drawing w^h this note, and I will briefly state my reasons for so doing. In the first place I do not think it merits the price you affix to it, *under any circumstances*. In the next place I never had the remotest suspicion that you c^d for a moment entertain the idea of writing *me* to supply money to create an honour in w^h I cannot possibly participate. The Queen allowed *you*, not *me*, to dedicate the work to *her!* The honour w^d have been yours exclus^y, but that you might not be deprived of any advantage likely to contribute to your reputation, I was willing to pay Mr. Schiavonetti *ten* guineas for etching a plate from the drawing in question.

Another reason for returning the sketch is that *I can do without it*, having already engaged to give a greater number of etchings than the price of the book will warrant; and I neither have nor ever had any encouragement from *you* to place you before the public in a more favourable point of view than that which I have already chosen . . .

I have imposed on myself . . . in believing you to be one altogether abstracted from this world, holding converse w^h the world of spirits!—simple, unoffending, a combination of the *serpent* and the *dove*. I really blush when I reflect how I have been cheated in this respect . . .

Why sh^d you so *furiously rage* at the success of the little picture of 'The Pilgrimage?' 3,000 people have now *seen it and have approved of it*. Believe me, yours is '*the voice of one crying in the wilderness!*'

Cromek's tactless, not to say impertinent, letter to Blake must have caused a permanent breach in their relationship. More important, Blake was discouraged by this experience from appealing directly to the public, and he only made one more attempt to do so, in his disastrous exhibition of 1809. The obscurity and poverty of Blake's last years are thus in part attributable to Robert Hartley Cromek.

The 1807 letter to Montgomery indicates that Cromek's feelings toward Blake were yet admiring, if ambivalently so, as late as a few weeks or days before Blake offered his vignette frontispiece to *The Grave* to Cromek. One of the best-known quarrels in literature thus seems to have boiled over very abruptly, though it had been long simmering. Doubtless the causes were that Cromek simply did not believe

Blake's claim that 'Imagination [*is*] the *only Truth*' and that he acted
on the assumption that he had 'been cheated' by Blake's claim to have
held 'converse w^h the world of spirits'. He was concerned with issues
which 'come home, more immediately, to my business & bosom' (as he
wrote on 16 December 1808). The letter to Montgomery indicates that
Cromek's admiration for Blake's genius was honest enough, though
his use of that genius was not. It was in significant part Cromek who
sent Blake like a prophet '*crying in the wilderness*'. As Cromek said in his
letter, this is 'the encouragement which Men of Genius receive from
Men of the World . . . the same encouragement as the Wheat receives
from the Tares'.

The price Cromek had to pay for the etchings of Blake's designs is
suggested by a letter his Italian engraver wrote him on Tuesday 21 July
1807:

Sir
    Thank[*s*] to God I have nearly completed the last judgment as you may see
by the proof which I send you by favour of your Sister, and on which I shall be
glad to know your opinion. As to what degree of plaisure I have found in
Engraving it you may easily conseive it from the accuracy of the outline, the *21*
truth of the light and shadow, and the magical way with which the effect of *July*
[*h*]armony is contrived in the Drawing[.]   *1807*
    It is useless for me to mentione the quantity of work that there is; you are an
Artist and can judge as well as myself, and therefore am persuaded that you
will find Sixty Guineas a very reasonable price.
Brampton   I remain Sir
    21! July 1807   Your[*s*] very Sincerely
                                L. Schiavonetti[1]

The price of etching Blake's 'Last Judgment' design is likely to have
been higher than those for the other plates, for 'the quantity of work'
for an engraver in it considerable exceeds that for the other plates. If
Cromek paid £60 for 'The Last Judgment', he may have paid about £40
for the others, or say £540 for all thirteen plates.

One of the earliest periodical puffs for Blake's designs for Blair's
Grave appeared in *The Monthly Literary Recreations* for September 1807:

    Shortly will be published, The Grave, a Poem, by Robert Blair. To be
printed in Imperial quarto, in Ballantyne's best manner, illustrated by twelve *September*
exquisitely finished etchings, by the celebrated Schiavonetti, from Original *1807*
Drawings, by William Blake, and a fac simile of Blair's hand writing, from the

---

[1] Quoted from the letter in my own collection.

Original Manuscript; with a Preface, containing Remarks on the Designs by
Henry Fuseli, Esq. R.A.[1]

Two aspects of this puff are particularly interesting (besides the
greater importance attached to Schiavonetti's name than to Blake's):
first, Cromek's name is not mentioned, and, second, the 'fac simile of
Blair's hand writing' was not published, though the portrait-frontis-
piece of Blake (omitted in this puff) was. This suggests that the
portrait was substituted for the handwiring facsimile some time after
the puff was written.

Sixteen months after his Birmingham expedition to promote his
edition of Blair's *Grave* and collect subscriptions for it, Cromek
placed an advertisement for it in Cowdray's *Manchester Gazette* for
7 November 1807 (p. 1) in terms very similar to those of the second
Prospectus of November 1805 and the Birmingham advertisements:

The Subjects proposed to be engraved:

7
November
1807

1. The good old man dying.
2. The strong and wicked man dying.
3. Christ descending into the grave, with keys of death and hell.
4. The valley of death.
5. Death's door.
6. The Counsellor, King, Warrior, Mother, and Child in the tomb.
7. The soul suspended over the body, unwilling to part with life.
8. The meeting of a family in Heaven.
9. A skeleton discovering the first symptoms of re-animation.
10. The soul exploring the caverns of death.
11. The last judgment.

☞   The original drawings may be seen at Mr Ford's, Bookseller, Market-
street-lane, where subscribers' names are received.

Notice that No. 9, 'A skeleton discovering the first symptoms of re-
animation', has not yet been put first and identified as the title-page
design. Note also that Phillips's portrait of Blake, painted in April
1807 and exhibited in May, had apparently not yet been given to
Cromek (see *BR*, 208) or been chosen as the frontispiece for the
edition.

In the list of subscribers the given names of some are reduced to
initials, that of 'Thomas Lawrence' to 'J. Lawrence', and Thomas
Hope and William Locke are omitted.

Cumberland twice described Blake's techniques. Once he wrote

[1] *Monthly Literary Recreations*, iii (Sept. 1807), 239.

out '*Blakes* Instructions to Print Copper Plates'.[1] Another time he gave 'Blake's directions for making lithographs':

White Lyas—is the Block[;] draw with Ink composed of Asphaltum dissolved in dry Linseed Oil—add fine venetian Tripoli & Rotten Stone Powder. Let it *1807* dry. When dry saturate the stone with water and Dab it with the broad Dabber, and cover it very thinly with best Printers Ink—and Print as a block— of Blake.[2]

Blake must have explained his method 'for making lithographs' about 1807, for these 'directions' are on a copy of his lithograph of 'Enoch' which was made about 1807. Further, the technique of printing from lithographs had been introduced into England only about 1800, and Blake was among the first English artists to experiment with it. He used the technique only once, with his 'Enoch' print, but George Cumberland's son used it to reproduce his father's *Scenes Chiefly Italian* (1821).

In the concluding number (1 August 1807) of *The Artist* (p. 11), Cromek managed to insert into 'an account of the principal Public Undertakings in the Arts of Design, which fall at present under the *1* knowledge of the Artist [*i.e. Prince Hoare*]', under Engravings, an *August* announcement of 'Designs for Blair's Poem of The Grave', with no *1807* indication of the designer.

On 17 November 1807 Cromek wrote to Archibald Constable, one of the publishers of *The Grave*: 'The Grave is going on very well. I shall soon write to Ballantyn[e] about printing it.[3] The most important object with me now is *Burns's Manuscript*. . . . I got 72 subscribers to *The Grave* at Manchester in less than 3 Weeks.'[4]

As late as 28 May 1808, when Cromek must have been on the verge

---

[1] See p. 11 above.

[2] Quoted from a photograph (generously sent me by its owner, the late Mr Edward Croft-Murray) of the inscription in Cumberland's hand on the verso of a copy of Blake's only lithograph, of 'Enoch' (1807).

Lias is a limestone rock found in the South of England which C. Hullmandel, *The Art of Drawing on Stone* [1824], 2, says 'is too soft and porous' for printing, compared with the German stone; 'Tripoli' or 'Rotten Stone' is a fine earth used as a powder for polishing metals. The ink here seems very unusual.

[3] James Ballantyne (1772–1833, Scott's printer) was announced as the printer of *The Grave* in the *Literary Panorama* for November 1807 (col. 304), but Thomas Bensley, who had been named in the 1805 prospectus, was the eventual printer.

[4] Quoted from a photocopy of the manuscript in the National Library of Scotland. The Burns MS was edited by Cromek and published in *Reliques of Robert Burns* (1808), with an advertisement for *The Grave*. *The Grave* had sixty-nine subscribers from Manchester.

of giving a firm print-order for Blair's *Grave*, he was still soliciting new subscriptions in the *Wakefield Star and West-Riding Advertiser*:

BLAIR'S GRAVE.

MR. CROMEK

Begs to inform the Subscribers at Wakefield and its Vicinity, to the New and
28 Splendid Edition of this POEM, that it will be published in London, on the 1st
May Day of July next; and that it will be delivered to them with all possible Speed.
1808
    Gentlemen who wish to possess this valuable Work, are respectfully apprised that on the Day of its Publication, its Price will be advanced from 21. 2s. to 21. 12s. 6d. Mr. Cromek will receive Names till the 1st of July at the Original Subscription Price, No. 64, Newman-Street, Oxford-row, London.
    The Work is printing in the most elegant Style, by *BENSLEY*, in Imperial Quarto, and illustrated by 13 Engravings, executed from the original Designs of William Blake.

    Notice that now the work is 'illustrated by 13 Engravings', though only six months before (7 November 1807) it was said to consist of only 'twelve . . . Engravings'. The new plate was not 'from the Original Design of William Blake' but from Phillips's portrait of Blake.
    Another Cromek advertisement for *The Grave* appeared in the *Bristol Gazette, and Public Advertiser* for 9 June 1808:

FINE ARTS

Thirteen very high-finished Engravings, in Imperial Quarto, executed by
9 *Schiavonetti*, V.A.[1] from sublime Compositions, by *Blake* illustrative of Blair's
June Poem, 'The Grave,' are now publishing by Subscription, in London. Impres-
1808 sions may be seen for a few days
                At Mr. Barry's Reading-Rooms,
                Bristol.
The Work has been honoured with the Subscriptions and Patronage of the President and principle [*sic*] Members of the Royal Academy of Painting, in London.
    The Engravings are completed,[2] and the Work will be published in about six weeks. Price to Subscribers £2. 2s. To Non-Subscribers, £2. 12s. 6d.

    The designs have been elevated from 'vigorous and classical' (28 July 1806) to 'sublime' and the publication date has been abruptly post-poned from 1 July (announced on 28 May 1808) to about 21 July, but the other details are much as before. It is notable, however, that Cromek gives no indication of where to subscribe.

---

[1] Schiavonetti was a member of the Venetian Academy.
[2] The plates are all dated 1 May 1808.

Three weeks later on Thursday 30 June, Cromek announced in the same journal that the exhibition of the engravings had been moved, and he carefully indicated the four agents for his subscriptions, but the announced date of publication is unchanged.

FINE ARTS.

MR. CROMEK begs to inform the lovers of the fine Arts in Bristol and its vicinity, that the series of thirteen highly finished ENGRAVINGS, executed by *24* S[*c*]*hiavonetti*, from the spirited and masterly sketches of *Blake*, illustrative of *June* Blair's poem, 'The Grave;' may be seen at Mr. HOBDAY's painting rooms in *1808* Small-Street, til[*l*] the time of their publication. The poem will accompany these prints, printed by Bensley, in his best manner, in large quarto.

Mr. HOBDAY has kindly undertaken to receive the names of those Gentlemen who wish to possess the work. Subscriptions are also received by Mr. NORTON, Mr. SHEPPARD, and Mr. BARRY, Booksellers.

'Till [*sic*] the 21st of July, the price will be 21.2*s*. after that period 21.12*s*. 6*d*.

Mr. Cromek cannot leave this city, without acknowledging his obligations to some of the principal gentlemen in it, who have not only promoted this undertaking with great zeal, but have also shewn much kindness to himself.

Bristol, June 24th, 1808.

On Saturday 2 July Cromek wrote to William Roscoe's son in Liverpool:

My work of 'The Grave' is on the verge of Publication—I am exceedingly busy about it. In about a month I shall serve the Birmingham Subscribers with their Copies, & shall then make the best of my way to Liverpool—*You* will *2nd* rejoice to be told that it has been a very lucrative & that it will be a very *July* honourable Speculation—[1] *1808*

Cromek's statements that the book was 'very lucrative' and 'very honourable' are particularly interesting in the context of his letter of May 1807 in which he claimed that he had commissioned more 'etchings than the price of the book will warrant' and tried to refute Blake's charge that he (Cromek) had imposed on Blake.

The first review of *The Grave*, by Leigh Hunt's brother Robert, was announced in the Hunts' new journal *The Examiner* for 31 July (p. 494): *31* 'Mr BLAKE's edition of BLAIR's *Grave* shall be noticed in our next.' *July* The article appeared on Sunday 7 August as *1808*

Blake's Edition of Blair's Grave[.]

On 11 August 1808 Cromek wrote from London to James Montgomery in Sheffield: 'I am ready to die with the fatigue of packing

---

[1] Quoted from a xerox of the MS in Liverpool City Library.

books. . . .' He apparently carried this letter with him on his trip North when distributing *The Grave* to subscribers, for he added a postscript in 'Manchester 28 Sept.': 'On hearing that your book [*i.e. copy*] of "The Grave" still remained in London, I sent for it to this Place. I now forward it & hope you will receive it safe—.'[1]

On Saturday 13 August 1808 Cromek in London sent to Thomas Bewick, Engraver, in Newcastle

a parcel containing the Copies of Blair's 'Grave' for the N. Castle Subscribers.

You will also receive your copy, of which I beg your acceptance. The work has produced a great effect amongst the best Judges here, and I hope it will meet with *your* decided approbation.

You will greatly oblige me by hiring a man to deliver the Books to the gentlemen to whom they are directed. I have marked on the back of each [*and in this letter*], what is to pay.

If you will collect the money in for me, you will do me a great Service, and I will do anything for you or any part of your family in London, with great readiness, in return.[2]

It may have been about September 1808 that a young Irish Law student in London sent a letter to his father about 'English Painters', in which he remarked that 'I have been always, from my childhood, . . . an enthusiastic admirer' of painting, perhaps encouraged by his father, who had some 'beautiful drawings of Mr. Westall'. He wrote particularly of 'Mr. Fuzeli' because 'you have heard so much' of him, though otherwise

I should certainly scarcely think he merited notice in this letter. He has modestly asserted, I am told, that he paints for posterity. I sincerely hope he will afford them more gratification than he does his contemporaries. He has a *September?* great admirer and defender, I believe the only one, in a Mr. W. Blake, a miser- *1808?* able engraver, and one of the most eccentric men of the age. This man has hailed him as the modern Michael Angelo. For my part, I have never seen a painting of Fuzeli, his Night-Mare excepted, which has certainly merit, which did not appear to be the crude efforts of a man writhing under an agonizing dream of indigestion.[3]

[1] Quoted from a photocopy of the original in Sheffield Public Library. Cromek sent George Cumberland's copy to him on 14 August 1808 (*BR*, 198).
[2] T. H. Cromek, 'Memorials of the life of R. H. Cromek' (1865), p. 14A, MS in the Possession of Mr Wilfred Warrington. Subsequent letters to Bewick of 25 June 1809 and 24 December 1810 (pp. 25, 56) make it clear that the Newcastle subscribers were slow to pay.
[3] Anon., *Letters from an Irish Student in England to his Father in Ireland* (1809), vol. ii, pp. 134, 139–40; the account is not altered in the Second Edition (1812), vol. ii, pp. 139–40, from which the details below are derived.
These amusing, anecdotal, undated letters were written 'by an Irish gentleman, who

He may have associated Fuseli with Blake because Fuseli had written an appreciation of Blake's designs for *The Grave* which was widely quoted in advertisements and reviews of it. The particular reference may have been to Blake's letter published in *The Monthly Magazine* in July 1806 in which he indignantly defended Fuseli's painting of 'Count Ugolino' and associated it with 'true art, such as it existed in the days of Michael Angelo and Raphael'. Blake had also ranked together 'Fuseli & Michael Angelo Shakespeare & Milton' in his manuscript Public Address (*Notebook*, p. 62), but it is likely that the student's information derived from gossip.

Cromek inscribed a subscriber's copy of Blair's *Grave*: 'T. Philips, Esq., R.A. from his greatly obliged servt R. H. Cromek, July 15th 1808' *15 July 1808* (now owned by Professor Robert N. Essick), probably in gratitude for the gift of the frontispiece painting.

James Montgomery was evidently favourably impressed by the copy of Blair's *Grave* which Cromek had sent him in August, for Cromek wrote to him on 16 December 1808:

Your Criticism on 'The Grave' M.ʳ Roscoe put into my hands at Liverpool. He *16 December 1808* was not less pleased with it than myself: It is very able and very friendly; but much as I value it, I value your Remarks on the *Reliques* infinitely more, because *they* come home, more immediately, to my business & bosom.[1]

At *The Exhibition of the Royal Academy*, [May] M.DCCCIX, The Forty First, the picture listed in the catalogue as no. 472 was 'Portrait of W. Blake— *W. Fraser*' of 17 Woodstock Street, Bond Street. Little more is known of W. Fraser beyond that he also exhibited pictures at the Royal Academy exhibitions of 1808 (at the same address) and 1811 (at 41, Bury Street, St James), and his picture has not been traced, so *May 1809* we can only guess whether it resembled the one by Phillips exhibited at the Royal Academy in May 1807 and engraved in Blair's *Grave*

lately prosecuted his legal studies in this country', i.e. in London (vol. i, p. iii); he is heir to an 'handsome property' from his uncle (vol. i, p. l), and he evidently came from north-western Ireland, for he travelled to London in 1807 by way of the Giant's Causeway, Belfast, and Dublin (vol. i, pp. 1–3). The editor remarks 'that the Original Letters . . . have undergone, for the sake of convenience and variety, some alterations of length and form' (vol. i, p. iii).

The author had visited Hayley at Felpham and remarked the two fine Romney portraits of Lady Hamilton in the Library (vol. ii, pp. 63–4) but not Blake's eighteen Heads of Poets there.

[1] Quoted from a photocopy of the original in Sheffield Public Library. Roscoe apparently gave this Montgomery letter to Cromek, for it does not survive with his other correspondence in Liverpool Public Library, and I have not traced it.

(1808). It might be the anonymous portrait of Blake in the collection of Professor Robert N. Essick, reproduced, *inter alia*, in *Blake Books* (1977).

The last reference to Blake in the letters to Hayley of E. G. Marsh concerns Hayley's decision to take most of the plates illustrating his *Life of George Romney* (1809) out of Blake's hands and place them elsewhere, chiefly with Caroline Watson. Blake had acquiesced in the decision, and on 28 March 1805 John Carr had assured Hayley that 'Mr Blake . . . observed that his feelings were not wounded, & that he was completely satisfied with your wishes' 'with respect to Caroline Watson's engraving' of new plates for Hayley's *Cowper*, but he probably would not have exhibited the same equanimity about Marsh's letter of Tuesday 9 January 1810: 'I have read with great interest your life of Romney and am sincerely obliged to you for so handsome a present. Caroline Watson's engravings are beautiful in the extreme; and you never made a happier exchange than when you employed her instead of Blake.'

9
January
1810

When he was collecting information in 1810 for his article in German about Blake, Crabb Robinson made transcripts on nine loose leaves watermarked AD/180[8?] (now in Dr Williams's Library), with minor careless variations from Blake's etched texts or from *Vaterländisches Museum*, of *'To the Muses' and 'Song [How sweet I roamed]' from *Poetical Sketches*; the dedication to Blair's *Grave*; 'The Little Black Boy', 'The Chimney Sweeper', 'Night', 'The Divine Image', and 'A Dream' from *Innocence*; 'Introduction', 'Earth's Answer', 'The Garden of Love', 'A Little Boy Lost', 'A Poison Tree', 'The Sick Rose', *'The Tyger', 'The Human Abstract', and 'Ah Sun Flower' from *Experience* (starred poems were printed in *Vaterländisches Museum*).

Perhaps a lost leaf contained *'Introduction', *'Holy Thursday', and 'Laughing Song' from *Innocence*, for these plus other lyrics headed 'Poems by William Blake' were transcribed in a little oblong 'M.S.' Commonplace book of Robinson, fos. 8–16. The poems in the volume are dated 1802 (the first) to 1866 (the last), and the one immediately after Blake's is dated 1816, suggesting that his poems were transcribed between 1801 and 1817. The order of the *Songs* poems in the 'M.S.' book (pl. 4, 19, 15, 9–10, 12, 20–1, 18, 30–1, 44, 50, 49, 39, 42, 47, 26 (NB), 43) follows the order in the loose leaves but is repeated in no extant copy of the *Songs*, though pl. 26, 'A Dream' from *Innocence*, is found thus eccentrically in *Experience* in Copies B–D. (On 20 April

1810 Robinson 'copirte Blake's Gedichte bey Mrs Iremonger', clearly from her Copy D.)

There are a number of minor errors in the transcriptions in the Robinson papers:

Title	*Striking Variants in Robinson's*	
	Loose Leaves	*'M.S.' Book*
'A Dream', l. 5	follorn (for 'fo[*r*]lorn')	
l. 8		'I heard I [for 'her'] say
l. 9		err (for 'cry'^a)
'The Little Black Boy'		
l. 27	ill (for 'I['']ll')	beard (for 'hair'^a)
'The Chimney Sweeper',		
l. 5	Dacte	Dacte (for Tom 'Dacre')
l. 16	wish (for 'wash')	
'Night', l. 30	eagels	Eagles (for 'angels')
l. 44	Grave after thee	Grieve after thee (for 'Graze after thee')
'The Divine Image'		omits ll. 12–15
'The Tyger', ll. 7–8	dares	dares (for 'dare')
'The Human Abstract', l. 3	could no where be	could no where be (for 'no more could be')

^a A rhyme word.

The reading 'Grazed after thee' caused difficulty also for the person(s) who made the MS facsimiles of the *Songs* about 1805 and 1821 and who read the phrase as 'graced after thee'.[1]

Robinson also wrote out (on a letter to him of 12 March 1810): (1) *America* pl. 5, ll. 1–18, pl. 8, ll. 1–13, 15–17, *pl. 10, ll. 5–12; (2) *Europe* *pl. 4, ll. 11–15 ('colourd'); and (3) most of the last paragraph of Blake's advertisement for his 'Exhibition of Paintings in Fresco', plus the manuscript date in the advertisement: 'May 15—1809' and the address of the exhibition: 'N° 28 Broad St.' (I have not found Robinson's transcript of the other passages from the advertment which he gives in *Vaterländisches Museum*.) Robinson may have seen Upcott's copies of *America* and *Europe*, and he may have acquired *Poetical Sketches* himself; he bought the *Descriptive Catalogue* on 23 April 1810.

[1] See 'Two Contemporary Facsimiles of *Songs of Innocence and of Experience*', *Papers of the Bibliographical Society of America*, lxiv (1970), 480.

In an article 'On Splendour of Colours, &c.' intended for the edification of young ladies of artistic inclination, Juninus wrote in the *Repository of Arts* for June 1810:

June
1810

Flaxman's *Illustrations of Homer, Æschylus, and Dante*, engraved by Piroli, of Rome; and Blake's plates from Blair's *Grave*, lately engraved, are excellent studies for a young artist. Blake has lately received much deserved commendation from Fuseli. Perhaps, this engraver has more genius than any one in his profession in this country. If he would study the ornamental requisites more, he would probably attain much higher celebrity than he has already acquired.[1]

See also
Addenda
(pp. 132–3)

11
August
1810

Cromek's obituary of Schiavonetti was praised in print next month by William Carey in his *Cursory Thoughts, on the Present State of the Fine Arts; occasioned by the Founding of the Liverpool Academy*, with special admiration for 'the taste and feeling' of the obituarist, who is also 'the publisher of *Blair's* Grave, with spirited engravings, by *Schiavonetti*, from *Blake's* masterly designs'.[2]

The mysterious Juninus showed surprisingly intimate knowledge of Blake and his profession in a dialogue, in *The Repository of Arts* for September 1810, between the well-informed Miss K and her pupil Miss Eve. Miss Eve draws a print from a portfolio which Miss K identifies as

The Fall of Rosamond, a stippled print. William Blake, *sculp*. Published by F. Macklin.[3] Underneath it are these lines:
'*Queen Eleanor*. Drink, ere this poniard searches every vein.
'*Rosamond*. Is there no pity?—None?—This awful silence
'Hath answer'd me, and I entreat no more.
'Some greater pow'r than thine demands my life.
'Fate summons me—I hear and I obey.
'O heaven! if crimes like mine may hope forgiveness,
'Accept a contrite heart!'———

[1] Juninus, 'On Splendour of Colours, &c', *Repository of Arts, Literature, Commerce, Manufactures, Fashions, and Politics*, ii (June 1810 Supplement), 408–9. The series by Juninus begins the issues of *The Repository of Arts* from 1809 through 1815.

[2] William [Paulet] Carey, *Cursory Thoughts* ... (Liverpool & London [1810]), p. 18; 'On Saturday the 11th [*of August 1810*], Mr. Carey's Essay, called "*Cursory Thoughts* ...*," was published by the Liverpool Booksellers, and on the 13th forwarded to Messrs. *R*. and *W. Dean*, Booksellers in Manchester', but a postscript was added later in August pp. [51–2].

[3] 'The Fall of Rosamond' was designed by Stothard, published 10 October 1783 by Thomas Macklin; the dialogue is quoted on the plate as it is by Juninus (except for punctuation, 'or' for 'ere', and 'mine' for 'thine', all improved by Juninus from the plate); the historical details are all new.

HULL's *Fall of Rosamond*, Act 5,

'Fair Rosamond, daughter of Lord Clifford and mistress of King Henry II.
said to have been concealed in a bower or labyrinth at Woodstock, to protect
her from the jealousy of the queen, died about the year 1170. By this lady the
king had two children, William Longue-espée, or Long-sword, Earl of Salisbury, and Geoffrey, Archbishop of York.

September
1810

'This print is solid, well drawn, and varied with much taste. How simple is
the design, and yet what elegance and feeling it displays!

'The same engraver executed a large print in the stroke manner from
Hogarth.[1] It represents a scene in the *Beggar's Opera*, first acted in 1727, with
the original performers, Mr. Thomas Walker, the first Macheath, Miss
Lavinia Fenton as Polly, Mrs. Egleton as Lucy, Mrs. Martin as Mrs.
Peachum, Mr. Hippesley as Peachum, Mr. Hall as Lockett, and Mr. Clark as
Filch. The point of time is when Polly appears on her knees before her father,
singing,

> 'O ponder well, be not severe,
> 'But spare a wretched wife;
> 'For on the rope that hangs my dear
> 'Depends poor Polly's life.'

'The Duke of Bolton, Miss Fenton's future husband, is represented in one of
the side boxes, as if admiring his destined spouse.

'This artist seems to have relinquished engraving, and to have cultivated
the higher departments of designing and painting with great success. His
works shew that he must have studied the antique with considerable attention.'

Miss *Eve*.—'If those ingenious men, the engravers, were to ask this man of
genius why he abandoned his profession, he might with truth answer to most
of those by whom it is followed, in the words of the poet:

> "I hear a voice you cannot hear,
> "That says I must not stay:
> "I see a hand you cannot see,
> "That beckons me away.["]'[2]

It is remarkable that Juninus and Miss K should have known that
Blake had 'relinquished engraving', for it is true that he signed no
commercial plate between 1805 (Hayley's *Ballads*) and 1814 (Flaxman's

---

[1] The *Beggar's Opera* plate was separately published 1 July 1790 by J. & J. Boydell,
24″ × 30″; the characters are identified in the text of Hogarth's *Works* (1790), where
the plate was also published, but the song is neither on the plate nor in the text of the
Works.

[2] Juninus, 'On Splendour of Colours, &c.', *The Repository of Arts, Literature, Commerce,
Manufactures, Fashions, and Politics*, iv (Sept. 1810), 130–1, part of a series which begins
each monthly issue of *The Repository*—see also June 1810.

Hesiod),[1] and he told Cumberland on 19 December 1808 that 'my time
... in future must alone be devoted to Designing and Painting'. His
cultivation of the 'higher departments of designing and painting' was
known chiefly to the few who saw his 1809 exhibition or the larger
number who saw reviews of it in *The Examiner* and elsewhere, but very
few of these would have agreed that he achieved 'great success' there—
The Examiner for 17 September 1809 called them 'a few wretched pictures ... "blotted and blurred," and very badly drawn'. Perhaps most
curious is Miss Eve's repetition of Rosamond's claim to supernatural
inspiration—'Fate summons me. I hear and I obey'—in her quotation
from Thomas Tickell's popular ballad 'Lucy and Colin', for Blake had
quoted the same quatrain about himself in his letter of 10 January 1802
to Thomas Butts. Juninus was clearly a sympathetic friend to Blake's
art and perhaps as well a friend to Blake.

It may have been not long thereafter[2] that fascicle 38 of Rees's
Cyclopaedia was published with 128 columns on the 'Italian School of
Engraving' and a substantial account of Schiavonetti:

> The chief of his *etchings* are, a set of twelve in small folio, from drawings by
> W. Blake, of which the subjects are taken from Blair's poem of the Grave.
> These are works of great merit, and (as we venture to pronounce) of lasting
> reputation ...
>
> Faithfully adhering to the character of art that is implied by the term *etching*,
> Schiavonetti is here slight and sketchy, and has produced his effects chiefly by
> the operation of aquafortis, with his usual fine feeling, and a congenial
> unstudied simplicity of style. The eye of discernment immediately sees that
> the same high finishing which he bestowed on his plates after Vandyke, was
> never intended, and that what was intended is precisely accomplished.

1811?
> Of this series of meritorious etchings, which were printed with Blair's poem
> and an able preface by the professor Fuseli, and published by Mr. Cromek,
> the subjects are 1. The Descent of Christ into the Grave; 2. The Descent of
> Man into the Vale of Death; 3. Death's Door; 4. The strong and wicked Man
> dying; 5. The good old Man dying; 6. The Soul hovering over the Body;
> 7. The Soul exploring the Recesses of the Grave; 8. The Counsellor, King,
> Warrior, Mother, and Child in the Tomb; 9. The Skeleton re-animated;
> 10. The Re-union of Soul and Body; 11. A family Meeting in Heaven; and
> 12. The Last Judgment.[3] These are preceded by a portrait of Mr. W. Blake,

---

[1] Blake's plate for Hayley's *Romney* (1809) was in fact finished by 1805—see his letters
of 1803–4.

[2] The date of composition of *c.* 1811 is derived from the facts that Schiavonetti
(d. 1810) is spoken of as dead and Cromek (d. 1812) and Bartolozzi (d. 1815) as if alive.

[3] The plates are given their titles and order from the description 'Of the Designs' in
Blair's *Grave* (1808), 33–6, rather than from the plates themselves, where they bear
somewhat different titles in a different order.

the poetic designer of the work, after T. Phillips, R.A. in which our engraver has manifested great judgment and taste. It is also an etching, treated in the vignette style, with small assistance from the graver and dry-point, where a certain degree of mellowness and blending were wanted, and the whole brought to a focus in the animated and thinking countenance which is the proper subject of the print. . . .

[*The folio engraving after Raphael's Cartoon is*] less elaborate than his prints from the pictures of Vandyke, though somewhat more so than his etchings after the poetical sketches of Mr. Blake.[1]

In an essay giving 'Hints on various Modes of Printing from Autographs' in the *Journal of Natural Philosophy, Chemistry, and the Arts*, xxviii (Jan. 1811), 56–9, George Cumberland remarked that the difficulty with many such modes of printing was that they would have had to be written backwards, and this 'would have demanded the talents of a Blake, who alone excels in that art'. *January 1811*

Blake's largest and most ambitious painting was 'The Ancient Britons', which he exhibited at his brother's house in 1809 and described at great length in his *Descriptive Catalogue* (1809), pp. 39–51. It was ten feet by fourteen (*BR*, 222), over one hundred times the size of his large designs for Milton and the Bible, and he was very proud of it: 'Mr. B. . . . defies competition in colouring.'[2] The painting is now lost,[3] but it aroused contradictory superlatives from four men who saw and commented on it. In his review of Blake's exhibition, Robert Hunt said that it was 'a complete caricature' (17 September 1809), and Robert Southey in 1847 called it 'one of his worst pictures,—which is saying much' (*BR*, 226), but in 1811 Crabb Robinson acclaimed it as 'His greatest and most perfect work' (*BR*, 451), and in 1870 Seymour Kirkup identified it as 'Blake's *Three Heroes of Camlan*' and called it 'his best work' (*BR*, 222). The subject illustrates his interest in Welsh and Druid matters which Blake developed after 1800, and according to Robert Southey

My old acquaintance William Owen, now Owen Pugh[e], who became rich [*in 1806,*] . . . found everything which he wished to find in the Bardic system, and

[1] Anon., 'Italian School of Engraving', Abraham Rees, *Cyclopaedia*, vol. xix (1819 [i.e. fascicle 38 issued in 1811?]), sig. 4b3ᵛ, 4b4ʳ.

According to the anonymous review of Rees's *Cyclopaedia* in *Philosophical Magazine*, lvi (1820), 218–24, the sections on French, Italian, and Other Schools of Engraving were written by John Landseer.

[2] *Descriptive Catalogue* (1809), Paragraph 87 (*William Blake's Writings* [1978], 854).

[3] A recreation of 'The Ancient Britons' seen on the wall of Blake's flat may be seen in Bo Lindberg's watercolour of 'Samuel Palmer climbing the stairs to Blake's flat in Fountain Court, Strand' (reproduced with 'Blake and the Ancients: A Prophet with Honour Among the Sons of God', *Huntington Library Quarterly*, xlvi [1983], plate 6).

there he found Blake's notions, and thus Blake and his wife were persuaded that his dreams were old patriarchal truths, long forgotten, and now re-revealed. They told me this. . . . [*BR*, 399]

Southey also said that the 'Welsh Triades', which Blake quotes (in his 'Exhibition of Paintings' advertisement) as the subject of 'The Ancient Britons', were translated for him 'no doubt by that good simple-hearted, Welsh-headed man, William Owen'.[1]

About a year after Blake's exhibition had closed, William Owen Pughe wrote in his diary on Wednesday 16 January 1811:

16. awn yn y prydnawn i weled vy mam: gadawwn ei lyvrau, ar y ford, i G. Chalmers. My mam druan yn wael iawn, yn gweddiaw am adu y byd hwn: doai vy çwaer Ann ac ei mab yno: gadwn gostrelaid gwin idi: gwystlwn vy
16 awran am $\frac{4}{2}$ i Dobree ar dyçwelyd; awn at W. Sharp, allan; a phan oeddwn wrth
January y drwi doai gwraig W. Blake i holi amdanaw o gylç y darluniad y 3 diangolion o
1811 Gamlan, a wnelai ei gwr imi: elai Anewrin i wahoddi I a C. Tuck i giniaw dydd Gwener.[2]

The relevant portion may be thus translated:

16. Went in the afternoon to see my mother . . . My poor mother is very ill and praying to leave this world . . . We promised to return again at 2 to Dobree; we were going out to W. Sharp and when we were at the door [*of his mother's House*] Mrs W. Blake came to ask about the painting of the 3 escapees [*or* prisoners] from Camlan that her husband was doing for me . . .

There are three points of particular interest about this diary entry. The first is that Mrs Blake knew Owen Pughe well enough to under-stand where to find him, though he was not then at his customary

---

[1] *BR*, 226. There was apparently no version in English of these Triads in Blake's time (see *William Blake's Writings* [1978], 820 n. 1), and, as we have no evidence that Blake knew Welsh, the translation must have been supplied to him by someone.

[2] Quoted from a reproduction of National Library of Wales MS 13248B, Pughe's diary for 1 Jan. 1811 to 13 April 1835. (A description of the forty-two volumes of Owen Pughe MSS may be found in the *Handlist of Manuscripts in the National Library of Wales*, Parts XXXII [?1978] and XXXIII [?1982], Supplement Series III, Numbers 32–3 of *The National Library of Wales Journal*, which specifies that the entries for '1811–22 appear to have been recopied by the diarist in 1824–5' [p. 537].) According to the *Dictionary of National Biography* ('1949–1950'), vol. xvi, p. 447, Owen Pughe attempted to reform Welsh orthography, substituting 'ç' for 'ch', 'v' for 'f', and 'z' for 'dd'. My learned friend and colleague Professor David Klausner assisted me with the transcription and provided the translation above.

The discovery of the Blake entry in Owen Pughe's diary was made by Professor James Hopkins, and he very kindly provided the information which enabled me to pursue the matter. Part of the present account is repeated from '"The Triumph of Owen": William Owen Pughe and Blake's "Ancient Britons"', *Cylchgrawn Llyfrgell Genedlaethol Cymru: The National Library of Wales Journal* xxvi (1985), 246–61.

lodging. The second is that William Owen Pughe commissioned Blake's painting, 'The Ancient Britons', a subject which is particularly suitable. Owen Pughe's authorship of *The Cambrian Biography*, or History of Celebrated Men Among the Ancient Britons (1803) makes the subject of 'The Ancient Britons' seem wonderfully appropriate. It is exceedingly likely, therefore, that Owen Pughe provided both the subject for the poem and the literary passage which it illustrates. There is, of course, no way of being sure whether the differences between the Welsh Triad and the English translation are due to Owen Pughe or to Blake—each is quite capable of making such changes. There is, for instance, nothing in the Welsh triad of the Romans whom Blake describes.

The date of the commission for 'The Ancient Britons' is obscure, for all we know of the painting are the descriptions by Blake and a few of his contemporaries. No preliminary or even clearly related drawing is known, though there surely must have been numbers of them. Almost certainly the design was commissioned after Blake returned from Felpham in 1803, probably after 1805, for there is no reference to it in the extensive records of Blake's life and correspondence of 1800–5. But a picture of this size argues considerable prosperity in the owner, if not in payment for it, at least in possession of a suitable place to hang it. As almost all Blake's other pictures are of cabinet or portfolio size for which his patrons paid him in advance (about a guinea per design), it is extremely unlikely that Blake would have embarked upon such a huge painting merely as a speculation, without a firm commission in hand. And it is virtually certain that William Owen had neither the cash nor the wall for such a work before 1806, when he inherited some property and changed his name to Pughe. Therefore it seems very probable that the commission for 'The Ancient Britons' was made by William Owen Pughe between 1806 and 1809, when the painting was exhibited. It is possible that William Owen and Blake knew one another before 1806, but Pughe's patronage must have been after that time. And apparently it was his only such commission, for no other work by Blake is known to have been owned by him.

The third important point about the diary entry is that though 'The Ancient Britons' had been exhibited in 1809, it was apparently not finished in January 1811, when Blake 'was [*still*] doing' it. (It is, of course, possible that Blake had made another version of the huge exhibition painting for Owen Pughe—he certainly made several versions of other designs, such as those for *Paradise Lost*—but, if so, no record of it has survived at all.) With such an enormous painting, it is not surprising that it was not quite finished when exhibited in 1809, or at any rate that Blake wished to add some more touches to it. But it does seem likely that the painting was eventually completed and delivered to William Owen Pughe, who had commissioned it. Presumably, therefore, it went to Wales, probably to his estate at Nantlynn, near Denbigh, and, if it has survived, one might expect to find it there.

Robinson's claim in *Vaterländisches Museum* in 1811 (*BR*, 441) that Blake's edition of Young's *Night Thoughts* was no longer to be found in the bookshops was premature, for on 27 December 1810 he acquired a copy, and it was offered, '*finely printed, with curious plates, designed and etched by Blake*' in boards, in Lackington's *General Catalogue* (1811), lots 264, 6569 (£2. 12s.), and in his *Catalogue of Books* (1815), lots 119, 8613 (£2. 2s.).

In his Diary for Sunday 24 May 1812 Crabb Robinson made notes about walking with Wordsworth across the fields to Hampstead Heath: 'I read W. some of Blake's poems[;] he was pleased with Some of them and consid^d B as hav^g the elements of poetry—a thousand times more than either Byron or Scott.' Many years later the publisher Edward Moxon sent Wordsworth a parcel of books which Wordsworth's friend Edward Quillinan happened to notice, and Quillinan wrote to Crabb Robinson: they included '*Blake's* Poems[1] . . . *some* of Blake's verses, illustrated in the book you possess, want in this publication the poetry of painting to support them . . .'[2] To this Robinson replied on 10 August 1848:

You speak more slightingly than I should [*have*] expected of Blake.[3] Recollect they are not to be considered as works of art. but as fragments of a shattered intellect. Lamb used to call him a 'mad Wordsworth'[.][4] Enquire of Mrs. W: whether she has not a copy of his *Catalogue*. If she has not, enquire of me hereafter.[5] Many years ago Mr. W: read some poems which I had copied and made a remark on them which I would not repeat to every one. 'There is no doubt that this man is mad, but there is something in this madness which I enjoy

---

[1] The poems might have been Wilkinson's edition of the *Songs* (?1843) or perhaps the seven poems reprinted in *The Harbinger*, vii (24 June, 8 July 1848), 57, 73.

[2] Quoted from the MS in Dove Cottage by Mark L. Reed, 'Blake, Wordsworth, Lamb, Etc.: Further Information from Henry Crabb Robinson', *Blake*, iii (1970), 78.

[3] Quillinan underlined 'Slightingly' and wrote in the margin in pencil: 'as usual a mistake of friend Crabbe's'.

[4] Lamb is not elsewhere recorded as having called Blake 'a "mad Wordsworth"'.

[5] Crabb Robinson may have given to Wordsworth one (?copy J) of the four copies of the *Descriptive Catalogue* which he had bought on 23 Apr. 1810.

more than the *Sense* of W: Sc: or Lord B:—['] I had lent him [*Blake*] when he died the 8vo Edit in 2 Vols: of W.W's poems. They were sent me by his widow with the pencil marginalia which I inked over. He admired W: W: 'tho an atheist' And when I protested against this sentence it was thus supported. 'Who ever worships nature denies God, for nature is the Devils work.' I succumbed, for he always beat me in argument. He almost went into a fit of rapture at the platonic ode.[1]

Much of this information about Blake is also given in Crabb Robinson's letter to Dorothy Wordsworth of 19 February 1826.

Only once after 1809 did Blake exhibit his pictures to the public. The spring exhibition of the Associated Painters in Water Colours included four pictures by him: 254, 'Sir Jeoffrey Chaucer and Twenty-seven Pilgrims'; 279, 'The Spiritual Form of Pitt guiding Behemoth'; 280, 'The Spiritual Form of Nelson guiding Leviathan'; 324, 'Detached Specimens of . . . "*Jerusalem*"'. The only known review of these pictures appeared in *The Lady's Monthly Museum* for June 1812. The anonymous author was clearly perplexed by works of such sublimity among genre scenes such as Holmes's 'Going to School', and landscapes, and historical pictures, and portraits, and it is notable not only that he mentioned Blake's works at all among 'productions, which the memory might feel most pleasure in dwelling on' but that he mentioned them in terms indicating such interest:

> No. 254. *Sir Geoffrey Chaucer and the Pilgrims*, by BLAKE, is a picture of mongrel excellence; yet has such a repulsive appearance, that we doubt most of our fair readers will scarcely view it with pleasure, unless they should be well acquainted with *Aunciente* tapestrye, to enter into its merits. That it is the work of genius, no one will deny; it possesses all the truth, the costume, and manners of the times; and the artist is perhaps worthy of the highest commendation for his industry, research, and correctness; but for our parts, we feel ourselves so perfectly satisfied with the same subject, as treated by Stothard, that we wish not to possess a picture whose greatest merit seems to be an imitation of the arts in their degraded state. Of the pictures 323 and 324 by the same artist, we must decline giving any criticism; we dare say they may be very fine; but they are also too sublime for our comprehension; we must therefore deprecate the mercy of the lovers of the Fuselian and the Angelesque.[2]   *June 1812*

This is a curious account in a number of respects. For one thing, what is meant by 'mongrel excellence'? I take it to mean the devotion

[1] See n. 2 on p. 68.
[2] Anon., 'The Water Colour Exhibitions', *The Lady's Monthly Museum*, NS, xii (June 1812), 344, a reference generously brought to my attention by my friend Mr Paul Miner.

of 'industry, research, and correctness' 'worthy of the highest commendation'[1] to 'an imitation of the arts in their degraded [*i.e.*
Aunciente *or mediaeval*] state' which forms an accurate though 'repul-
sive appearance'. To assert that it 'is the work of genius, no one will
deny' is very high praise, but the praise must have turned to jangling in
Blake's ears when it was coupled with preference for 'the same subject, as treated by Stothard', a preference so marked 'that we wish not
to possess a picture [*such as Blake's*] whose greatest merit seems to be
an imitation of the arts in their degraded state.'

The criticism of 'the pictures 323 and 324' is more perplexing on different grounds. If it refers to No. 324, Blake's 'Detached Specimens of
... "*Jerusalem*"', this is the only known allusion to them—we are not
even sure which *Jerusalem* plates were included in the exhibition. The
reference to them as 'too sublime for our comprehension' does not
assist much in their identification.

However, it seems likely that the numbers are mistaken—No. 323
has nothing to do with Blake. Probably the reviewer meant to refer to
No. 279–80, which are by Blake, the Spiritual Forms of Pitt and
Nelson. These are sufficiently sublime and idiosyncratic to perplex
the friendliest critic. Blake's early companion J. T. Smith spoke of
them as 'allegorical . . . pictures which the present writer, although he
has seen them, dares not describe' (*BR*, 451). The association of Blake
with his friend Fuseli and his admired Michael Angelo at least
indicates a context appropriate for Blake and a company in which he
would have been proud to be found.

When Blake's sometime patron and *bête noir* R. H. Cromek died in
March 1812, his widow was left in difficult circumstances, and
Stothard wrote in an undated letter that 'Mrs Cromack has (with a
view to Shivonetty [*Niccolo Schiavonetti*] proceeding on [it (*the engraving
of Stothard's Canterbury Pilgrims design*) imme]diately) sold blayrs grave
for one hundred & twenty pound [*to Ackermann*]',[2] who published it in
1813. On 30 December her neighbour Ralph Rylance of 34 Newman
Street wrote to William Roscoe, the Liverpool friend of Fuseli and
Cromek, that 'Mrs Cromek, the widow, is selling her late husband's
books and prints'. When Roscoe responded showing interest in

---

[1] Blake would have been pleased with the praise of his accuracy, for he boasts of his
Chaucer design in the *Descriptive Catalogue* (1809), paragraph 18, that 'the costume is
correct according to authentic monuments'.
[2] Quoted from the MS in an extra-illustrated set of Mrs Bray's *Life of Thomas Stothard*
(1851) in Boston Public Library; the letter is normalized in the book on pp. 141–3.

Cromek's prints and drawings, Rylance wrote again on Wednesday 3 February 1813 in phraseology which smacks of Cromek himself:

Dear Sir

The following is a list of the Principal things in Mrs Cromek's collection of Prints and Drawings.

Blake's original Designs for Blair's Grave with other curious Drawings of his, valued at thirty Pounds and likely to sell for a great deal more if ever the man should die. . . . These Sir are now on sale, and I suppose Mrs C. is rather urgent for the disposal of them, though she had assigned over the Chaucer engraving to her father who is to defray the further expenses and reimburse himself 'out of the first & readiest' as Burns says.[1]

3 February 1813

These 'original Designs for Blair's Grave' were probably the twenty (or perhaps forty) which Blake had made for the very modest price of £21. I do not know what 'other curious Drawings of his' Cromek may have had. Mrs Cromek's price of £30 was probably both modest and unrealistic. At any rate, Roscoe does not seem to have accepted the offer of Mrs Cromek's Blake drawings, which he had probably seen seven years before (see 16 July 1806), and they are next (and last) traced as a group in the Edinburgh sale by C. B. Tait of the property of the late Thomas Sivwright of Meggetland, 1–19 February 1835, lot 1835.[2]

On 24 May 1812 Crabb Robinson 'read W[*ordsworth*]. some of Blake's poems'. On 1[?] September 1862, Samuel Palmer wrote to Anne Gilchrist:

You have of course this anecdote—about Songs of Inn and Exp. Wordsworth said to a friend [*?Crabb Robinson*], 'I called the other day while you were out and stole a book out of your library—Blake's songs of Innocence'[.] He read and read and took it home and read and read again.[3]

Blake was commissioned by Longman to engrave seven plates to illustrate John Flaxman's article on 'Sculpture' for Abraham Rees's great *Cyclopaedia*, which had been appearing in Parts since 1802. For the earliest of these plates, he made a copy of the cast of the 'Laocoon' in the Royal Academy, working patiently among the students making their apprentice-drawings. According to p. '108' of the twenty-three pages remaining from the fragmentary ledger of 'Rees's Cyclopædia'

---

[1] Quoted from reproductions of the letters in Liverpool Public Library.

[2] The context is given in 'Thomas Sivwright and the Lost Designs for Blair's *Grave*', *Blake*, xix (1985–6), 103–6.

[3] *Letters of Samuel Palmer*, ed. R. Lister (Oxford, 1974), vol. ii, pp. 668–9. Crabb Robinson said on 19 Feb. 1826 that he gave Wordsworth 'some poems in MS' by Blake; for Wordsworth's opinion of the *Songs*, see *BR*, 536.

of July 1803–September 1839 among the Longman archives now in Reading University, on 'Aug 19 [*1815*] M.ʳ Blake was [*paid*]—for a plate of Sculpture [£]10 10'. The entry, like many others, has been deleted, perhaps indicating that it was transferred to another ledger, now lost. If Blake was paid at the same generous rate for the other six plates he made for the *Cyclopædia* in 1816–19, he must have received £73. 10s. 0d. for them all told. This payment, together with his other known receipts for commercial engravings of the time—Wedgwood's catalogue (1816), £30; and Flaxman's Hesiod (1814–17), also for Longman, £207. 8s. 0d. —brought his income for professional work to over £50 a year, a total which the Blakes probably found quite adequate. All these commercial commissions probably originated in the kindness of John Flaxman.

19 August 1815

On the same page of the ledger, among repeated entries for 'Beer' and 'Carr[*iage*]', is an enigmatic entry for '25 [*May 1815*] to Stamp for pay to Blake— – – 8[*d.*]', perhaps for the revenue stamp on a promissory note to Blake.

The information about the Blake entries and a xerox of them were generously provided by June Fullmer, who tells me that there is no other Blake reference in these records.

On 21 December 1817 Dawson Turner, the Yarmouth banker and autograph collector, wrote to William Upcott: 'You took, I think, from Yarmouth a list of 2 or 3 books to be got for me. Lackingtons, I see have a copy of the 1ˢᵗ edition of Blake's Blair's Grave at a price that seems to me cheap.'[1] Perhaps Upcott had talked about his father's friendship with Blake and his collection of Blake's works, urging Turner to write to Blake himself, for Blake wrote to Turner on 9 June 1818, evidently in reply to an enquiry, describing 'Those [*works*] I printed' for Upcott's father and detailing those still for sale. Turner is not known to have bought any work by Blake, but he did bind Blake's letter carefully with his autograph collection.

21 December 1817

The spread of interest in etching techniques like Blake's was remarked in Cumberland's note to his son George on 22 January 1819:[2] '—Tell *Blake* a Mr Sivewright of Edinburgh[3] has just claimed

---

[1] Quoted from the MS in the Huntington Library, pointed out to me by my friend Professor D. H. Weinglass. 'Lackingtons' is doubtless the Lackington Catalogue of 1817. On 25 May 1818 Turner thanked Upcott for sending 'the other books' but did not specify which they were.

[2] British Library Add. MSS 36,501, fos. 360–1. The blurred date-stamp was given, probably erroneously, as 1809 in the 1969 edition of *Blake Records*.

[3] He is probably the same as 'John Sivewright Teacher of Music' (*c.* 1770–1846),

in some[?] Philosophical Journal of Last Month As his own invention Blakes Method—& calls it Copper Blocks I think.'[1] 22 *January 1819*

A copy of the Upton engraving by Blake and Linnell in the collection of R. N. Essick is inscribed 'March. 1819—Unfinished Proof. must be returned to M.r J. Linnell.'[2] *March 1819*

On Thursday 7 January 1819 Isaac D'Israeli wrote to a dealer named Dyer:[3] 'M.r D'Israeli wants as soon as possible a copy of Blake's Young',[4] i.e. the *Night Thoughts* (1797). *7 January 1819*

What his father called Blake's 'designs' (*BR*, 243) Isaac D'Israeli's

author of *A Collection of Church Tunes & Anthems* (Edinburgh, *c.* 1805); John Sievwright, Engraver, who (according to Miss Marion Linton) appears in the Edinburgh directories for 1805–15; 'Mr Sivright' in Lizars's account in fn. 1, immediately below.

[1] Cumberland's information may have come (perhaps through a friend) from (1) Anon., 'Art. V.—*Account of a new Style of Engraving on Copper in Alto Relievo, invented by W[illiam Hone]*. LIZARS. Drawn up from information communicated by the Inventor', *Edinburgh Philosophical Journal*, ii (April 1820), 19–23, in which Lizars says he 'was much indebted' 'during these experiments' to 'Mr Sivright of Meggetland' (a suburb of Edinburgh), but says nothing of 'Copper Blocks'; (2) The reprint of the bulk of Lizars's account in *Gentleman's Magazine*, xci (1821), 625–6, citing *Edinburgh Philosophical Journal*; (3) Anon., 'A new Style of Engraving, invented by Mr. Lizars', *London Journal of Arts and Sciences*, i (1820), 78–9, which does not refer to 'Copper Blocks', Sivright, or *The Edinburgh Philosophical Journal*; and (4) Charles Pye, '*Mr. Pye on Engraving on Metal and Stone. On a new Process of Engraving on Metal and Stone*', *London Journal of Arts and Sciences*, i (1820), 55–8, which describes Pye's own experiments made 'five years' earlier than the 'account of the Process of Engraving on Copper Blocks in alto relievo by Mr. Lizars' 'in the Edinburgh Philosophical Journal', but which does not mention Mr Sivright. None of these accounts mentions *both* 'Copper Blocks' and Mr Sivright, as Cumberland does.

There is a further, chronological difficulty, for all four of the articles were published in 1820 and 1821 (Lizars's account did *not*—as Keynes, *Blake Studies* [1971], 246 asserts— appear in the *Edinburgh Philosophical Journal* for June–October 1819). Without yet another date for Cumberland's letter (after January 1819) or an earlier account of Sivright's Copper Blocks in some Philosophical Journal, we are left with a mystery as to where Cumberland found his information. 'Mr. Lizars of Edinburgh, succeeded so well |*in experiments with relief etching like Blake's*] that the newspapers of the day called it a "splendid invention"' (B. J. Lossing, *Outline History of the Fine Arts* [N.Y., 1840], 301–2, but I have been unable to trace these 'newspapers of the day'.

[2] R. N. Essick, *The Separate Plates of William Blake* (1983), 186.

[3] It is probably the same Dyer from whom Francis Douce acquired *Marriage* (B) in April 1821. I know no London dealer of the time named Dyer, but Gilbert Dyer (1743–1820) was an Exeter bookseller from 1788.

[4] Quoted from a photocopy of the MS in the Pierpont Morgan Library. In the same letter D'Israeli complains that 'two portfolios' he had of Dyer 'are *sheep-skin*, & not morocco'. He gives no indication of what was in the portfolios, but it is possible that they contained some of the 160 Blake plates he owned by 1835 (*BR*, 243–4), for even by 1824 Dibdin said D'Israeli has 'the largest [*Blake*] collection of any individual' (*BR*, 289). In particular, they may have contained *Europe* (A) pl. 1–2, 4–6, *America* (a) and pl. d, 'The Accusers' (H), *Song of Los* (B), *Visions* (F) pl. 1, and 'Joseph of Arimathea Preaching' (F) which were 'somewhat irregularly' bound together for many years (see *Blake Books* [1977], 156–7).

son identified in 1862 as coloured etchings.[1] Benjamin Disraeli also remarks that 'there is not the slightest foundation for any of the statements, contained in the [*unidentified*] letter, to which you refer. My father was not acquainted with Mr Blake . . .' In his account of Blake's drawing of the Visionary Head of the Ghost of a Flea, Allan Cunningham (1830) said: 'He looked earnestly into a corner of the room, and then said, here he is—reach me my things—I shall keep my eye on him. There he comes! . . . as he described him so he drew him.' (*BR*, 498)

Blake's old friend Johnny Johnson refers to this passage in a poem (pp. 12–14) in the possession of his great-granddaughter Miss Mary Barham Johnson, entitled 'The Day-Dream: or Cowper in the Shades. a poem by *John Johnson L.L.D. (Cowper's Kinsman)* late Rector of Yaksham with Welborn, Norfolk. (Written in *1832*, the last year of his life.)' In it, Cowper is welcomed to heaven by the great English poets such as Milton, Dryden, and Pope, and especially by Shakespeare:

64

Thus mutual, in soul-searching look,
 They rivetted remained;
And I my chalky pencil took—
 O what would Blake have gained?

. . .

75

Now symptoms of commencing speech
 By Shakespear's image shewn
Call'd on 'my things[x]' for rapid sketch
 Of Cowper lately flown . . .

'*Reach me my things*' was the constant call of poor Blake the painter, to his faithful Catherine whenever the Ghosts of the Mighty Dead stood before him. See the delectable Life of that extraordinary Genius of Allan Cunningham &c[.]

Among Blake's Visionary Heads were two inscribed:

Imagination of a Man who M.[r] Blake has rec.[d] instruct in painting &c. from

---

[1] Raymond Lister, 'A Letter from Benjamin Disraeli to Anne Gilchrist', *Blake*, xiv (1980), 99.

The Portrait of a Man who instructed M.ͬ Blake in Painting &c. in his
Dreams
Imaǧination of a Man who.ᵐ M.ͬ Blake had rec.ᵈ instruction in Painting &c
from[1]

On a tracing of a Visionary Head is inscribed: 'The Egyptian Task
Master slain by Moses', 'Seen in a Vision by Wᵐ Blake & Drawn
while the Same remained Before hi*m*, My Self J. Varley being
Present. in the Front room first floor No. 3 Fountain Court near
Exeter Change.'[2]

A curious later account records one such seance: '"Call up, and
paint the Founder of the Pyramids," said some one to the artist-
visionary. "There he is," replied Blake, "a stately man, in purple
robes, with a book full of golden leaves on which he sketches his
designs."'[3] The instigator was probably Varley, and the drawing is
inscribed 'The Man who built the Pyramids Drawn by William
Blake [*Monday*] Oct.ͬ 18. 1819 15 Degrees of Cancer ascending.'[4]

*18
October
1819*

Blake's last home, in a couple of upstairs rooms off the Strand in
Fountain Court, was cramped and dim. '"I live in a hole here," he
would say, "but God has a beautiful mansion for me elsewhere"'
(*BR*, 567).

---

[1] Martin Butlin, *The Paintings and Drawings of William Blake* (1981), no. 755. The
second is on the verso of the first, and both inscriptions are probably by Varley.

[2] In Queen's University, Kingston, Ontario, reproduced in ibid., pl. 911.

[3] Anon., 'I. Blake's Poetry', *Monthly Magazine*, NS, ii (1839), 700, a review of the *Songs*
generously pointed out to me by my friend Dr Raymond Deck. Anon. is probably John
A. Heraud, the editor of *The Monthly Magazine*; he goes on to say: 'Such is the character
portrayed in ... *The Judgement of the Flood*. Book ix.' The unidentified author of *The
Judgement of the Flood* (1834) is John A. Heraud. In the passage quoted from Book iv,
ll. 134–8 (p. 78), 'the transcendent architect' 'Barkayal' (a name derived from *The Book of
Enoch*)

> drew his purple robe about his loins,
> Displaying in his hand his gold-leaved book,
> And instant 'gan to sketch his vast conceits,
> Creations which alone his mind might dare.
> He was the 'Founder of the Pyrami[*d*]s'.

No other reference to The Man who built the Pyramids before 1839 is known, though
Cunningham in 1830 had given anecdotes of the Visionary Heads, and Jane Porter in
1841 referred to the Man who built the Pyramids (*BR*, 263). Either Anon.-Heraud had
made up his account of Blake's vision and based it on *The Judgement of the Flood* (1834), or
Heraud had learned the story before he wrote his epic and based this passage in Book iv
on it. The similarity of the two passages is too striking to be accounted for by mere coincidence.

[4] The original in the Blake–Varley sketchbook is lost, but a copy is in the Tate Gallery, reproduced in M. Butlin, *William Blake* (1971), p. 59.

He saw and drew his own residence at Felpham differently to what it appeared to anyone else. It was in this spirit that, as we are informed by Dr. Wilkinson, when Mr. Rudall, the Flautist, called upon him at his poor lodging near Clare Market, the mystic told his visitor that he had a palace of his own of great beauty and magnificence. On Mr. Rudall's looking round the room for evidence, Blake remarked, 'You don't think I'm such a fool as to think this is it.'[1]

Blake did not live 'near' Clare-Market (just south-west of Lincoln's Inn Fields) after his apprenticeship, but Clare-Market might loosely be described as in the neighbourhood of Fountain Court.

26 October 1819   According to his Journal, on 'Tuesday 26 [*October 1819 Linnell*] . . . Pro[*ceeded with the*] Heads of Wallace & E$\underline{d}$ [*I*]' which he was copying from Blake's design.[2]

30 October 1819   At the end of October Blake made another drawing which Varley identified as 'Wat Tyler By Wm Blake from his Spectre as in the Act of Striking the Tax gatherer on the head, Drawn [*Saturday*] Oct. 30, 1819, 1 h a.m.'[3]

1 November 1819   And two days later Linnell recorded again, 'Mon 1st [*November*] . . . Heads from Blake's Designs of Wallace & Edward 1$^{\underline{st}}$.'

18 October 1820   John Linnell wrote in his Journal for 'Wed 18 [*October 1820*] . . . Began a small Drawing on a wood Block / of Polypheme (from N. Poussin) for Dr Thornton / to receive a guinea for it—.' In the block of 'The Giant Polypheme, from a Famous Picture by N. Poussin' in Thornton's Virgil, the plate is signed '*Blake, del.*', making it very difficult to know who in fact made the drawing on which this particular print was based.

John Linnell had deeply impressed a young man some four years younger than himself named Edward Denny (b. 1796), the son of a baronet and a man of substance, and Linnell had apparently made Denny acquainted with Blake and his works. From August through November 1821 Linnell was busy painting portraits of Edward Denny and five other members of his family; that of Edward Denny shows a dreamy young man with his finger marking his place in a little book[4]—

---

[1] According to J. Spilling, 'Blake the Visionary', *New Church Magazine*, vi (1887), 209.

[2] The rediscovered MSS of John Linnell's Journal in the Ivimy MSS contain a number of references to Blake not found in the transcripts by John Linnell Jr. and Herbert Palmer quoted in *BR*, and these new references are incorporated in the text above. All the Blake references in Linnell's Journal are given in Appendix I below.

[3] Reproduced in the book catalogue No. 282 of E. Parsons & Sons (1918), lot 453.

[4] Linnell's portrait of Edward Denny (1821) is reproduced in Katharine Crouan, *John Linnell: A Centennial Exhibition* (Fitzwilliam Museum 5 Oct.–12 Dec. 1982; Yale Center for British Art, 26 Jan.–20 Mar. 1983), No. 76.

he looks strikingly like a Romantic poet such as Shelley. On 30 October Linnell sent some of the portraits to Denny at his home at King's End House, Worcester. On 2 November, Denny wrote that the pictures had arrived, and in passing he remarked:

When you see Mr. Blake be so kind as to tell him to keep the drawings he is making for me, when they are finished, till he either sees or hears from me— ...

and Believe me, dear Sir,
your's truly obliged,
Edward Denny.–[1]

2
November
1821

This is the first known reference to a direct connection between Blake and Denny, but it is plain that already Denny was an admirer of Blake. Unfortunately, we do not know what drawings Blake was making for Denny in 1821, for Denny is not known to have owned any drawings by Blake.[2] Apparently the drawings pleased Denny, for he purchased other Blake works in November 1826.

John Linnell scrawled a long draft reply on the letter itself, including a fascinating reference to a curious theatrical performance:

Mr Varley, Mr Blake & myself were much entertained Thursday Evening last by wittnessing a representation of Oedipus at the West London Theatre as it much exceeded our expectations as to the effect of the Play & the performance of the Actors. I see it sneered at in one of the public[?] papers but you know what [a bad(?) set *del*] ∧petty motives govern all∧ ∧most of∧ the Public criticism.

November
1821

Linnell had taken his friends to a box[3] at the West London Theatre in Tottenham Street[4] where they saw *Oedipus* by John Dryden and

---

[1] Quoted from the transcript by my friend Mark Abley of the letter among the Ivimy MSS; Mr Abley also supplied most of the context here.

[2] According to the index to Martin Butlin's magisterial *Paintings and Drawings of William Blake* (1981).

[3] In his Journal, Linnell recorded that he went on 'Th[*ursday November*] 2 To see Œdipus', but he said nothing about his companions, and in his Cash Account Book he noted under 8 November 1821 payment of four shillings 'to Dr Thornton for Box Ticket'—for Œdipus[?]'.

Linnell was clearly keenly interested in Greek plays, and the impulse to attend this production may have been his. On 8 May 1819 he paid £1. 10s. 0d. 'for Greek Theatre 3 vol. 4to', and on 24 April 1821 he paid four shillings for 'Sophocles—Greek'.

[4] For details of the theatre itself, see Raymond Mander & Joe Mitchenson, *The Lost Theatres of London* (1976), 202. It was not a patent theatre and was not therefore entitled to perform legitimate drama, but, 'being of too humble pretensions to create jealousy, [*it*] is permitted to play tragedy, comedy, or farce, in as legitimate a manner as the

Nat Lee, first acted in 1678. However, the play was advertised as being the *Oedipus* of Sophocles, and, not surprisingly, at lease some in the audience reacted with indignation to the imposture. The anonymous reviewer in *The Times* for Friday 2 November 1821 wrote:

ROYAL WEST LONDON THEATER.

A numerous audience was attracted yesterday evening to this theatre, by as barefaced an imposition as was ever practised on a public audience since the days of the bottle-conjuror. It was ostentatiously announced in the play-bills, and also in some of the public prints, that the *Œdipus Tyrannus* of Sophocles would be acted last night at this theatre, 'being its first appearance these 2440 years'.[1] Of course many persons, attracted by the accurate chronological knowledge of the supposed translator, went in the expectation of seeing the ancient tragedy stalking for once on modern boards in all the pomp and pride of the Athenian buskin, and of beholding the far-famed chorus tracing and retracing its steps among them to the notes of 'Doric flutes and soft recorders' as it poured forth the lyric measures of the bard of Colonus. In this expecta- tion, which the numerous translations of the *Œdipus Tyrannus* into English prose and verse did not render altogether unfounded, they were most miser- ably disappointed; for instead of listening to the simple yet majestic strains of Sophocles, they were indulged with a cut-down edition of the bombastic yet powerful tragedy of Lee and Dryden upon the same subject. That piece, which must always affect an audience very strongly, certainly has made its appearance on the stage within the last 2440 years . . .

Mr. Huntley . . . ranted through the part with tolerable emphasis, tearing the ears of the groundlings as violently as Lee himself could have wished it done, even at the moment when he was mad enough to 'put out each fiery spark', and to bid 'gods meet gods, and jostle in the dark'. Mrs. Glover's delineation of *Jocasta* was very powerful, and met with deserved applause; but we have seen her to greater advantage than we did last night in her Grecian costume. The other performers were of such a stamp as is generally found in the minor theatres. The tragedy, in spite of 'being its first appearance for these last 2440 years', was given out for repetition amidst thunders of applause, which we expect the play-bills of today will inform us proceeded from an

company is capable of doing' (*The Percy Anecdotes Original and Select* [1822], p. 160, cited in Allardyce Nicoll, *A History of English Drama, 1660–1900* [1955], iv, 228).

[1] The chronology is indeed striking, for Sophocles (496–406 BC) must have produced the play in 619 BC, one hundred twenty-three years before his birth. The advertisement quoted below, however, specifies '2240 years', which puts the first performance more plausibly in the year 419 BC.

audience, distinguished no less for its numbers and its fashion, than for its intelligence and discrimination.

The reviewer's dire prediction was at least partly fulfilled, for in *The Times* for Wednesday 7 November appeared the following advertisement:

NEW ROYAL WEST LONDON THEATRE,

Tottenham-street, Charlotte-street, Fitzroy-square.
Œdipus Tyrannus, by Sophocles, revived after a lapse of 2240 years, and received (as at Athens) with shouts of applause. It will be repeated till further notice.
THIS and every EVENING, ŒDIPUS. Œdipus, Mr. Huntley; Jocasta, Mrs. Glover. After which, THE WAGER LOST; in which Mrs. Glover will perform.
Boxes 4s., pit 2s., gallery 1s. Private boxes for families may be had nightly.

At least the date in this advertisement is two centuries less preposterous than that in the review.

Blake was certainly familiar with Sophocles, for his 'Philoctetes and Neoptolemus at Lemnos' (1812) was made some nine years before from Sophocles' *Philoctetes*,[1] and his intimate friends John Flaxman and John Linnell were admirers of Sophocles and made designs from his plays. It is agreeable to find that Blake was 'much entertained' by the performance, even though the play was some 2,300 years younger than it was advertised to be.

In his Journal Linnell recorded that on 'Sunday 14 [*April 1822*] M^r *14 April 1822*
Varley & Mr Blake Dined here'. Blake evidently regularly dined with the Linnells on Sundays.

Henry Howard, the Secretary of the Royal Academy Council which voted on 28 June 1822 to give Blake £25, was a particular admirer of Blake. In 1864 Samuel Palmer wrote: 'Howard the R.A. said he would give one of his fingers to design figures [*?such as those in the Blair designs*] like Blake.'[2]

Perhaps by the time of the 1823 *Job* agreement Blake had made his reduced pencil sketches the size the engravings were to be, transferred the outlines to copper, and given the sketches to Linnell, who wrote on the wrapper: 'These are Mr Blakes reduced Drawings & studies for the Engravings of the Book of Job Done for me John Linnell.'[3]

---

[1] Martin Butlin, *The Paintings and Drawings of William Blake* (1981), No. 676.
[2] *Letters of Samuel Palmer*, ed. R. Lister (1974), vol. ii, p. 700.
[3] The drawings with their wrappers are now in the Fitzwilliam Museum.

May On 'Tuesday 18' May 1824 Linnell went 'to M[r] Vine—M[r]
1824 James[?]—Blake— —'. Mr Vine was a distinguished patron, sometimes of Blake, and Mr James may have been as well.

A friendly reviewer of Montgomery's book in *The Eclectic Review* for
June 1824 was puzzled about 'The Chimney Sweeper' which it quoted:
June 'We know not how to characterize the song given from Blake's "Songs
1824 of Innocence". It is wild and strange, like the singing of a "maid in
Bedlam in the spring;" but it is the madness of genius.'[1]

Linnell commissioned Blake to assist him in engraving the portrait
of the distinguished engraver Wilson Lowry which Linnell had
painted. The progress of the work on the plate is recorded by Linnell
in his Journal. On 24 July 1824 Linnell 'made outline for M[r] Lowry's
Engraving'. About 5 August he 'rec[d] of M[rs] Lowry 15£ on acc[t] of the
engraving of M[r] Lowry to be done in October the price to be 30 gs the
remainder to be paid on delivery of the Plate—'. On 15–17 November
he was busy 'Pro engraving M[r] Lowry's Portrait', on 20 November he
'del[d] a Proof to M[rs] Lowry', on 22–6 November he worked 'Pro Plate
of M[r] Lowry', on 29 November he 'del[d] the Plate of M[r] Lowry—Ball
of acc[t] £16.10[s], on 6 December he 'retouchd & del[d] the Plate of M[r]
Lowry'. Though the Journal does not record Blake's part on the plate,
Linnell paid £20 'Cash on account of Picture of M[r] Lowry, to Blake',
£5 each on 18 August, 10 November, 25 December 1824, and 28 January 1825 (*BR*, 604), and the plate, published 1 January 1825, bears the
names of both Linnell and Blake as engravers.

On 13 November 1824, Johnny Johnson wrote to Bernard Barton,
13 who was then much interested in Blake, that 'Blake, and Caroline
November Watson failed just as much, in their Engravings of Romney's fine head
1824 of Cowper, in Crayons' as engravers of other Cowper subjects did.[2]

According to Gilchrist, Palmer reported Blake as saying 'that we
were two centuries behind the civilization which would enable us to
estimate his [*Fuseli's*] *Ægisthus*' (*BR*, 281–2), and on 22 July 1879
Samuel Palmer wrote: 'Blake *told me* about 1825 that we were one century behind the civilization which would enable us to appreciate
Fuseli's Œdipus with his daughters painted [*in 1787*] the year before
Fuseli became an A R A—.'[3]

[1] Anon., 'Art. VIII. *The Chimney-Sweepers' Friend, and Climbing-Boys' Album* ...
Arranged by James Montgomery ... Price 9s. London, 1824', *Eclectic Review*, NS, xxi
(June 1824), 559–60 (the entire review is on pp. 558–62). The review was first noticed by
Geoffrey Keynes and recorded in a note added in MS to his own copy of his *Bibliography*
(1921) now in Cambridge University Library.
[2] Quoted from the MS in Princeton University Library.
[3] *Letters of Samuel Palmer*, ed. R. Lister (1974), vol. ii, p. 968.

Blake became a frequent visitor at the Linnells about 1824, and the whole family became fondly familiar with his domestic opinions. Mrs Linnell wrote on 20 August 1839 to her daughter Hannah: 'I thought of Mr Blake who used to say how much he preferred a cat to a dog as a companion because she was so much more quiet in her expression of attachment . . .'[1]

On his son's death, Palmer wrote to Gilchrist about September 1861: 'if any one say that *I* overpressed the dear boy's brain or urged over study I *might* reply as Mr Blake did about the beauty of the view from his Hampstead window.'[2]

Palmer wrote a memorandum on 9 October 1824 of his first visit to Blake, when Blake said he began his Dante designs 'with fear and trembling'. Pamer replied, '"O! I have enough of fear and trembling." "Then," said he, "you'll do."' (*BR*, 291) This was a favourite story with Palmer, and he repeated it a number of times, including in a letter of 4 August 1879 to Phillip Gilbert Hamilton: 'I am very glad that you like my [*etching of the*] *Bellman*. When I was first introduced to dear Mr. Blake, he expressed a hope that I worked "with fear and trembling". Could he see me over an etching, he would behold a fruition of his desire copious as the apple-blossoms of that village [*Shoreham*], of which this *Bellman* is in some way a "cropping-up" (geologically speaking).'[3]

9 October 1824

After 1826 Blake and Samuel Palmer were firm friends. Palmer had certainly been deeply impressed by Blake's ideas about art, and it is at least imaginable that he had seen or heard of passages in Blake's *Notebook* such as the couplet on Sir Joshua Reynolds's presentation of his portrait to the Academy at Florence:

> The Florentines said 'Tis a Dutch English bore
> Michael Angelos Name writ on Rembrandts door'
>
> [*Notebook*, p. 32]

[1] Ibid., vol. i, p. 403 n. 3.

[2] Ibid., vol. ii, p. 618; 'Hampstead' may be a mistake for Fountain Court, for Blake never lived in Hampstead, though he apparently stayed with Linnell in Hampstead. In a letter of 14 September 1845 (vol. i, p. 438), Palmer speaks of teaching his son to read *Songs of Innocence*. George Richmond said that 'Blake often spoke of the beauty of the Thames, as seen from the window, the river looking "like a bar of gold"' (see *BR*, 566).

[3] *The Parting Light: Selected Writings of Samuel Palmer*, ed. Mark Abley (1985), 230. The editor remarks (p. 229) that there are 'two published excerpts from what seems very likely to be a single letter, the manuscript of which has been lost', one of them in A. H. Palmer's *Life and Letters of Samuel Palmer* (1892), 377–8 (reprinted in *The Letters of Samuel Palmer*, ed. R. Lister [1974], vol. ii, pp. 969–71) and the other in John Roget, *A History of the 'Old Water-Colour' Society* (1891), 275, 280, from which the Blake passage comes.

and the little poem on the 'reserve & modesty' of Stothard:

> The Fox the Owl the Beetle & the Bat
> By sweet reserve & modesty get Fat
>
> [*Notebook*, p. 36.]

At any rate, after 1827 Palmer made a note in his copy of Richard Payne Knight's *An Analytical Inquiry into the Principles of Taste* (1808) in response to Knight's praise of Salvador Rosa and Raphael at the expense of Michelangelo's Sistine Chapel:

Those artists who are so base that they do not attempt grandeur of form and yet lyingly pretend to grand effect are now called modest; but those who, as William Blake, do attempt and achieve both will, with him, by blind cunning and stupid wilfulness be set down impudent madmen: for our taste is Dutch; Rembrandt is our Da Vinci, and Rubens our Michelangiolo![1]

The attitudes and vocabulary of this passage are densely Blakean.

Palmer's son A. H. Palmer wrote that 'No one could imagine Palmer arguing with Blake as Richmond did' (*BR*, 292), but Palmer apparently *did* argue with Blake on occasion, for on 8 September 1878 he wrote:

I remember, young as I was, presuming to demur to an assertion of Mr. Blake's that our old cathedrals were not built to rule and compass; but I now see that, like many of his art statements, although literally a stretch or violation of truth it contained or suggested a greater truth.[2]

4 March 1825 On 'Friday 4 [*March 1825 Linnell went*] . . . to Dixon's proving Job. with Mr Blake'. As this is the first time proofs were pulled, presumably this is the first time the plates were thought to be in a relatively finishing state.

---

[1] A. H. Palmer, *Life and Letters of Samuel Palmer* (1892), 35–6; Palmer's copy of Payne Knight's book has not been traced. A. H. Palmer does not date his father's annotations—or for that matter Payne Knight's book—but he does associate them with 1826, and he quotes some later passages among the annotations 'written some forty years later', or at least by 1841 (Samuel Palmer died in 1881). The reference below to 'our most lamented William Blake' suggests a date (?not long) after Blake's death in August 1827.

In another note to Payne Knight, Samuel Palmer wrote (pp. 36–7) that 'Michaelangelo's and Da Vinci's works are models of light and shade so profound, subtle, intense, and commanding that after *their* contemplation, the Venetian and Flemish pictures present only in their effects the miserable varieties of imitation, spiritless and castrated, blind wanderings and glaring impudence. To prove this, any perceiving mind need only . . . look over Rembrandt's original etchings by the side of the *Illustrations of Job* by our most lamented William Blake.'

[2] *Letters of Samuel Palmer*, ed. R. Lister (1974), vol. ii, p. 957.

'The Divine Image' from *Songs of Innocence* was reprinted in the Swedenborgian *Dawn of Light* in April 1825—it had previously *April* appeared in Malkin's life of Blake in 1806 (*BR*, 427–8). *1825*

In the July 1825 issue of *Dawn of Light* appeared 'On Another's *July* Sorrow' from *Songs of Innocence* which had not been seen in type *1825* before.[1]

In a notebook, Blake made a sketch of two seated women and a naked man, which is inscribed by Richmond: 'drawn by W Blake to help me in my picture of "Abel". 1825'.[2]

One of Blake's young disciples in 1824 was Francis Oliver Finch, who said that Blake 'struck him as *a new kind of man*, wholly original, and in all things' (*BR*, 294). Samuel Palmer wrote to Anne Gilchrist in January 1863: 'of all the circle perhaps, [*Finch*] was the most inclined to believe in Blake's spiritual intercourse'.[3]

George Richmond made a sketch of 'Henry Fuseli from recollec- tion after death', 'Drawn from recollection 11[?] May 1825 / Henry *May* Fuseli aged 87'; it is also inscribed 'Mr B & H Fuseli were great *1825* friends'; on another leaf in the same notebook is a sketch inscribed by Palmer 'Drawn by Mr Blake to shew me what Fuseli's mouth was when a young man', and above it is 'A portrait from memory of Fuseli by Mr B.'[4]

On 10 December 1825 Blake told Crabb Robinson that 'One of the figures' in the Canterbury Pilgrims engraving 'resembled one in one of Aders' [*fifteenth century*] pictures[.] ["]They say I stole it from this picture, but I did it 20 years before I knew of the picture—however in my youth I was always studying this kind of paintings. No wonder

---

[1] There were other early printings of Blake's poems, mostly from *Songs of Innocence* (— *I*) in Swedenborgian periodicals:

'Introduction' (*I*)	*Boys' and Girls' Magazine*	July 1843
'The Blossom' (*I*)	*Boys' and Girls' Magazine*	Aug. 1843
'Nurse's Song' (*I*)	*Boys' and Girls' Magazine*	Sept. 1843
'Laughing Song' (*I*)	*Boys' and Girls' Magazine*	Oct. 1843
'The Lamb' (*I*)	*The Retina*	21 Oct. 1843
'A Dream' & 'The Lily' (*I*)	*New Church Magazine for Children*	Nov. 1843
'The Blossom' (*I*)	*New Church Magazine for Children*	1843
'A Dream' & 'Cradle Song' (*I*)	*Little Keepsake for 1844*	1843
'The Lamb' & 'The Shepherd' (*I*)	*New Church Magazine for Children*	1843
'The Divine Image' (*I*)	*New Church Advocate*	Dec. 1844
'Evening Hymn'	*Boys' and Girls' Library*	1844
'The Lamb' (*I*)	*Boys' and Girls' Library*	1844

[2] *The Complete Portraiture of William & Catherine Blake*, ed. G. Keynes (1977), 143.
[3] *Letters of Samuel Palmer*, ed. R. Lister (1974), vol. ii, p. 674.
[4] *The Complete Portraiture of William & Catherine Blake*, ed. G. Keynes (1977), 142–3.

there is a resemblance"' (*BR*, 310). On 27 June 1862 Samuel Palmer
wrote to Anne Gilchrist about the *Marriage* pl. 24 that it 'gives Blake's
Idea of Nebuchadnezzar in the Wilderness. I have very old German
translations of Cicero [*1531*] and Petrarch in which among some wild
and original designs, almost the very same figure appears. Many years
had elapsed after making his own design before Blake saw the wood
cut.'[1]

Crabb Robinson saw Blake again on 17 December 1825 and
recorded in his Diary that Milton had appeared to Blake and that 'he
resembled [All] the prints of him' (*BR*, 317). In his Reminiscences,
Robinson was much more specific about the appearance of Milton: 'I
ventured to ask, half ashamed at the time, which of the three of four
portraits in *Hollis's* Memoirs (Vols in 4to) is the most like—He answ[d]
["]They are all like, At different Ages—I have seen him as a youth And
as an old man with a long flowing beard[.] He came lately as an old
man . . .["]' The book referred to is *Memoirs of Thomas Hollis, Esq. F.R.
and A.S.S.* [ed. Francis Blackburne, 2 vols.], London [privately]
Printed 1780. Half a century later, Samuel Palmer wrote to George
Richmond in March 1879:

> Touching Milton . . . I asked William Blake whether there was any one por-
> trait of him indicative of his greatness. Yes, he said—there was a print in
> Hollis's life of Thomas Hollis and I think he added that it was from a plaster
> cast or bust. Now a friend has lent me a collection of 24 engravings or etchings
> of Milton placed in the order of his age,—and among them are three etchings
> by Cipriani each in an oval wreath of laurels or what no*t*, The original of each
> having been in the possession of Hollis. *One alone* renders Milton as one
> would love to imagine him, & this is from a plaster cast.—Now every part of
> this etching except the head is unmistakeably by the same artist (Cipriani) as
> the two others, & the head, it seems to me, unmistakeably not. The lips are
> finely chiselled, the expression is noble, & they combine with a peculiar treat-
> ment of the hair in attesting themselves to be the burin work of William Blake.
> The dress, wreath, & ray-like background are just in the manner of the other
> two, the wreaths being very well etched in all,—but everything is quite differ-
> ent from this mysterious head: mysterious because if Blake did it for Cipriani
> he must have done so when three years of age—the inscribed date of the etch-
> ing being 1760. But what if the original head received some damage on the
> copper & was sent years after its original publication to Basire [*whose shop
> signed ten of the Hollis plates*] or to Blake for repair? I do not think the head had
> become worn, for the rest of the etching does not indicate it.[2]

---

[1] *Letters of Samuel Palmer*, ed. R. Lister (1974), vol. ii, p. 660.
[2] Quoted from a transcript by Ruthven Todd (ending 'from Geoffrey Grigson, 2: xii:

Palmer describes three of the Milton plates first printed in the *Memoirs of Thomas Hollis*, the crucial one being adapted 'FROM A BVST IN PLAISTER ... IN THE POSSESSION OF THOMAS HOLLIS' 'DRAWN AND ETCHED MDCCLX [*1760*] BY I. B. CIPRIANI', but though the face does seem different in graphic style and engraving technique from the others in the book, the differences are not so idiosyncratic as to make it possible to say with confidence either that they are by William Blake or that they are not by Cipriani.

On 9 February 1826 Linnell wrote to his father from Cheltenham about a 'scrape' relating to his painting of 'The Burial of Saul', and as an afterthought he remarked: 'I shall be glad to hear from Ed. Chance how the Job goes on & what has occurred.'[1] Edward Chance was Linnell's nephew, who was helping to supervise the printing of Blake's *Illustrations of the Book of Job* at just this time. For instance, on this same day, 9 February 1826, Linnell's wife Mary wrote to him that 'Edward ... has been every day to Lahees & to [*the Linnell's house in*] Cirencester Place[;] from all I can learn the printing is going on well by a man of the name of Freeman[.]'

9 February 1826

Blake gave Linnell numbers of his works, from the manuscript *Vala* (*BR*, 332–3) and the unique printed copy of *The French Revolution* to very minor drawings. Professor Robert N. Essick owns Fuseli's sketches for the frontispiece of Lavater's *Aphorisms* (1789) and the last plate (1801) (engraved by Blake) inscribed, apparently by Linnell, 'Given by W. Blake to J. Linnell / by Fuseli' and 'Mich! Angelo / by Fuseli / original Drawing had from W.ᵐ Blake'.

At the Saunders & Hodgson sale on 26–9 April 1826 of the *Bibliotheca Splendissima*: A Catalogue of a Select Portion of The Library of Mrs. Bliss, Deceased, Removed from her Residence at Kensington, were sold lots:

10 Blake's (W.) [*For Children*: The] Gates of Paradise [Copy A], 16 *plates, red morocco, gilt leaves* [for 8*s.*]

1943') in his copy (now in the Brotherton Library, Leeds University) of Gilchrist's *Life of William Blake*, ed. Ruthven Todd (1942), p. 17; the original Palmer MS is untraced. (Geoffrey Grigson wrote to me on 18 July 1980: 'I have no recollection of the Samuel Palmer letter you mention.') Palmer clearly did not know that the Cipriani plates were first printed in 1780 in the Hollis volume. Blake's own portrait of Milton (1800) for Hayley's library at Felpham (see *BR*, 69) is clearly related to the Cipriani print based on the bust. The context is developed more fully in 'A Portrait of Milton Engraved by William Blake "When Three Years of Age"? A Speculation of Samuel Palmer', *University of Toronto Quarterly*, li (1981), 28–35.

[1] Quoted from the transcript by my friend Mark Abley of the letter among the Ivimy MSS.

26–9
April
1826
11 —— Songs of Innocence and Experience [Copy P], 2 vols, *coloured engravings, red morocco gilt leaves* [for 20*s.*]

. . .

371 Young's (Edw.) Night Thoughts [Copy D], *with engravings from Blake's designs, coloured, calf extra, marble leaves* 1797 [*for £4. 4s. od.*]

as well as No. 41, Blair's *Grave* (1808) [£1. 11*s.* 6*d.*] and No. 370, a plain copy of *Night Thoughts* [£1. 19*s* o*d*]. The first three volumes had probably been bound for Mrs Bliss about 1805, and a manuscript coloured copy of Mrs Bliss's *Songs* was made about 1825. P. A. Hanrott acquired the first two lots.

It may have been about April 1826, when the Royal Academy exhibition was being arranged, that Samuel Palmer wrote to John Linnell:

10 Broad St. Bloomsbury
Thursday morng.

Dear Sir

They told me at the Academy that your pictures were all received. Mr. Blake is better, and is getting strength;[1] he has been visited by Dr. Thornton, who says

?May
1826

that Mr. Harrison has lost the opportunity of selling two or three copies of the Job through not having one to shew.[2] Mr. Behnes also, who called on Mr. Blake, wants a copy—not a proof I believe—and says he intended becoming a subscriber,[3] but that is no matter. . . .

P.S. If there be any message to Mr. Blake or elsewhere, the bearer will wait.—[4]

Crabb Robinson wrote to Dorothy Wordsworth on 19 February 1826 that 'Coleridge has visited B. & I am told talks finely about him'. According to a later report, 'Charles Augustus Tulk took Coleridge to see Blake's picture of "The Last Judgement" and . . . the author of *Christabel* poured forth concerning it a flood of eloquent commentary and enlargement.'[5]

[1] Blake wrote of suffering from 'the old Shivering fit' and general illness in letters of ? March, 10 Nov. 1825; 1 Feb., 31 March, 19 May, 2, 5, 14, 16, 29 July 1826; Feb., 15 March, 12 April, 3 July 1827.

[2] William Harrison wrote to Linnell on 31 Jan. 1826 ordering a copy of *Job* about which Dr R. J. Thornton had told him. Harrison is known to have acted as 'Agent for Dr. Thornton' (*BR*, 320 n. 3, 271), but not for Blake or Linnell.

[3] This is apparently the dealer John Bohnes, who paid for his 'Plain' copy on 29 June 1826 (*BR*, 592, 599) and offered it in his *Catalogue* (1829) for £3. 3*s.* o*d.*

[4] Quoted from the MS in the possession of A. H. Palmer II in *The Letters of Samuel Palmer*, ed. R. Lister (1974), vol. i, pp. 10–11.

[5] J. Spilling, 'Blake Artist and Poet', *New Church Magazine*, vi (1887), 253; his source here is not identified, but it is presumably a letter from Garth Wilkinson which he cites elsewhere (*BR*, 209, 210, 254). For Blake's 'Last Judgment' design painted about 1826, see *BR*, 386.

On 'Sat 30 [*September 1826 Linnell*] . . . lent a Copy of Job (proofs) to Master[*?*] Shorto' the artist. It was being lent to Shorto in the hope that he might find a customer for it in Salisbury, but he returned it sadly on 5 January 1827. *30 September 1826*

Two weeks later, on 'Friday 13 [*October 1826 Linnell*] . . . Sent a Copy of Job (proofs) to Bohn' the Bookseller. This copy (for which there is no receipt in the *Job* accounts) or the one for which 'Mᵣ Bohnes' paid £2. 12s. 6d. on 29 June 1826 (*BR*, 592) may be the copy in John Bohn's *Catalogue* (1829) offered for £3. 3s. (Later Linnell also 'exchanged' copies of *Job* for goods with Bohn—see *BR*, 597, 601.) *13 October 1826*

On 'Frid[*ay*] 10 [*November 1826 Linnell*] sent to Mᵣ Denny a Copy of Job proofs 5 gs also—a Copy of Blair's Grave 2.12/6' in response to Denny's letter to Blake of 4 November requesting these works. *10 November 1826*

George Cumberland had been moved by Blake's letter of 12 April, and he wrote to his son on Friday 20 July 1827:

for Blake I have spared no pains but have no success. They seem to think his prices above their reach, yet they seemed very anxious to have his works. My best regards to him. His Job I have placed with a third bookseller Mr Lewis of Clifton.[1] *20 July 1827*

Eighteen-year-old George Richmond came in just after Blake died and 'closed the poet's eyes and kissed William Blake in death' (*BR*, 343). Sir Arthur Richmond (1879–1968) told Ruthven Todd that his grandfather closed Blake's eyes 'to keep the vision in'.[2] Richmond also made a drawing (in the Keynes Collection) inscribed 'G R W Blake from recollection after his death 1827' and 'He Died Sunday the 12 August 1827 at 6 in the Evening & was Buryed the Friday following'. *12 August 1827*

Edward Price wrote to Linnell from Trentham on Monday 3 September 1827, three weeks after Blake's death, about Blake's *Job* engravings:

Lady Stafford will not be here for a month so I have not been able to put before her Ladyship Blake's Etchings, and I fear I shall not be able to get subscribers as many of my friends who have seen them, have only made the remark that they were 'striking but extravagant' and not one has yet expressed a desire to buy, but I will omit no opportunity of shewing it whenever I meet with the One Man in a Thousand who understands Painting.[3] *3 September 1827*

---

[1] British Library Add. MSS 36,412, fo. 10.

[2] Ruthven Todd in *Blake Newsletter*, vi (1972), 24.

[3] Quoted from the transcript by my friend Mark Ablcy of the letter among the Ivimy MSS.

Elizabeth Lady Stafford, the wealthy Countess of Sutherland in her own right, was married to the even wealthier George Grenville Leveson-Gower, Marquis of Stafford, who was famous as a politician and an improver of their huge estates (including most of the County of Sutherland). Both Lord and Lady Stafford were keenly interested in the arts; he was President of the British Institution, she was a painter in water-colours, and both collected art eagerly. A purchase from the Staffords might have led to important commissions for Linnell and perhaps to purchases of other works by Blake. However, if Lady Stafford was shown the *Job* engravings on her return, she apparently showed no interest in them, for her name does not appear in Linnell's *Job* accounts (*BR*, 598–605).

There are numerous letters from Edward Price to Linnell among the Ivimy MSS, but he is not known to have any other connection than this one with Blake. Clearly he was simply one of many acquaintances through whom Linnell tried to sell copies of Blake's *Job*.

On Wednesday 14 November 1827 Samuel Palmer concluded a letter to George Richmond: 'Remembering me kindly to all friends you may see, if you think of it, would you, Sir, do me this kindness in particular to present Mrs. Blake with my most affectionate and respectful remembrances.'[1]

14 November 1827

Catherine Blake may have been feeling in somewhat straitened circumstances in the winter of 1827, for on 'Saturday 8 [*December 1827 Linnell*] ... gave Mʳˢ Blake 5£ boroᵈ[?]'. It was probably not until about a year later that her situation was eased by generous patronage from unexpected friends.

8 December 1827

On 'Thursday 24 [*January 1828 Linnell*] ... sent to Mʳ Johns at Plymouth a copy of India proofs of the *Job* & one plain imp[*ression*]—'. A. B. Johns acknowledged receipt of 'the two copies' on 31 January.

24 January 1828

In a letter of 24 June 1828 to George Richmond, Samuel Palmer asked: 'Will you offer my best remembrances to Mr. and Mrs. Linnell and if you happen to see them to Mrs. Blake, Mr Walter Mr Tatham Mr. and Mrs. Calvert and Mr. Sherman.'[2]

24 June 1828

By September 1828 Catherine Blake had moved from Linnell's house to Tatham's, and perhaps in gratitude she gave him a copy of

September 1828

---

[1] Quoted from the MS in the possession of Mr Anthony W. Richmond by Raymond Lister, 'The Writings of Samuel Palmer', *Gazette des Beaux-Arts* (1973), 254.
[2] Quoted from the MS in the possession of Anthony W. Richmond in *The Letters of Samuel Palmer*, ed. R. Lister (1974), vol. i, p. 22.

Blake's Canterbury Pilgrims engraving[1] which is inscribed 'This print was coloured by the Artist, W. Blake, and given by Mrs Blake to F. Tatham Esqr.' And about the same time Tatham made the fine portrait which he inscribed 'Mrs Blake' and 'Frederick Tatham Septr 1828'.[2]

In a journal letter of September and October 1828, Samuel Palmer wrote to George Richmond:

> I have been sketching a head from life, and life size on gray board, in colours, and heightened with Mrs. Blake's white,[3] which is brighter, and sticks faster than chalk; and it seems such a quick way of getting a showy, but really good effect, that I was thinking you might do five or six at Calais . . . Mr. Linnell has given my Father impressions of those Inferno plates dear Mr. Blake had lived to execute: nothing can be finer: they are Art in its sublime nakedness (not as being unfinish'd) and in its eternal abstraction from cloggy corporeal substances. They are not of this World.[4]

September October 1828

One of Blake's Visionary Heads, a portrait of Nebuchadnezzar, was engraved for Varley's *Zodiacal Physiognomy*, a prospectus for which was issued about October 1828. A tracing of the face, probably made by Linnell, in the collection of G. Ingli James is inscribed 'Nebuchadnez[z]ar / Coin as seen in a Vision / by Mr Blake'.[5]

Tatham's kindness to Catherine Blake is shown in his letter to an unnamed patron who had evidently read in J. T. Smith's life of 'Blake' (1828) that 'Blake died in . . . No. 3, Fountain-court, Strand' (*BR*, 476) and that 'his beloved Kate survives him clear of even a sixpenny debt; and in the fullest belief that the remainder of her days will be rendered tolerable by the sale of the few copies of her husband's works, which she will dispose of at the original price of publication . . .' (*BR*, 476).

[1] Seen in the collection of David McC. McKell Jr.

[2] The drawing in the BMPR is reproduced in *The Complete Portraiture of William & Catherine Blake*, ed. Geoffrey Keynes (1977), pl. vii.
Tatham also made a water-colour portrait which he inscribed:
Frederick Tatham
This drawing was made from a Mrs Wilson who lived in a hut upon Epping forest. I drew her because she was so like William Blake—indeed this portrait of Mrs Wilson is much more like Blake than any hitherto published except that by Phillips engraved in Blairs Grave.
(BMPR: 1867-10-12-240, reproduced in *The Complete Portraiture*, pl. 43a-b.)

[3] The composition of Mrs Blake's white is not known.

[4] Quoted from a typescript of the mislaid MS in the possession of Anthony W. Richmond in *The Letters of Samuel Palmer*, ed. R. Lister (1974), pp. 34, 43. The Dante prints must be engraver's proofs, for the first commercial printing of the work was apparently in 1838.

[5] R. N. Essick, *The Separate Plates of William Blake* (1983), 247.

When the patron wrote to Catherine at 3 Fountain Court, Strand, in the Spring of 1829 offering to purchase Blake's books, Tatham generously replied for her:

34. Alpha Road. Regent's Park. London. April 11. 1829
Sir,

In behalf of the widow of the late William Blake, I have to inform you that her circumstances render her glad to embrace your Kind offer for the purchase of some of the works of her departed husband. The character you appear to have read and appreciated was so little exaggerated, that even more could be said of such an eminent, but neglected genius. His devotion to his art, his originality, his mechanical invention, his research, his ingenious candour, his simplicity of character, his retired endurance of the scoff of the foolish, his patience under many wicked persecutions, together with many other, and peculiar attributes, rendered him as unique as transcendant, and as singular as unequalled. There were those who were even more intimate with

11 him than the author of the short life you have read, and it will be the object of
April some of them, at some future period, to give forth such biographical informa-
1829 tion as shall bespeak him a just example for imitation, and a model seldom surpassed, but by the Saint, the Prophet, or disciple.

To emulate the character of such an individual, in a letter, can only be a trifling attempt, and to eulogize with a deserved strength might by some be said to be bordering on adoration; but permit me to remark that although I am strange to you, I cannot but extol, and by intimacy, sanction the object of your admiration, as also the motive of your Kindness displayed in relieving a forlorn and destitute widow, from some of her inevitable cares.

But to answer your enquiry, which would have been done before, but that in consequence of M.ʳˢ Blake's removal from Fountain Court to N.º 17. Upper Charlotte S.ᵗ Fitzroy Square, a wrong address was put on the letter at Fountain Court and it was only received by her the day before yesterday.[1] The works for Sale are as follows:————

M.ʳ Blake's industry was such that I have often heard him say that he has written more than Milton and Shakspeare put together; he has engraved large quantities of plates, and has painted an immense number of elaborate and laborious fresco-pictures, highly finished as Miniatures.

The artists of the 14ᵗʰ and 15.ᵗʰ centuries have done much, but they had friends, pupils, and every assistance; but this man had to struggle with poverty in a Commercial Country, and has produced these *mountains* of *labour*, with the assistance only of a fascinated and devoted wife, who, as a beautiful damsel, loved, as a woman, cherished, as a wife, obeyed,—as a willing slave

---

[1] For six months after Blake's death, Catherine lived with John Linnell (a fact which Tatham consistently ignored or concealed), and the patron's letter was presumably forwarded from Fountain Court to Linnell's house and by Linnell to Catherine.

incessantly laboured, and as an aged nurse, attended, and alleviated his last sickness; and now, as bereaved, deplores but patiently acquiesces.

This elevated widow is now seeking a support during the remainder of her exemplary course, through the medium of the enlightened and the generous with no other hope than that she will ultimately be joined to that partner once more, whose loss she pitiably laments, and whose praises it is her only pleasure to reiterate. Affected as I now am at the recollection of his admirable qualities, and the loss of his friendship and advice, I can only add, that, should you, Sir, be inclined to possess, for the embellishment of your own collection, and the benefit of the widow, any of the enumerated works, they shall be carefully sent to you upon your remitting the payment, and I will take proper care that your Kindness shall be rewarded with the best impressions, and that you shall be used in a manner that shall not cause you to regret your absence from the scene of purchase.

And communicating either with myself or M.ʳˢ Blake, you will Receive her ample thanks and the acknowledgements

   of your obedient and humble Servant
    Frederick Tatham.[1]

Extravagant as parts of this letter seem, they are confirmed by other evidence. Blake told Crabb Robinson on 18 February 1826 that he had 'written more than Voltaire or Rousseau—Six or Seven Epic poems as long as Homer and 20 Tragedies as long as Macbeth'. The description of his frescoes being as 'highly finished as Miniatures' is taken from his *Descriptive Catalogue* (1809) paragraph 12—'All Frescoes are as high finished as miniatures'—though we may doubt that their number was 'immense'. The collaborative life of Blake by The Ancients was never written, of course, but Tatham wrote a life himself (see *BR*, 507–35). The patron to whom Tatham was writing here may have been the Earl of Egremont in Petworth, Sussex; at any rate, a few months later he put Catherine out of need by his payment of £84 for Blake's design from Spenser's *Faerie Queen*.

John Linnell had vigorously cultivated patrons for Blake, among them 'Lord Egremont, Sir Thomas Lawrence, Mr. Tatham, and others' (*BR*, 339). Of these, Lord Egremont was an old acquaintance,

---

[1] Quoted from a facsimile (generously provided me by my friend Professor Dennis Read) of the transcript by Thomas Hartley Cromek in his 'Recollections of Conversations with Mr. John Pye London 1863–4' pp. 56–8 in the possession of T. H. Cromek's great-grandson Mr Paul Warrington. (I have omitted the quotation marks down the left margin, the words '(Copy)' and '[M.ʳˢ Blake]' at the top, '(Signed)' at the bottom, and the redundant 'inclined to to possess' at the juncture between p. 57 and p. 58. The tantalizing dashes after paragraph 3 evidently indicate an omission.) The original letter is not known to survive, and its addressee and sequel are only the subject of speculation.

for Blake had known him when living near Felpham, Lord Egremont
had been one of the Justices of the Peace who tried Blake on 4 October
1803, and his wife had commissioned Blake's 'Vision of the Last Judgment' (1808) and 'Satan Calling Up His Legions' (1808). Perhaps in
response to private appeals from Linnell or the public one of J. T.
Smith,

Lord Egremont visited her and, recalling Blake's Felpham days, said regret-
fully, 'Why did he leave me?' The Earl subsequently purchased, for the handsome sum of eighty guineas, a large water-colour drawing containing 'The
Characters of Spenser's *Faerie Queene*,' grouped together in a procession, as a
companion picture to the *Canterbury Pilgrims*. [*BR*, 363]

Apparently the picture (see Plate V) was delivered to Lord Egremont
on Saturday 1 August 1829[1] with the following note:

*1
August
1829*

The widow of the late Wm Blake begs permission to inform the Earl of Egremont, that the Picture of Spenser's Fairy Queen has upon it 2 coats of *white
hard Varnish*, it would be better for one more, but the weather being so chilly
& damp it would not be safe to apply it now. She takes the liberty to offer her
most humble thanks to his Lordship for his patronage & liberality & con-
siders herself in gratitude bound ever to pray for his Lordships prosperity &
increase.

N.° 17 Upper Charlton S^t
Fitzroy Square.[2]

After having left this note, it apparently occurred to Catherine that the
picture would be damaged if varnished by an ignorant hand, and three
days later she wrote again:

N.° 17 Upper Charlton S^t
Fitzroy Square
August 4. 1829.

My Lord,
   The Note I had the honour to address to y^r Lordship accompanied the
Picture, which I left at Grosvenor Place on Saturday last August the first,
together with a descriptive Paper.
   Any Artist or person accustomed to Pictures can apply a coat of White

---

[1] The date derives from the next letter.
[2] Both letters are still, like 'The Faerie Queene', in Lord Egremont's residence,
Petworth House, Sussex.
   The letters of 1 and 4 Aug. 1829 seem to provide evidence that Mrs Blake moved to 17
Upper Charlton Street about June 1828, later moved in with the Tathams, and then
returned to Charlton Street, where she died. See *BR*, 354, 534–5, 567–8.
   The hand in which the second letter is signed seems to be less carefully formed, and
perhaps different from, the one that wrote the message.

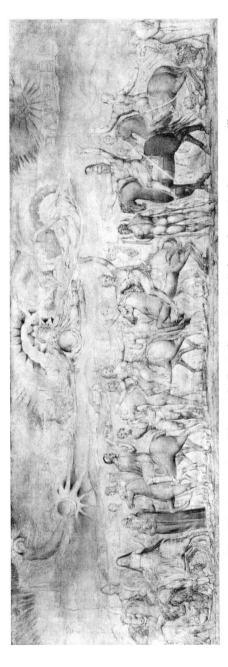

Pl. 5 The Procession of Spenser's *Faerie Queene* (*c.* 1825), from the original tempera still at Petworth House (Petworth, Sussex). The design, echoing Blake's design and engraving of the Procession of Chaucer's Canterbury Pilgrims (1808ff.) was bought for the munificent sum of £84 by Lord Egremont after Blake's death, and Catherine wrote to Lord Egremont about varnishing it (see pp. 92–4).

hard Varnish supposing the Weather to be settled & Warm. Oil or any thin varnish will inevitably turn the Picture Yellow. M! Blake had a great dislike to his pictures falling into the hands of Picture Cleaners. But [as it *del*] as the Picture [has *altered to*] having already had 2 Coats may not require [var(*?*) *del*] another for 2 or 3 years & perhaps more your Lordship need not at present trouble y'self on the matter[.]

4 August 1829

I remain My Lord
Y! Lordships most obliged &
humble Serv'
C Blake

to the Earl of Egremont
&c &c &c

The '*descriptive Paper*' left with 'The Faerie Queene' was presumably similar to Blake's descriptions of the 'Vision of the Last Judgment' written for the wife of the Earl of Egremont and to his accounts in the *Descriptive Catalogue* (1809) of her 'Satan Calling Up His Legions' (paragraphs 94–9) and of the Canterbury Pilgrims (paragraphs 13–64). However, no such '*descriptive Paper*' about 'The Faerie Queene' is traced—indeed, this is the only known reference to it—so we cannot judge whether it was in Blake's hand, composed before his death in 1827, or was in Catherine's hand, perhaps dictated to her in a vision after his death.

The gift-price of eighty guineas which Lord Egremont paid for 'The Faerie Queene' is likely to have kept Catherine out of want for the rest of her life.

On 'Thursday 26*th* [*November 1829 Linnell*] . . . Sent Copy of Job, Proofs to Miss James'. On 13 October Linnell had gone 'to M' Vines M' James &c═'; Mr James may be a dealer in colours, and Miss James is probably his daughter or sister. As no 'James' appears in the *Job* records, this copy may have been a gift.

26 November 1829

Three weeks later, on 'Thursday 17 [*December Linnell*] . . . Sent Book of Job to M' Allen to see'. In Linnell's *Job* accounts, this is recorded as '1 Copy plain to Mr Allen given', without date (*BR*, 602).

17 December 1829

A clear connection of Blake and Thomas Taylor is seen in the commonplace book of William George Meredith (1804–31), the nephew of Thomas Taylor's patron William George Meredith (?1756–1831), who wrote:

Wednesday. Dec! 30. 1829.

T. Taylor gave Blake, the artist, some lessons in mathematics & got as far as the 5.*th* proposit? wch proves that any two angles at the base of an isoceles triangle must be equal. Taylor was going thro the demonstration, but was interrupted by Blake, exclaiming, 'ah never mind that—what's the use of going

30 December 1829

to prove it, why I see with my eyes that it is so, & do not require any proof to make it clearer.'[1]

This association could have been at almost any time, but an early date, perhaps in the 1780s, seems most plausible.

Another anecdote of the two men was reported *c.* 1867–9 in the Reminiscences of Taylor's long-time friend Alexander Dyce (1798–1869):

Taylor, so absurd himself in many aspects, was ready enough to laugh at the strange fancies of others,—for instance, at those of that half-crazed man of real genius, Blake the artist. 'Pray, Mr. Taylor,' said Blake one day, 'did you ever find yourself, as it were, standing close beside the vast and luminous orb of the moon'?—[']Not that I remember, Mr. Blake: did you ever?'—'Yes, frequently; and I have felt an almost irresistible desire to throw myself into it headlong.'– 'I think, Mr. Blake, you had better not; for if you were to do so, you most probably would never come out of it again.'[2]

Cunningham was evidently asked by a John Edwards to show him a specimen of Blake's handwriting, and on 1 January 1830 Cunningham wrote to John Murray Jun[r], who was the publisher of his *Lives*: 'I enclose the Autograph of William Blake which I obtained only this morning. Will you have the goodness to put it into the hands of Jn Edwards and inform him at the same time when you will send it home[*?*]'[3] With it is a small piece of paper with the careless signature of 'W. Blake', perhaps by the poet. The signature may come from the Blake letter which Cunningham borrowed from Linnell and never returned (see *BR*, 375 n. 1). No surviving Blake manuscript seems to be conspicuously missing a signature, and this may be all that survives of Blake's missing letter.

1 January 1830

Catherine's new-found financial security is indicated by the fact

---

[1] Reproduced from the MS now in McMaster University Library in James King, 'Studies in the Society's History and Archives C: Thomas Taylor, The Meredith Family, and The Society (i)', *Journal of the Royal Society for the Encouragement of Arts, Manufactures and Commerce* (March 1973), 255 and discussed in James King, 'The Meredith Family, Thomas Taylor, and William Blake', *Studies in Romanticism*, xi (1971), 157. For 'simple paths', 'obtuse Acute Scalene', and 'intricate ways biquadrate Trapeziums Rhombs Rhomboids Parallelograms, triple & quadruple', see *Vala*, p. 33, ll. 32–5.
[2] Quoted from a reproduction (of the MS in the Victoria & Albert Museum) kindly sent me by Professor R. J. Schrader, who quoted it in his edition of *The Reminiscences of Alexander Dyce* (1972), 134–5. Can Dyce have been familiar with the *Marriage* pl. 19, where 'I found myself on a bank by moonlight' and 'flung myself . . directly into the body of the sun'?
[3] Quoted from the manuscript in Yale University.

that when 'The following [*seven*] New Cases from Applicants was then
read' to the 'Special Meeting of Directors [*of The Artist's General Benevolent Institution*] Jany 5 1830', 'Thos Phillips Esq in the Chair', 'The Case of Mrs [Mary(?) *del*] C Blake was withdrawn at her desire—'[1]

5 January 1830

John Clare wrote a sonnet, perhaps between 1824 and 1831, to

BLAKE

Blake though insulted by a kings decree
Thy fame stirs onward like the mighty sea
That throws its painted gems upon the shore
To deck crowns heirs with glitter little more
While all thats truly noble & sublime
Is rolling onward to the throne of time
Time the insulted arbiter of fame
Merits reward & tyrants lasting shame
That rusts crowns into baubles—kings to dust
Then Blake thy glory kindled in its trust
& like the sea thy hearts own element
Shining in light & earths amaze it went
Pursuing on a worth ennobled way
Heroe-inspiring theme of glorys dauntless day[2]

1830?

Note that many of the terms such as 'Thy fame . . . like the mighty sea', 'the sea thy hearts own element', and Blake's example as 'heroe-inspiring' seem more appropriate to Cromwell's Admiral Robert Blake than to the poet, though neither Robert nor William seems to have been literally 'insulted by a kings decree'.

Blake's friends were of course eager to see the published accounts of him, and on Monday 17 February 1830 George Cumberland wrote to his son George: 'I have read Blake's Life in the Family Library of Allan Cunningham and it seems he died amusing himself harmlessly in his own way. I think it pretty true and suspect it was written by Mr Linnell. I could add a creditable anecdote or two and you perhaps several.'[3]

17 February 1830

---

[1] Quoted from the manuscript 'DIRECTORS / ARTIST'S / GENERAL BENE-VOLENT / INSTITUTION / MINUTES' 'BOOK / N.? 2', 28, in the Institution's offices in Burlington House, Piccadilly, London. I was able to find no other reference to Mrs Blake either in this volume (for Jan. 1829–June 1842) or in the previous one (for 1815–Jan. 1829).

[2] John Clare, *The Midsummer Cushion*, ed. A. Tibble & R. K. R. Thornton (1979), 446; the whole volume is from a MS fair copy of *c.* 1831.

[3] British Library Add. MSS 36,512, fo. 260, misdated 17 *July* 1830 in Geoffrey Keynes, 'George Cumberland 1754–1848', *Book Collector*, xix (1970), 56.

Linnell recorded in his Journal that on 'Sat 20 [*February 1830 he went*] ... to Mr Callcott with Mr Allan & Shewed Mr Callcott the Drawings by Mr Blake of Dantè——'. Linnell may have been trying to interest the painter Sir Augustus Wall Callcott in the Dante drawings either for himself or for Lord Egremont, whose artistic interests Callcott apparently served in London. On 30 July 1830 Callcott delivered £6. 6s. 0d. to Linnell for Lord Egremont's copy of *Job* (*BR*, 596), and about 18 March 1831 he apparently wrote to Lord Egremont for Linnell about the Dante designs (*BR*, 409). *20 February 1830*

According to Linnell's Journal, on 'Thursday 11 [*March 1830*] ... Mr Ollyer, Mr Allason / & Mr Allan came to see Mr Blake's Drawings', but neither Mr Ollyer (Ollier) nor Mr Allason is otherwise known to have expressed an interest in Blake, though Mr Allen was given a copy of Job about 1831 (*BR*, 602). *11 March 1830*

On Thursday 25 March 1830 the painter William Etty sent some anecdotes about the generosity and humanity of his old master Sir Thomas Lawrence (who had died some ten weeks earlier) to the poet Thomas Campbell which Etty thought 'likely to be of use to you ... in the important work in which you are engaged'.[1] *25 March 1830*

Mr Blake, the artist who made the designs for 'Blair's Grave' engraved by Schiavonetti, and lately made designs also from 'Job,' was a year or two ago in great pecuniary distress, which came to the knowledge of Sir Thomas, and he, Mr Blake, came to a friend's of mine, who lives near Charing Cross, one morning, with tears of joy and gratitude in his eyes—on being asked the cause, he told my friend that Sir Thomas had sent him a 100£ [*in*] bills that [*sic*], which had relieved his distresses, and made him and his wife's heart leap for joy.—[2]

Ignoring 'a year or two ago' (for Blake had died three years previously), we cannot easily date this incident. Perhaps it occurred in July

---

[1] 'The office [*of Lawrence's biographer*] was undertaken by his friend, Mr. Thomas Campbell', but 'circumstances prevented' Campbell from carrying it out, and he therefore delegated the task to his 'coadjutor' D. E. Williams in a letter of 10 Nov. 1830, along with the 'documents' which he had collected, presumably including the above letter from Etty. However, as Williams reported: 'The instances in which Sir Thomas exhibited the kindness of his heart to others, were so very numerous, that a selection even of the strongest cases, would, I fear, occupy too large a portion of space for me to insert them in this work' (D. E. Williams, *The Life and Correspondence of Sir Thomas Lawrence, K^t.* (1831), vol. i, pp. vi, vii, ix–xii, 349), and the Etty letter must thus have been cast aside.

[2] Quoted from a xerox of the letter generously sent me by its owner, Professor Robert Essick, who has since printed it in 'William Blake and Sir Thomas Lawrence', *Notes & Queries*, ccxxiii (1978), 211–13. Lawrence bought Blake's Blair, *Job*, 'The Wise and Foolish Virgins' (Lawrence's 'favourite drawing'), 'The Dream of Queen Katherine', and perhaps the *Songs* but not the *Paradise Regained* designs which were offered him— see *BR*, 169, 338–9, 400, 591.

1822, when Lawrence had just learned of Blake's distress through the application made for him to the charity of The Royal Academy (of which Sir Thomas was President), for Blake called on Sir Thomas on 13 July 1822. On 7 June 1825 Blake hoped that Sir Thomas 'has a good opinion of my willingness to appear grateful tho not able on account of this abominable Ague'.

3 April 1830 Linnell made a note in his Journal for 'Sat 3ᵈ [*April 1830*]—Sent a plain Copy of Job to Mʳ Bernard Barton of Woodbridge Suffolk—with a letter' in response to a poem about Linnell which Barton had sent him. Linnell's long letter to Barton and Barton's reply are on *BR*, 394–8.

29 November 1830 On 'Monday 29 [*November 1830 Linnell*] . . . sent a Copy of proof of Job to the Princess Sophia at Kensington Palace'. Other *Job* accounts refer to 'one plain Copy to Mr Leonard by Mr Varley to shew Princess Sophia' in October and November 1834 (*BR*, 597, 602), suggesting that the Princess did not take the 'Copy of proof of Job' sent in November 1830.

1 December 1830 Two days later, on 'Wed.—December 1ˢᵗ [*1830 Linnell went*] to Dᵒ [Mʳ Le Beaume 31 Southampton Row *where he had gone with Varley the previous day*] & took a Copy of proofs of Blake's *Job*', but Mr Le Beaume is not recorded in the *Job* accounts as having taken a copy.

2 December 1830 Next day, 'Thursday 2ᵈ [*December 1830 he*] . . . sent a Copy of Job to Mʳˢ *Dowson*', whose children he was painting at the time, but there is no Dowson in the *Job* accounts either.

27 January 1831 Throughout the first month of 1831, Linnell had been, as he recorded in his Journal for 'Thursday 27ᵗʰ . . . Dantè tracing some every Evening'.[1]

29 January 1831 Two days later, on 'Sat 29 . . . Mr Bull pro. Engraving backgᵈ &c of Dʳ Gooch / Job 2.12 6d. Paid him 1£. more in Cash & a copy of Blake's Job—Cash 1 10—reckoning 2–10–0 for 6 days'. On the endpaper of the Journal is:

Mʳ Bull	Cʳ	Dʳ	Dʳ
1 week	2–10–0	Cash	0–10———
		Dᵒ	1—
		Book of Job	2.10—
			4———

[1] The same day Linnell went 'to Mʳ Blakie's John Street Fitzroy Sq—' to settle the disputed bill for painting Linnell's house; 'To Mʳ Rice[?] previous to going to the Galleries Consulted him respecting the Demand of Mʳ Blakie.' I think, however, that the presence in Linnell's Journal of references to the picture painter Mr Blake and the house painter Mr Blakie has not caused confusion between them. On 11–13, 17–19 Jan 1830 Linnell had 'Pro [Tracing of] Dantè [*or* Dante] [by Blake]'.

And in the *Job* accounts (*BR*, 601), under 'Copies of the Book of Job. exchanged', is '1 Copy of J. Bull in exchange for work'.

An anonymous early review of 'Lives of the Most Eminent British Painters. By Allan Cunningham. Vol. I. & II. London. Murray, 1830', *Library of the Fine Arts*, i (February 1831), 35, pointed out that 'In the *February* second volume Mr. Cunningham has given us accounts of the lives of *1831* West, Barry, Blake, Opie, Morland, Bird, and Fuseli, all painters of great though unequal merit[.]'

On 'Monday 20 [*June 1831 Linnell*] . . . sent Parcel to Mr Lizars at Edinburgh—Containing Book of Job plain' and other works. This is *20* the 'Copy plain' recorded as sent in June 1831 and is perhaps the same *June* as the one paid for by 'H. W. Lizars Edinburgh for a friend' in August *1831* 1832 at the rate of £2. 12s. 0d. (or £2. 10s. 0d.) (*BR*, 602, 597, 600).

And next day, 'Tuesday 21 . . . sent Proof of Dr Gooch & P. & pla[i]n of of [*sic*] Job to Dr King'. This is the copy entered in the *Job* *21* accounts (*BR*, 602) as '1 copy Dr King Brighton upon sale or return / *June* returned'. *1831*

In October 1831 a harsh series of Anonymous '*Remarks on Williams's Life of Sir Thomas Lawrence*', *Library of the Fine Arts*, ii (October 1831), 214, commented that:

practise is the life and soul of painting; ideas may be grand, but they offend the eye and mind of taste if not portrayed with becoming felicity. Look at the *October* instances of Barry, Fuseli, and Blake,—men redolent with the finest ideas and *1831* imagination; but they wanted practice in the handicraft of their art, which the confined patronage they received debarred them from attaining.

In his Journal for October 1831, Linnell recorded:

Tuesday 18 . . . Mrs Blake died at 7 in the morning *18–19* Wed 19 to F. Tathams &c—see F. Tatham's letters *October* *1831*

For Tatham's letter announcing Mrs Blake's death to Linnell at 'at ½ past 7', see *BR*, 411.

According to his Journal, Linnell went on 'Sat 7 [*April 1832*]—to Mrs Callcott / to Mr Rogers left Blake's Drawings of Paradise Reg.^d for *7* him to look at'. Gilchrist mentions that Linnell offered the Milton *April* drawings to Chantrey, who declined them (*BR*, 339), but he does not *1832* mention the great patron Samuel Rogers, who is not known to have owned anything by Blake.

A week later Linnell went on 'Sat 14 . . . to Mr Rogers bro.^t away *14* Blake's Drawings of Paradise reg.^d—'. *April* *1832*

20   On 'Monday 20 [*August 1832 Linnell*] . . . sent to Sussex Hotel for M^r
August Lizars also a Book of Job plain 2.2 o . . .'. Lizars appears in the *Job*
1832 accounts under August 1832 (*BR*, 597, 600), as having taken a 'Book of
Job plain' 'for a friend' at £2. 10s. 0d. and £2. 12s. 6d.

According to W. M. Glenning, 'Fancy and Imagination', *Arnold's
Library of Fine Arts*, NS, i (March 1833), 372,

> The best designs of Fuseli are, to my thinking, far more imaginative than
> those of any other modern master. There may not be even a single exception.
> Reynolds and West had, perhaps, more vigorous fancies, but they were never
> so abstractedly ideal as Fuseli. Blake too was possessed of strong imagination.
March But like the imaginations of men in the infancy of the world, it was little under
1833 the dominion of reason. Consequently other men could not adequately com-
> prehend it. Because as reason and feeling are the only common ties between
> mind and mind, if these do not attend the footsteps of imagination, it will be in
> vain for other imaginations to follow out the remote and devious track it takes.

According to his Journal, on 'Thursday 21 [*November 1833 Linnell*]
. . . sent in the Evening by M^r N^s[?] messenger . . . 1 Book of Job . . . to
21   Colnaghi'. The only copies of *Job* for Colnaghi in the *Job* accounts are
November for July 1827 and Spring 1829 (*BR*, 601), both 'in exchange'; probably
1833 this copy also was for goods received from Colnaghi.

APPENDIX I: LINNELL MANUSCRIPTS REDISCOVERED

———

BLAKE RECORDS quotes extensively from the journal, letters, and account books of John Linnell, mostly from transcripts by his son John Linnell Jun. and his grandson Herbert Palmer in the Ivimy MSS (*BR*, 256 n. 2). In 1970 the original manuscripts were rediscovered, also in the Ivimy MSS, in trunks of papers recently recovered, and I transcribed the Blake references from the originals, once more through the kindness of my friend Miss Joan Linnell Ivimy. In the process, I discovered that John Linnell Jun. and Herbert Palmer had been on the whole commendably accurate but that they had omitted a number of minor references to Blake (inserted in the text above) and made some small, involuntary changes.

For the sake of completeness and accuracy, these recovered references to Blake in the original manuscripts are repeated here[1] under Part A: Linnell's Journal, 1818–38, Part B: Letters to Linnell about Blake, 1825–35, and Part C: Linnell's General Account Books, 1818–79. In each section, the previously unpublished references to Blake are distinguished with an asterisk by the marginal date to indicate that they are also given with annotation in the text above.[2]

Part A: LINNELL's JOURNAL

John Linnell's Journal was kept in little books which, so far as Blake is concerned, are as follows: (1) A vellum book marked on the cover '3 / 1817 to 1822 / 3', paginated in ink 29–264 (259–62 missing); (2) Vellum spine marked '18 / 23 / to 27', marbled boards, not numbered; (3) Green spine with '1828 to 30' over green marbled boards; (4) Brown calf spine with '[*18*]31 / to / 33' over brown marbled boards; (5) Three-quarter brown leather marked '7', '[*18*]34 / to / 36' (though it begins on 6 May 1833); there are successive volumes for '8' (1 April 1836 to 27 Dec. 1837), '9' ('[*18*] 38 / 40'), '10' ('1840 to Aug 1841'), '11'

---

[1] Naturally the Blake references quoted in *BR* from Linnell's original manuscripts, such as the Job accounts in Yale, are not reprinted here.
[2] Except for those after 1833.

('Sept 1841 to Dec 1848'), '12' ('January 1849 to June 22nd 1854'), '13' ('June 1854 to Dec 1857'), 14 (1858–66), and '15' ('1867 to 1879').

Linnell entered something in the Journal almost every day but Sunday (it is largely a business journal); most of the Sunday entries I noticed were for Blake. There are often sketches in the margin to indicate the drawing he is talking about (e.g. Vol. '3', pp. 86–7). It is in pencil and sometimes hard to read.

The entries are laconic, e.g. 8 September 1818, 'Hannah born', 7 November 1823 'second Son Born ½ past 8 morning'. It is not an exhaustive account of Blake's business affairs, or even of Linnell's dealings with Blake, for there are a number of dates when we know that Blake and Linnell were together (e.g. 6 June 1820, 25 March 1823) for which there is no Journal reference to Blake.

Linnell often paid for goods and services by barter rather than by cash; for example, on 27 October 1818 he 'gave Dr Thornton the Skull of a Tyger & D?. of a Boar / Jaw Bone of a Fish—& one pound for the air pump / which is all he would receive for his attendance', apparently at the birth of Linnell's daughter Hannah. There is of course much which is of interest in the Journal beyond the affairs of William Blake. For instance, on 8, 15, 22, 25, and 29 March 1819 he went in the 'Evening to Mr Coleridge's lecture on Philosophy'.

Friday 19 June 1818 'to Mr Rogers with Mr Cumberland Junr'.

Tuesday 23 June 1818, 'recd a Copper Plate from Mr Pontifex for to Engrave Mr Uptons Portrait on—'.

24 Wed. 24 [*June 1818*]—to Mr Blake (Evening) deliverd to Mr Blake the Picture
June of Mr Upton & the Copper Plate—to begin the engraving— . . . .
1818

10 Friday 10 [*July 1818*]—went with Mr Blake to Lord Suffolks to see Pictures /
July to [*Pall Mall to*] see Leonard Da Vinci's Last Supper— / to Mr Vine's deliverd
1818 Pictures of Moon light & Scotch Forrest . . .

21 Friday 21 [*August 1818*] . . . to Colnaghi's with Mr Blake . . .
August
1818

24 Monday 24th [*August 1818*] . . . Mr & Mrs Blake to Tea &c . . .
August
1818

9 Wed—9 [*September 1818*]— . . . to Mr Blake Evg / to Mr Pontifex to ask for
September Money . . .
1818

Friday 11 [*Sep)tember 1818*]—went with Mr Cumberland to Mr Flaxmans & to
Mr Stothard & museum— / to Mr Blake Evening / Paid him 5£— . . .

Sat 12 [*September 1818*] . . . Mr Blake Brought a proof of Mr Upton's / Plate /
left the Plate & named 15£ as the / Price of what was already done by him— /
– / Mr Varley— & Mr Constable stay'd with Blake / – / Mr Farr—Came from
Mr Pontifex & Paid me 10£—on acc^t / of Mr Upton's Picture— . . .

Friday 18 [*September 1818*] . . . to Mr Blake with Mr Varley—Ev^g— . . .

Sat 19 [*September 1818*]—Began upon Mr Upton's Plate— / Engraved all day
on it / Dr Thornton called & Mr Blake / went with Mr Blake to Mr Varley's
Evg— . . .

Linnell continued to work on 'Plate of Mr Upton' on 2–3 October, 16,
18–21, 24 November, 7 December 1818, 21–3 January, 2–3, 5, 8–9, 11,
15–19, 22–4 February, 3–5, 10 March 1819, and proofs were pulled on
13 March, 3, 15, 16 May 1819.

On 20 March 1819 Linnell went 'To Mr Pontifex with Mr Upton's
Plate— / left it for the writing engraver'. On 26 April 1819 he went to
the copperplate-printer James Lahee, and on 15 May 1819 he went 'to
Lahee—for Proofs of Mr Upton . . . to Mr Sawyer for Proof of Upton
Plate—' on the same day. He took two more proofs from the Upton
plate on Tuesday 18 May, and on the 21st he went 'to Mr Pontifex with
two proofs of Mr Upton⹀approved—'. (NB There is also a 'Painting
of Mr Upton in May 1819, and some of the work above may in fact be
painting on the picture.) On 28 May 1819 he went 'to Mr Pontifex—
agreed to endeavor to give more of flesh color to the face of M^r
Upton's Plate—& then it shou d be considered finished—'. He worked
again on the Upton plate on 3 June 1819.

Thursday 17 [*June 1819*] . . . to Mr Denny—[1] to Mr Blake—to Mr Stewart—to
Miss Pocock . . . to Mr Pontifex del^d Proof of Mr Upton . . .

On 30 June 1819 he 'Sent by A[?]. Varley. The Copper Plate of M^r
Uptons Portrait. to Mr Pontifex', with the imprint presumably freshly
added of 'London Published July 1st 1819 by R Pontifex Lisle Street'.[2]
On 17 July 1819 he settled with Pontifex for the Upton plate, and on
26 August he received £40 from Pontifex.

[1] On 19 Sept. 1821, Linnell went to visit Denny near Worcester and made five portraits of his family for £162. 5s.

[2] The third and final state of the plate was bought in 1985 and first recorded by Professor Robert N. Essick; in the previously known states the publisher was not identified,
though of course Linnell's Journal points clearly to Pontifex.

20　Friday 20 [*August 1819*] . . . with Mr Blake to see Harlow's Copy of Transfigur-
August　ation . . . with Mr Holmes to Mr Blake, Ev^g . . .[1]
1819

23　Sat 23^d [*October 1819*]— . . . Began a Painting in oil colors of two Heads Size of
October　life from Drawings by W. Blake of Wallace & Edward 1st—for Mr Varley . . .
1819

26　Tuesday 26 [*October 1819*] . . . Pro Heads of Wallace & Ed$^{\underline{d}}$ . . .
October
1819

1　Mon 1st [*November 1819*]— . . . Heads from Blake's Designs of Wallace &
November　Edward 1$^{\underline{st}}$ . . .
1819

24　Monday 24th [*April 1820*] to Spring Gardens with Mr Blake / Met the Duke of
April　Argyll . . .[2]
1820

On Wednesday 12 April 1820 Linnell had been 'to Council Meeting at
Sp. Gardens', apparently for the Society of Painters in Oil and Water
Colours.

8　Monday 8$^{\underline{th}}$ [*May 1820*] to Mr Wyatt. with Mr Blake / To Lady Ford—saw her
May　Pictures . . .
1820

11　Thursday 11$^{\underline{th}}$ [*May 1820*] . . . to Mr Denny's to Tea with Mr Blake & M^r
May　Varley— . . .
1820

On 2 October 1820 Linnell went 'with Dr Thornton to Dartmouth
St *W*est[*minste*]^r to the Lythography Press—to prove a Head of
Virgil—' engraved by Blake.

9
October　Monday 9 [*October 1820*]—to Dr Thornton—M^{r}Blake &c. . . .
1820

'Wed 18 [*October 1820*] . . . Began a small Drawing on a wood Block
/ of Polypheme (from N. Poussin) for Dr Thornton / to receive a
guinea for it—'. Blake made the engraving of this plate.

3　Sat 3$^{\underline{d}}$ [*February 1821*]— . . . Dr Thornton dined with me—we went to M^r
February　Blakes . . .
1821

[1] A. H. Palmer's transcript quoted in *BR*, 259, gives:

August 20. With Mr Blake to see Harlowe's copy of *Transfiguration*
　　21. With Mr Blake to Mr Carpenters. with Mr Homes to Mr Blake Evening.

I cannot explain the discrepancies.

[2] The A. H. Palmer transcript quoted in *BR*, 264, continues: 'dunned him for money
due on portrait. "The Duke of Argyll appointed tomorrow"', but these are interpola-
tions by Palmer. I find nothing written about dunning the Duke of Argyle (though the
implication is likely), and the words 'the Duke of Argyll appointed tomorrow' appear
under 25 April 1820 in the Journal.

Friday 9 [*February 1821*]— ... Mr Blake came Evening— ...

9
February
1821

Thursday 8th [*March 1821*] to British Gall. &c. with Mr Blake— / Dined with me ...

8
March
1821

Tuesday 27 [*March 1821*] ... to the Theatre Drury Lane with Mr Blake ...

27
March
1821

Monday 30 [*April 1821*]—with Mr Blake to water color Exhib. &c / to Fulham ... [*to see a patron*].

30
April
1821

Mond[*ay*] 7 [*May 1821*] ... with Mr Blake to Somerset House Ex: ...

7
May
1821

Sunday 29 [*May 1821*]—to Hampstead with Mr Blake[1] ...

29
May
1821

Friday 8 [*June 1821*] ... to Drury Lane Theatre with Mr Blake ...

8
June
1821

Sunday 26 [*August 1821*] to Hendon to Mr Woodburns with Mr Blake ...

26
August
1821

Sat 8 [*September 1821*] Traced outlines from Mr Blakes Designs from Job ∧all day∧— / Mr Blake & Mr Read with me all day— ...[2]

8
September
1821

Monday 10th [*September 1821*] Traced outlines from Mr Blakes drawings of Job—all day / Mr Blake finishing the outlines—all day. / Mr Read left London for Salisbury / who had lived with us since Friday every day / Mr Blake took home the drawings of Job—

10
September
1821

Tues 11—Mr Blake brought a Drawing of Cain & Abel.
Wed.—12 Began a Copy of Cain & Abel— ...

11—12
September
1821

Friday—14 [*September 1821*] Pro[*ceeded with*] & fin^d Cain & Abel ...

14
September
1821

Sat 27 [*October 1821*] Mr Blake came to see me Ev g— ...

27
October
1821

---

[1] This is given as Sunday 27 May 1821 in *BR*, 272.
[2] The entries for 8–14 Sept. are somewhat garbled in A. H. Palmer's transcript in *BR*, 275:
Sat 8 Mr Blake & Mr Read with me all Day
Mr Blake finishing the outlines all day Monday 10th.
11. Mr Blake took home the Drawings of Job. 11 Mr Blake brought Drawing of Cain & Abel.
12. Began a copy of Cain & Abel. Finished 14th.

*11
November
1821*

Sund[*ay*] 11. [*November 1821*]—Mr Blake dined with us . . .

*9
December
1821*

Sunday 9 [*December 1821*] Mr Blake dined here . . .

*14
April
1822**

Sunday 14 [*April 1822*] Mr Varley & Mr Blake Dined here . . .

*8–9
May
1822*

Wed 8 [*May 1822*][1] . . . to M^r. Vines with Mr Blake.

Thursday 9.[1] Mr Blake began copies from his Drawings from Miltons P.L. . . .

*13
July
1822*

Sat 13 [*July 1822*] to Sir Thos. Lawrence with Mr Blake— . . .

*17
April
1823*

Thursday 17 [*April 1823*] with Mr Blake to British Museum to see Prints . . .

*24
April
1823*

Thursday 24 [*April 1823*] to British Museum. with M^r. Blake . . .

*5
May
1823*

Monday 5 [*May 1823*] to Royal Academy Exhibition with Mr Blake . . .

*25
June
1823*

Wed. 25 [*June 1823*] with Mr Blake to British Gall. &c.— . . .

*14
May
1824*

Tuesday 18 [*May 1824*] . . . to Mr Vine—Mr James[?]—Blake— — . . .

On 24 July 1824 Linnell 'made outline for Mr Lowry's Engraving'. About 5 August 1824 he 'rec^d of Mrs Lowry 15£ on acc^t. of the engraving of Mr Lowry to be done in October the price to be 30 gs the remainder to be paid on delivery of the Plate—'. On 15–17 November he was busy 'Pro engraving Mr Lowry's Portrait'. 20 November 'del^d a Proof to Mrs Lowry'; 22–6 November 'Pro Plate *of* Mr Lowry', 29 November 'del^d the Plate of Mr Lowry—Bal of acc^t £6. ^s10'; 6 December 'retouchd & del^d the Plate of M^r. Lowry' which he had engraved with Blake.

*4
August
1824*

Wed 4 [*August 1824*] Mr Varley. Mr Tatham & Son & Mr Blake dined with me at Hampstead . . .

[1] Not April 1822, as in *BR*, 275.

Friday 28 [*January 1825*] . . . to Capt Buller—Rennie—Blake—Bank—Neale— &c . . .

Friday 4 [*March 1825* . . . to Dixon's proving Job. with Mr Blake . . .

Sat 5 [*March 1825*] . . . with Mr Blake to Lahee's proving Job . . .

Wed 9 [*March 1825*] to Mr Blake, Read, Capt Buller[1] &c . . .

Friday 8 [*April 1825*] to City—Blake &c . . .

Tuesday 3 [*May 1825*] . . . to Mr Blake. to Exhibition . . .

Sat 6 [*August 1825*] to Mrs Aders 11 Euston sq with Mr Blake

Monday 8   D—   D°. with S. Palmer . . .

Monday 7 [*November 1825*] to Mr Blake . . .

Sat 10 [*December 1825*] dine at Mr Aders. with Mr Blake & Mr H. C. Robinson . . .

At this dinner, Crabb Robinson reported that Blake 'brought with him an engraving of his Canterbury pilgrims for Aders[.] One of the figures resembled one in one of Aders's pictures[.] ["]They say I stole it from this picture, but I did it 20 years before I knew of the picture—however in my youth I was always studying this kind of paintings".' This was probably the head of John the Baptist on a golden dish attributed to Van Eyck but probably by Petrus Christus. Blake would have known of the painting before he saw it, for on 10 November 1825 Linnell 'Agreed with Mr Aders to engrave a Plate of Part of the Van Eyck Picture 20 Inches by 7″ to be done in about three months, for 100 gs— see agreement—'. On Monday 14 November he 'Engraved a small Plate of one figure from the centre Picture by Van Eyck done as a Specimen of the style—& for a prospectus for the whole work'. He 'Bro^t away the Picture from Mr Aders—to Hampstead' on 19 November, and on 21 November he 'Began the outline for the Plate from Van

[1] For 'Capt Buller', as in 28 Jan. 1825, A. H. Palmer gives 'Cafe Bollo' (*BR*, 300).

Eyck'. On 19–24 November he 'Fin$^{\underline{d}}$ in the Evenings the Small Plate of one figure'. On 23 November he 'dined at Mr Aders rec^d verbal order to begin the Plate'. He sent Aders his terms on 26 November, worked on the outline on 28–30 November, and continued with it through April 1826; on 15 April 1826 he 'Sent a proof to Mr Aders of the Plate from Van Eyck'.

17
May
1826
Wed 17 [*May 1826*]—to Father's—to Mr Blake &c— . . .

12
July
1826
Wed 12 [*July 1826*] to Mr Blake . . .

13
July
1826
Thursday 13 [*July 1826*]—to Mr Blake, Dr Young &c . . .

30
September
1826*
Sat 30 [*September 1826*] . . . lent a Copy of Job (proofs) to Master[?] Shorto [*the artist*] . . .

13
October
1826*
Friday 13 [*October 1826*] . . . Sent a copy of Job (proofs) to Bohn . . .

10
November
1826*
Frid[*ay*] 10 [*November 1826*] sent to Mr Denny a Copy of Job proofs 5 gs also— a Copy of Blair's Grave 2.12/6 [*in response to Denny's letter of 4 November*] . . .

9
January
1827
Tuesd[*ay*] 9 [*January 1827*]—to City— / to Mr Blake—5£ . . .

7
February
1827
Wed 7 [*February 1827*]—to Mr Blake. to speak to him @ living at C[*irencester*]. P[*lace*] . . .

8
February
1827
Thurs 8 [*February 1827*] . . . left with Sir Tho Lawrence Blake's Drawings of Par. Reg^d pr[*ice*]. 50£ . . .

23
February
1827
Friday 23^d [*February 1827*] . . . Sent a copy of Job. (proofs) to Dr Gooch— prom^d to take them for the Kings Library . . .

17
April
1827
Tuesday 17 [*April 1827*] to Mr Ottley with Mr Blake[1] . . .

15
May
1827
Tuesday 15 [*May 1827*] to Bank—Mr Blake &c— . . .

[1] Linnell saw Ottley frequently at this time, on 20 and 24 April, 1 and 11–12 May, etc.

Wed 11 [*July 1827*]—to Somerset House— / Mr Blake &c— ...   11
                                                               July
                                                               1827

Tuesday 17 [*July 1827*]—to Bank, Mr Blake, Cochrane &c. ...   17
                                                                July
                                                                1827

Friday 3 [*August 1827*] to Mr Blake— ...   3
                                              August
                                              1827

Friday 10 [*August 1827*] ... to Mr Blake / not expected to live. ...[1]   10
                                                                             August
                                                                             1827

Sunday 12 [*August 1827*]—Mr Blake died—   12–14
Monday 13   to Mrs Blake— / to B. Palmer— @ Mr Blake's Funeral   *August*
Tuesday 14   to Sir Thos Lawrence @ Mrs Blake ...   *1827*

Thursday 16 [*August 1827*] ... sent Mr Blake's Jerusalem to Mr Ottley— ...   16
                                                                                 August
                                                                                 1827

Sat 18 [*August 1827*] to Mrs Blake ...   18
                                            August
                                            1827

Tuesday 21 [*August 1827*] ... Mr F. Tatham came @ Mrs Blake ...   21
                                                                      August
                                                                      1827

Wed 22^d [*August 1827*]—to Mrs Blake to arrange @ moving Printing press &c—   22
....   *August*
                                                                                 1827

Thursday 30 [*August 1827*] Mrs Blake's press moved to C^r Place[2] ...   30
                                                                            August
                                                                            1827

Tuesday 11 [*September 1827*] Mrs Blake moved to Cirencester Place ...   11
                                                                           September
                                                                           1827

Saturday 8 [*December 1827*] ... gave Mrs Blake 5£ boro^d[?] ...   8
                                                                     December
                                                                     *1827**

Wed 16[3] [*January 1828*] Mr Cumberland Came & paid Mrs Blake for the card   16
Plate 3 gs & for the copy of Job 2.12.6 ...   *January*
                                                                                 1828

---

[1] Below is a very slight sketch which is reproduced in *The Portraiture of William &
Catherine Blake*, ed. Geoffrey Keynes (1977); I see no sign of the skull-cap or pillow
reported by A. H. Palmer.
    [2] Not 29 August, as in the A. H. Palmer transcript quoted in *BR*, 351.
    [3] Not the 17th as in A. H. Palmer transcript (*BR*, 365).

24   Thursday 24 [*January 1828*] . . . sent to Mr Johns at *P*lymouth a copy of India
January proofs of the *Job* & one plain imp[*ression*]— . . .[1]
1828*

17   Monday 17 [*March 1828*] . . . two Ladies called to [*see*] the Book of Job & gave
March Mrs Blake—4^s . . .
1828

> On 26 July 1828 'Mr Varley Came to agree about Etchings [for his
> Zodiacal Physiognomy (1828)] @ 10 gs. for a Plate with four
> squares[?] in each'. On 31 July Linnell 'made Etching of four heads
> for Mr Varley / Scorpio Aries Libra & Taurus', and on 4 August he
> 'Etchd Heads for Mr Varley / of Cancer & Leo'. On 29 October 1828
> he 'Began 2$^{\underline{d}}$ Plate of Physiognomy for Mr Varley—', on 31 October he
> worked on 'Varley's Plate', and on 5–7 November he was concerned
> with '2^d Plate of Physiog^y for Mr Varley'. One of the Cancer plates was
> after Blake's design.

8   Monday 8$^{\underline{th}}$ [*September 1828*] . . . Mr Calvert came & brought impressions of
September Blake's wood Cuts . . .
1828

19   Friday 19 [*September 1828*] to Dr Johnson's Mrs Blake & Varley . . .
September
1828

27   Tuesday 27 [*January 1829*]—to Mrs Blake——who s^d that Mr Blake told her he
January thought I sh^d pay 3 gs. a piece for the Plates of Dante— . . .
1829

26   Thursday 26$^{\underline{th}}$ [*November 1829*] . . . Sent Copy of Job, Proofs to Miss
November James . . .
1829*

17   Thursday 17 [*December 1829*] . . . Sent Book of Job to Mr Allen to see . . .
December
1829*

10   Wed^y 10$^{\underline{th}}$ [*February 1830*] . . . Sent to Mr Cooper. R.A. a scetch by Mr Blake &
February a letter of his also—for his Collection of Autographs . . .
1830

20   Sat 20 [*February 1830*] . . . to Mr Callcott with Mr Allan & Shewed Mr Callcott
February the Drawings by Mr Blake of Dantè . . .
1830*

25   Thursday 25$^{\underline{th}}$ [*February 1830*] . . . Mr Haviland Burke Called @ Mrs Blake /
February from the Bishop of London [*i.e. Limerick*], Showed me / a letter from the
1830   Bishop enquiring / how he c^d best serve Mrs Blake / advised him to recom-
         mend to the B— / to purchase the works of M^r B— / from M^{rs} B [*i.e. not from*
         Tatham] . . .

---

[1] For A. B. Johns's reply of 31 January 1828, see *BR*, 366.

Tuesday 2ᵈ [*March 1830*] . . . Mʳ H Burke Called & appointed tomorrow to go to Mʳˢ Blake—with me . . .

2
March
1830

Wedʸ 3 [*March 1830*] . . . went with Mʳ H. Burke to Mʳˢ Blake & selected two Drawings 8 gs. two Prints of Job & Ezekiel 2 gs & the colorᵈ Copy of the Songs of Innocence & Experience making 20gs—which the Bishop of Limerick sent Mʳ Burke to lay out with Mʳˢ Blake . . .

3
March
1830

Thursday 11 [*March 1830*] . . . Mʳ Ollyer, Mʳ Allason / & Mʳ Allan came to see Mʳ Blake's Drawings . . .

11
March
1830*

Sat 3ᵈ [*April 1830*]—Sent a plain Copy of Job to Mʳ Bernard Barton of Woodbridge Suffolk—with a letter . . .

3
April
1830*

Friday 3ᵈ [*August 1830*]¹—to Town with Mʳ Varley overston[?] Mʳˢ Blake—Carpet Shop &c . . .

3
August
1830

Monday 29 [*November 1830*] . . . sent a Copy of proof of Job to the Princess Sophia at Kensington Palace . . .

29
November
1830*

Wed.—December 1ˢᵗ [*1830*] . . . to Dᵒ [Mʳ Le Beaume 30 Southampton Row *where Linnell went with Varley on 30 November*] & took a Copy of proofs of Blake's *Job* . . .

1
December
1830*

Thursday 2ᵈ [*December 1830*] . . . sent a Copy of Job to Mʳˢ *Dowson* . . .

2
December
1830*

Monday 10ᵗʰ [*January 1831*] . . . Pro every morning & Evening with tracings of Mʳ Blake's Drawings from Dantè—began them 10 Days back or thereabouts . . .

10
January
1831

[*Tuesday and Wednesday 11–12 January 1831*] Pro Tracing of Dantè by Blake . . .

11–12
January
1831*

[*Thursday 13 January 1831*] Pro tracing of Dante . . .

13
January
1831

[*Monday and Tuesday 17–18 January 1831*] Pro tracing of Dantè . . . [*Wednesday 19 January 1831*] Dᵒ . . .

17–19*
January
1831

[*Wednesday 26 January 1831*] Pro Dantè . . .

26
January
1831*

Thursday 27ᵗʰ [*January 1831*] . . . Dantè tracing some every Evening . . .

27
January
1831*

¹ In John Linnell Jun.'s transcript quoted in *BR*, 401, this is given under 3 Sept.

29
January
1831*
Sat 29 [*January 1831*] . . . Mr Bull pro. Engraving backg^d &c of Dr Gooch / Job 2.12 6d. Paid him 1£. more in Cash & a copy of Blake's Job—Cash 1 10— reckoning 2–10–10 for 6 days . . . [*And on the end paper is:*

Mr Bull	C^r	D^r	D^r
1 week	2–10–0	Cash	0–10——
		D°	1——
		Book of Job	2.10—
			4——

2
February
1831
Wed. 2.^d [*February 1831*] . . . Dante some every day . . .

7
February
1831
[*Monday 7 February 1831*] Tracing Dante also—morning & Evening— . . .

19
February
1831
[*Saturday 19 February 1831*] Dante tracing also . . .

20
June
1831*
Monday 20 [*June 1831*] . . . sent Parcel to M^r. Lizars at Edinburgh——Containing Book of Job plain [*and other works*] . . .

21
June
1831*
Tuesday 21 [*June 1831*] . . . sent Proof of Dr Gooch & P. & pla[*i*]n of of [*sic*] Job to Dr King . . .

18—19
October
1831*
Tuesday 18 [*October 1831*] . . . Mrs Blake died at 7 in the morning
Wed 19   to F. Tathams &c—see F. Tatham's letters . . .

7
April
1832*
Sat 7 [*April 1832*]—to Mr Callcott / to M^r. Rogers left Blake's Drawings of Paradise Reg^d. for him to look at . . .

14
April
1832*
Sat 14 [*April 1832*] . . . to Mr Rogers bro.^t away Blake's Drawings of Paradise reg^d— . . .

20
August
1832*
Monday 20 [*August 1832*] . . . sent to Sussex Hotel for Mr Lizars . . . also a Book of Job plain 2. 2 o . . .

1
July
1833
Monday 1st [*July 1833*] to Mr Geo Stephen[1] Coleman[*?*] St. to meet Miss Blake / @ Administering to her Brothers Effects / with Mr S. & Miss B—to Proctors. &c . . .

4
July
1833
Thursday 4 [*July 1833*] . . . to Miss Blake, Painters [*or* Pimlico], &c . . .

---

[1] On 23 Sept. 1823 Linnell had gone 'to Mr Geo Stephen Broad St B^dings Began a sketch on Ivory in water Colors of his little Boy—(price to be 5 g^s[)]'.

Friday 26 [*July 1833*] to Lisson Grove to look at F. Tatham's effects. on   *26*
sale . . .   *July*
                                                                                1833

Thursday 21 [*November 1833*] . . . sent in the Evening by M^r N^s[*?*] messenger   *21*
. . . 1 Book of Job . . . to Colnaghi . . .   *November*
                                                                                           1833*

Friday—7 [*September 1838*] . . . changed with Mr Hilly[*?*] Bookseller King   *7*
S$^{t[?]}$—C[*ovent*] gardens 6 plain Copies of Job[1] for Encyclopedia Britan. . . .   *September*
                                                                                          1838*

Part B: LETTERS TO LINNELL ABOUT BLAKE

On Tuesday 18 October 1825, Mrs Linnell wrote to her husband:

I must now give you an account of my Sunday Visitors, Hannah came on
Saturday night, which was the only night she has slept here, on Sunday morning Mr Blake came as usual, and brought some good news respecting the Job.
He has taken them to Mr Flaxman you [*i.e.*, who] was delighted beyond   *18*
expectation, and paid for a copy of them, his approbation M^r B— thinks will   *October*
be of considerable advantage, I then took a Lesson on what I had in hand (I   *1825*
mean the copy. from Mich- Angelo,) which I think will be of service to me for
though I have done but little, yet I feel a want of advice from those more
skilled in the art. Just before we sat down to dinner my Father made his
appearance so that we had plenty of company till about six oclock, when they
all departed.

Two days later, on Thursday night,[2] Mrs Linnell wrote to John again:

Mr Blake has been to see us to day instead of Sunday, and brought a Sketch   *20*
Book, of Copy from Prints & which he made when about 14^{yrs} old. I have kept   *October*
it to show you. . . .   *1825*

On Thursday 10 February 1826 Mary Ann Linnell wrote to her husband:

Thursday Evening

My Dear Mr Linnell
   I should have written before but have not seen Edward untill this evening
having sent for him by Mrs Barling in order to hear respecting the Job &c—He
has been every day to Lahees and to Cirencester Place[,] from all I can Learn   *10*
the printing is going on well by a man of the name of Freeman, there has not   *February*
been any Letters or messages left at Cirencester Place.   *1826*

---

[1] This is not in the *Job* accounts, which, however, seem to stop about 1832.
[2] It is postmarked 21 Oct. 1825.

Robert Balmanno enclosed a letter to John Linnell 'with a parcel':

23 Mornington Place
22 Apr: 1826

Dear Sir

I have received Mr Blakes Illustrations of the Book of Job and perused the work with great attention and much interest.

You will not be offended if I say, your binder has put you to great expense in doing them up, and has thereby, *to me*, very greatly lessened the pleasure I should have taken in them. The back is so squeezed and pinched, the prints *22* crack and cockle every time they are turned over, and *must* in a short time be *April* much damaged. I can not handle the book without pain. With your permission *1826* therefore I will return it, and ask you for a set on plain paper, *loose*, & without fly leaves between. This reduction of the expense, and the Artists allowance, which I am in the habit of receiving, will reduce the cost to what I contemplated & understood when I subscribed viz! 2 Guineas, one of which I paid to Mr Blake a considerable time ago. I am Dr Sir

Your very obed Servt
J Linnell Esqre   Robt Balmanno

On Monday 24 April 1826, Robert Balmanno wrote to Linnell again:

Dr Sir

I am favord with your note and beg to inform you that I have not the hon[o]ur of being an Artist, but my labours for the benefit of the profession having been exerted rather zealously, for many years, I thought I might, from *24* an Artist, have asked the usual allowance (which has been invariably conceded *April* to me by Printsellers,) without its being considered as a very great favor.— *1826* When Mr Blake shewed me one of the Plates some years ago, I understood the work was for his own benefit & that the price was to be two Guineas, and I gave him what I believed to be half the Subscription: this I intimated to you, but as you have not noticed the circumstance, I will not trouble you to send me the work in any shape, I will see Mr Blake himself & arrange with him. I am your obed Hu Servt

Robt Balmanno
23 Mornington Place 24 Apr 1826

On Saturday 4 November, Edward Denny wrote to Linnell:

Dear Sir

I do not know exactly Mr Blake's residence, and therefore I have enclosed this letter to you, hoping that you will be so obliging as to deliver it to him—I should be very much obliged if you could write me a line to tell me when the *4* Book of Job will be completed, and whether Mr Blake is engaged in any other *November* *1826* work—I think I remember your telling me, that he had some notion of illustrating Dante, I should be glad to know if he has begun it yet, or whether he ever intends to do so . . . how is Mr Varley? . . .[1]

The enclosure to 'Mr Blake' said:

Sir

If you have a copy of Blair's Grave, with your illustrations, to dispose of, I should be much obliged to you if you could let me have it, or if you have not one yourself, would it be asking too much, to request you would be so kind as to procure a copy for me, and if you will send to me directed to me '*at Bar-* *bourne House, Worcester*' I shall feel particularly thankful to you—I hope you will be very particular in letting it be as good an impression as you can, as I am very much interested in it, I was shewn the work a day or two ago, and think it one of the most beautiful and interesting things I have seen of your's—I am also much interested in the progress of your illustrations of the Book of Job, having seen the unfinished plates some time since in the possession of M^r. Linnell, and hope you will tell me how it is going on, and when it is likely to be completed, perhaps also you would let me know whether you are engaged in any other performance at present—

> Believe me, Sir,
> Your's very truly obliged
> Edward Denny

Barbourne House—Worcester
November 4th 1826—

Will you let me know the price of the Grave, at the same time that you send it to me[?][2]

Linnell himself carried out the commissions Blake had been asked to perform, and some two weeks later Denny wrote to Linnell again:

Dear Sir

I thank you for your ready compliance with my wishes, and beg you will pardon my tardiness in writing to you—I am much obliged by your letter, and the very interesting information it contains— What shall I say, what *can* I say of the book of Job—I can only say that it is a *great work*—and tho' I can not venture to pass my humble comments upon any thing so truly sublime—I do indeed feel its exquisite beauty and marvellous grandeur— It is a privilege to possess such a work and ∧still greater to∧ be able to feel it— it is, I think, the

4 November 1826

20 November 1826

[1] The letter is addressed to 'M^r J Linnell / N° 6 Cirencester Place / Tichfield Street / London', marked 'Post-paid', with a round postmark: 'WORCESTER / NO 3 D 2 / 117' and a rectangular stamp: 'D / PAID / 4 NO 4 / 1826'. In it Denny remarks that he has not been in London for 'so long'.

[2] The cover is addressed merely to 'Mr Blake', and there is no postmark, etc., because the letter was enclosed with that above and was intended for delivery by hand. It is watermarked R BARNARD / 1825.

most perfect thing I ever have seen from the hands of Mr Blake, and if his Dante is superior, he will, I may almost say, outdo himself—I hope indeed he may complete this valuable work—

I am very sorry to hear that Mr Blake has been in danger, and sincerely hope that he is now in perfect health—

I congratulate you on success in your own affairs, and shall be happy to see what you have been doing when I next visit London— I send you a draft upon Puget & Bambridge for £7.17..6 the price of the Job and the Grave—and will you oblige me by informing me of your having received it—

> I remain dear Sir
> Your's very truly
> Edward Denny

Barbourne House—Worcester
Novr 20th 1826

Blake sold an extraordinarily beautiful copy of *Songs of Innocence and of Experience* (copy AA) to Mrs Charles Aders in July 1826 for £5. 5s. od. (*BR*, 583), and Linnell apparently had it bound for her—indeed, probably the sale was made through him. Eight years later, when in somewhat narrower circumstances, Mrs Aders wrote to Linnell:

24 Savage Gardens June 17th [*1834*]^1

My dear Sir

I much hoped to have been able to see you before this, but as usual illness has prevented me.—The fact is, I wish to explain to you my feelings & wishes about Blakes songs of Innocence & I cannot resist the desire to have Mr Aders' portrait, but am not now so well able to dispose of money as I was, (at any rate for my luxuries or fancies) and wish therefore that you would take that

17 June 1834 work in part payment, it cost me as you know 6£ that is £5..5s..od to Mr Blake & 16s to you for the Book in which they are— I have also another work of Blakes for which I gave to Mr. Tatham 5..5..0 [—] perhaps you might like to have that also— What I have said above is in confidence to you, & I feel sure your delicacy will treat it as such— If you agree to my plan you will have the kindness to send for the Songs—and Michael Angelo's whenever you please[;] perhaps some day it may please God that I may be rich enough to purchase the latter[.]

> Yours very sincerely
> Eliza Aders^2

---

^{1} The letter is postmarked 'NIGHT / JU 17 / 1834' and addressed to 'J. Linnell Esqr. / Porchester Terrace / Bayswater'.

^{2} Quoted from the transcript by my friend Mark Abley from the letter among the Ivimy MSS.

Linnell evidently was not tempted by the Blake work which had come from Tatham—perhaps the drawings of 'Los Walking on the Mountains of Albion' and 'Christian with the Shield of Faith, Taking Leave of His Companions'—from *Pilgrim's Progress* which she is known to have kept in an album[1]—but he did take the *Songs*. Next year he had an unfortunate misunderstanding with Mrs Aders about the prices of these works, and on 8 August 1835 she wrote to him that she had understood the price of her portrait was to have been £26. 5s. 0d.; 'when therefore you took Blakes Songs of Innocence &c at 6Gs I of course concluded I had only 20£ to pay'. She declined to pay more but said that a friend might do so, 'in which case when you receive the money you will send us the 6 Gs for Blakes work' (*BR*, 583 n. 1).[2]

On Tuesday March 10th [1835], S. Boddington, apparently a dealer, wrote to Linnell:

> There was not time to shew you my small Blakes coloured by himself—will *10* you do me the favour to call again soon . . . *March*
> S. Boddington[3] *1835**
> Tuesday Morning Mar—10th

By this time, Samuel Boddington apparently owned copies of *America* (P), *Descriptive Catalogue* (E), *For the Sexes* (C), *Songs of Innocence and of Experience* (c), *Jerusalem* (H), and coloured copies of *Europe* (M), and Young's *Night Thoughts* (J); Hannah Boddington had a copy of the *Songs* (b), and Thomas Boddington had a copy of *For the Sexes* (D) in which he put a copy of his bookplate dated '1833'.

In an undated letter to Linnell, perhaps from the artist Henry James Boddington (1811–65), there was another request for Blake information:

> My dear Sir   will you be so good as to tell me ye price of a proof copy of *?1835**
> *Blakes Job* such as we had of you before.
> Yrs very truly
> H[?] Boddington
> 5 Norfolk Crescent
> Hyde Park[4]

---

[1] Martin Butlin, *The Paintings and Drawings of William Blake* (1981), Nos. 784 and 829 (20).
[2] Linnell did acquire *Songs* (AA), for he inscribed it: 'Given to James Thos Linnell by John Linnell senr, April 28 1863'.
[3] March 10th was a Tuesday in 1818, 1829, and 1835. The paper is not watermarked.
[4] The paper is not watermarked.

Linnell may have replied by sending a copy of *Job*, perhaps the 'plain Copy' which Samuel Boddington paid for on 30 March 1835 (*BR*, 597) in addition to a proof copy. At any rate, on an unidentified Tuesday Boddington replied:

Mʳ Boddingtons Compᵗˢ to Mʳ Linnell & returns the *bound* copy of Blakes *?1835** book of Job.—& also the copies of his work which Mʳ L's Servant says he was desired to ask for that Mʳ L. might see that they were all right[.]

    when Mʳ Linnell sends the work again Mʳ Boddington begs if convenient that it may come between 9. & 10 when Mʳ B. will pay for it & the Blake's work if Mʳ L. will be so good to send a receipt[.]

    Mʳ B. would be glad to see the [book *del*] case which Mʳ Linnell shewed him he had had made to hold the engravings in as they came out[.]

    Tuesday Evᵍ

Linnell had become a profound admirer of the 'dear kind and accomplished Lady Torrens', and in 1820 he painted an admirable portrait of her and her six children.[1] In April 1826, Linnell sold a copy of *The Book of Job* to her (*BR*, 590, 599), and on 9 December 1832 her son A. W. Torrens, a captain in the Grenadier Guards, asked Linnell to send 'by the bearer the "*Book of Job*", as you kindly promised to do'.[2] Captain Torrens apparently admired but did not buy Blake's *Job*, so three years later Linnell gave him a copy. Captain Torrens replied appreciatively:

> Windsor.
> *17. April 1835.*

Dear Mr. Linnell,
    I received the book of Job, & return you many thanks for the present, in the
17 name of my wife.[3]—The note you were so good as to send with it, is no mean
April part of the value of the gift, containing as it does from so eminent an artist such
1835 strong approbation of the copy which was inadvertently left in the book ...
    Yr. very trly obliged,
    Arthur W. Torrens.

Clearly the Denny and Torrens families were appreciative patrons of William Blake. If only we had records of the rest of their dealings with and opinions of Blake.

---

[1] It is reproduced in colour in Katharine Crouan's catalogue of *John Linnell* (1982), No. 75.

[2] *William Blake*: The Critical Heritage (1975), 226.

[3] Of course neither Arthur Torrens nor his wife appears in the records of payments for *Job* (*BR*, 598–605), since the copy they received was a gift.

Part C: LINNELL'S GENERAL ACCOUNT BOOKS

Up to 8 August 1821 the entries in Linnell's General Account Books are from a little book 5 × 7½″ with the Ivimy MSS headed '1', 'CASH / 1813 / to / [*Feb. 18*]22'. The entries are in ink, very legible, and they are remarkably detailed, with columns of 'Cash Received' on the left hand page (verso) and 'Cash paid' on the right (recto). Many of the entries are of interest beyond the context of William Blake, such as:

1814 'for a Portrait of F.B. 10.10.0' from W. Beckford;

13 Nov. 1815 'of Mr Constable for a Drawing in Black-lead of Trees', £1;

27 December 1816 'of Mr Cumberland for A Small Painting of Windsor Forest & Lesson's on the Same', £5;

14 June 1817 'to Dr Spurzheim for his Book on Insanity—14*s*'—this may be the copy Blake annotated.

The leaves are foliated for fos. 2–65 at the top right corner. A pencil note at the bottom left of fo. 2 says: 'The 1st entries are written by Charles Tatham who gave John[?] this book'.

Other Linnell Account Books in the Ivimy MSS are:

2, 'Cash Account', 2 January 1822 to 31 December 1836, 5½ × 7¾″;

'3', 'Cash Book', '1837 / to / 1848', in brown calf, 5 × 7¼″;

'4', 'CASH', 1849–64, maroon morocco, 4 × 6″;

'5', 'CASH', '1864 to 1879', very pale brown cloth with a clasp, 4¼ × 6¼″;

'LEDGER', covering 1812–19 chiefly but with some entries for 1827, in vellum, 4½ × 6⅞″;

'LEDGER', '1819 / To / 1853', vellum, 4⅛ × 6⅛″.

The Blake entries for 1821–36 are not repeated here because they were quoted in *BR* (1969) from the original manuscript and not, like those of 1818–21, from a transcript. The entries for 1838–75 from the Ledgers are all new.

The entries below for 1818–75 in chronological order are from the Cash Books, which are of course organized by date. The entries which follow them in alphabetical order of debtor are from the two Ledgers, which are organized by name. '[*Receipt*]' means a separate receipt for this sum is given in *BR* (1969).

	[£, *s. d.*]	
12 [*August 1818*] to Mr Blake on account—	2 — —	[*Receipt*]

[£ s. d.]

[*11 September 1818*] to Mr Blake on account of
the plate of Mr Upton—   5 — —   [*Receipt*]

12 [*September 1818*] of Mr Pontifex by the
Hands of Mr Farr—on acc.^t of Mr Upton's Por-
trait—   10 — —

9 [*November 1818*] to Mr Blake on account—   5 — —   [*Receipt*]

[*17 July 1819*] of acc.^t for Engraving & Painting
Mr Upton's Portrait—   45 11 —

27 [*August 1819*] to Mr Blake for a Book of
Designs   2 — —   [*Receipt*]

31 [*December 1819*] to Mr Blake for 2^d n.^o of Jer-
usalem   14 —   [*Receipt*]

[*10 December 1820*] to Mr Blake for Prints—   1 — —

[*4 February 1821*] to Mr Blake—Bal of Jerusalem   —15 —

30 [*April 1821*] to Mr Blake for A Copy of his
Marriage of Heav. & Hell   2 2 —   [*Receipt*]

[*4 August 1821*] to Mr Blake for a Design—   1 1 —

     8   to Mr Blake on acc.^t for A Book of
Europe & America (not fin^d)   1 — —

 *   *   *   *   *   *

[*1 November 1838*] of Evans for Dante—   1   1

[*6 February 1839*] of Bryant for 2 plain Copies
Book of Job   2 10

7 [*December 1840*] of Mr Richmond for a plain
set of Blake's Job——   2   2

13 [*December 1842*] to Mr White for a Copy of
Blakes Songs Col^d   10 — —

[*6 February 1843*] of Mr Dilke for a Copy of
Dantè 1.12 & Job 1.10   3   2

[*14 February 1843*] of Mr Dilke by Mr Cole for a
Copy of Job—   1 10

[*8 November 1844*] of C. W Dilke for two copies
of job—   3   3

[*17 August 1845*] of Mr Richmond for book of
Job—   4· 4·

March 1 [*1859*] of J H Chance for a copy of
Blake's Job   2. 2

[*£ s. d.*]

Jan. 8 [*1863*] of Mr J H Chance for two french
proof copies of Blakes Job—— 6 6

[*16 April 1863*] to D° [*James Chance*] for a Drawing by Blake for William 3 13 6

    [*received*] of William 3 13 6

[*3 December 1863*] to Macmillan & co for three
copies of life of Blake—trade 3 8

[*28 December 1863 another copy for* 1 2 8]

[*20 May 1864*] of J. H. Chance for two copies of
Job 4.4. & 4.10 6—less 25 per C.— 6.10. 6

16 [*September 1864*] of H. Chance for copies of
Job—see acc^t—— 15 7 6

5 [*September 1865*] of H Chance for a Copy of
Job sold from his Stock in hand 3 15

[*13 December 1865 for a copy of Gilchrist from Macmillan* 1 2 8]

11 [*April 1866*] of J. H. Chance for 2 Dantè & 1
Job 11.15. 6

[*4 August 1866*] By copies of Job see bill &c [— — —]

[*30 October 1872*] of J H Chance balance for Job
& Frame &c 13 9 9

11 [*October 1873*] of Chance for Two India Sets
of Job 15 15

[*7 April 1874*] to Holdgate Bro^s for printing Job.
100 Sets See bill[*?*] &c[1] 66 —

[*25 June 1875*] of James Chance for Copy of Job
old proofs— 15 15

    The Ledger is an account book with a page for each payer and an
index of names at the beginning. There are many payments to Mr
White the engraver for laying on the ground for copperplates, for payments to James Linnell, for quarter's rent, &c. At the beginning (fo. 2^v)
of the earlier Ledger is an undated note: 'Blake—I owe him 2£', perhaps referring to the £2 paid Blake on 12 August 1818.

  [1] A receipt in the Ivimy MSS from Holdgate Bros, Steel & Copper-Plate Printers, 39,
London St, Fitzroy Square, dated 23 March 1874 is made out to Mr Linnell for 'paper
and printing as estimated Illustrations "Book of Job" 100 ea[*ch of*] 22 plates 2200 a[*t*] 3£
[*per hundred:*] £66.0.0.'

1816	Mr Pontifex	Dr	£ s D	
	—for Mr Upton's Church—			

		£	s	D
June	to a Painting of Mr Upton Pastor of the church Meeting at Black Friars—as p^r agr!	12	12	—
	Plate Engraved D^o from the above—	52	10	—
		65	2	
	Deducted for mistake	5	2	—
	Ball[ance]	60	—	—

[*The bill was paid in September 1816 and July 1819 by goods and cash*]

        Aders

[*December 1825*] Blake, Cant. Pilgrim		2	2
. . .			
Proof of Job——		5.	5
Songs of In & Ex—		5	5

        Lady Torrens

Sep^r	Copy of Book of Job	5	5	
[*1825*] Cash ——			5	5

		D^r	C.
1824	Mrs Lowry	£	£

Engraving on Copper the Portrait of the late Wilson

Dec^{ber} Lowry as agreed.—	31	10.	
Cash on acc^t		15	—
By Copper Plate & writing		—	10
Decr 25 Cash—		16	—
		31	10

      [*Geo Stephen Esq*]

Aug— [*1824*] to Mr Blake for C. Pilgrims		I	I
Oc^{tr} Framing & Glazing Pilgrims	2	2	
[*?August 1827*] Book of Job—	5	5	
[*September 1828*] Book of Job returned—		5	5

      [*Sir Geo Pocock*]

[*December 1826*] By Book of Job proof	5	5	
Frame & Case	5	5	

	D^r	C.
	£	£

[*Daniel Esq*]

[*1826*] proofs of Job—   5 5

    [*W. S. Davidson Esq*]

[*?July 1826*] 1 set of proofs of Job—   5 5

    [*James Brown Surveyor*]

Oct^r [*1829*] Book of Job—   5 5

    [*Mr Dowson*]

[*1831*] Book of Job—   5 5

    [*Messrs Payne & Foss Booksellers, Pall Mall*]

July [*1845*] one Blakes Job   5 5
    one Dante   2 2

[*January 1846*] one Job   [——]
    one Dante on Sale   [——]

1848 P. & F returned M[*ichael*] A[*ngelo prints by Linnell,*] Job & Dante

*   *   *   *   *   *   *   *

In the Ivimy MSS is a separate receipt:

Mr Linnell To Thos Palmer—		£ s d
1826		

Jan—1 Chald^n Coals to Mr Blake 56/————————   2.16 —
    Metage Shoot^g &c————————   5 —

                               3—1—0

Deduct for ready money———— ————   1—6
    Rec^d Jany 31st 2 19 6

                         Thos Palmer

This confirms the entry in Linnell's account book under 27 January 1826 for '1 chaldron of coals sent to Mr Blake' (*BR*, 589). 'Metage' is the duty paid for the official weighing of a load of coal, and 'Shooting' is the act of emptying the load.

APPENDIX II: BLAKE'S LIBRARY

FREDERICK Tatham wrote that Blake 'had a most consummate knowledge of all the great writers in all [*sic*] languages. To prove that, I may say that I have possessed books well thumbed and dirtied by his graving hands, in Latin, Greek, Hebrew, French, and Italian, besides a large collection of works of the mystical writers, Jacob Behmen, Swedenborg, and others. His knowledge was immense . . .' (*BR*, 41 n. 4.) None of Blake's books 'in Latin, Greek, Hebrew, French, and Italian' and by Jacob Boehme have survived (except for one in Italian), or at any rate been identified and traced, and we cannot now locate Blake's copies of numbers of books which we may be confident he owned,[1] such as the Bible. He must have had many books, but the few about which we may be confident are merely these:

1 *The Tragedies of Aeschylus*, tr. R. Potter, The Second Edition, With Notes. In Two Volumes (London: W. Strahan and T. Cadell, 1779) [Pierpont Morgan Library]. Blake signed his copy.

2 Francis Bacon, *Essays, Moral, Economical, and Political* (London: J. Edwards and T. Payne, 1798) [Cambridge University Library]. Blake made his extensive annotations about 1798.

3 *The Tvvo Bookes of Francis Bacon. Of the proficience and aduancement of Learning, diuine and humane* (London: Henrie Tomes, 1605) [untraced]. Blake said that he annotated 'Bacon's Advance of Learning' 'when very Young', and he quoted in 1799 from the 'first Edition'.

4 James Barry, *An Account of a Series of Pictures, in the Great Room of the Society of Arts, Manufactures, and Commerce, at the Adelphi* (London: Printed for the Author, 1783) [Cambridge University Library]. The copy in which Blake's portrait sketch of Barry was found presumably belonged to Blake.

5 [George Berkeley] G.L.B.O.C. [i.e. George Lord Bishop of Cloyne], *Siris: A Chain of Philosophical Reflexions and Inquiries Concerning the Virtues of Tar Water, And divers other Subjects connected together and arising one from another* (Dublin: R. Gunne, 1744) [Trinity College, Cambridge]. Blake annotated his copy about 1820.

6 Robert Blair, *The Grave, A Poem. Illustrated by Twelve Etchings Executed from Original Designs* (London: R. H. Cromek, Cadell & Davies, J. Johnson,

---

[1] All but Hallet's are recorded in *Blake's Books* (1977), 681–702. Notice that more than half these books are untraced.

T. Payne, J. White, Longman, Hurst, Rees, & Orme, W. Miller, J. Murray; Edinburgh: Constable & Co, 1808) [untraced]. Cromek said in 1808 that he had sent Blake '2 Copies' of the book for which Blake had made the designs.

7 Edmund Burke, *A Philosophical Enquiry into the Origins of our Ideas of the Sublime and Beautiful* [untraced]. Blake said he had annotated 'Burkes treatise' 'when very Young', but we do not know which of the eight editions before 1776 he had.

8 Edward Bysshe, *Art of Poetry* [untraced]. Catherine Blake was evidently using a one-volume edition of 'Bysshes Art of Poetry' for geomancy, as Blake recorded in his Notebook, but we do not know which of the one-volume editions of 1702, 1705, 1708, 1710, 1724, 1725, 1737 they had.

9 Cennino Cennini, *Trattato della Pittura Messo in Luce la Prima Volta con Annotazione dal Caveliere Giusseppe Tambrone* (Roma: Paolo Salviucci, 1821) [untraced]. Blake annotated his copy about 1822.

10 Thomas Chatterton, *Poems, Supposed to have been Written at Bristol, by Thomas Rowley, and Others, in the Fifteenth Century*, The Third Edition (London: Payne & Son, 1778) [Cambridge University Library]. Blake wrote his name on the title-page.

11 Francois Antoine Chevrier, *The Political Testament of the Marshal Duke of Belleisle* (London: P. Vaillant and D. Wilson, 1762) [Mr Charles Feinberg]. Blake signed the half-title.

12 George Cumberland, *Thoughts on Outline, Sculpture, and the System that Guided the Ancient Artists in Composing their Figures and Groupes: Accompanied with Free Remarks on the Practice of the Moderns, and Liberal Hints Cordially Intended for their Advantage. To Which Are Annexed Twenty-Four Designs of Classical Subjects Invented on the Principles Recommended in the Essay* (London: Robinson and T. Egerton, 1796) [untraced]. Cumberland said he gave away nineteen copies of his book, including one to 'Mr Blake' who had helped with the engravings.

13 Dante Alighieri, *A Translation of the Inferno in English Verse, with Historical notes; and the Life of Dante, To Which is Added, A Specimen of a New Translation of the Orlando Furioso of Ariosto By Henry Boyd* (Dublin: Printed by P. Byrne, 1785) [Cambridge University Library]. Annotated by Blake about 1800.

14 Allessandro Vellutello's *Dante* (1551, 1554, 1564, 1571, 1578, or 1596) [untraced]. Blake used the Sessi Vellutello Dante when working on his Dante illustrations, according to the *Literary Gazette* obituary (1827).

15 Dante, tr. Henry Francis Cary (London, 1814 or 1819) [untraced]. The same obituary said Blake was using 'Mr. Cary's translation'.

16 Jacob Duché, *Discourses on Various Subjects* [2 vols.] (London: T. Cadell, H. Payne, C. Dilly, and J. Phillips, 1779) [untraced]. 'Mr. William Blake' is in the subscription list.

17 William Falconer, a Sailor. *The Shipwreck, A Poem. The Text Illustrated by*

Additional Notes . . . with A Life of the Author, by James Stanier Clarke (London: William Miller, 1804) [untraced]. Blake thanked Hayley on 4 May 1804 'sincerely for Falconer, an admirable poet, and the admirable prints to it by Fittler'.

18 John Gay, *Fables, With a Life of the Author and embellished with Seventy Plates* [2 vols.] (London: John Stockdale, 1793) [untraced]. The 'Blake Mr.' in the subscription list is probably the poet, who engraved some of the plates for it.

19 William Gordon, *The History of the Rise, Progress, and Establishment of the Independence of the United States of America: Including an Account of the Late War; and of the Thirteen Colonies, from their Origin to that Period*. In Four Volumes. (London: Printed for the Author; and sold by Charles Dilly and James Buckland (1788)) [untraced]. The subscription list includes 'William Blake esq'.

20 Joseph Hallett Junior, *A Free and Impartial Study of the Holy Scriptures recommended: Being Notes on Some Peculiar Texts* . . . [3 vols., each with a different title-page] (London: J. Noon, 1729, 1732, 1736) [untraced]. Blake's copy, with his signature and the date (1799), was offered with the Library of H. Buxton Forman by Anderson Gallery, 26 April 1910, lot 46, and has not been traced since.

21 Alexander Hay, *The History of Chichester; interspersed with Various Notes and Observations on the Early and Present State of the City, The most Remarkable Places in its Vicinity, And the County of Sussex in General: with an Appendix, Containing the Charters of the City, at three different Times; also an Account of all the Parishes in the County, their names, patronage, appropriations, value in the king's books, first-fruits, &c. Dedicated, by Permission, To William Hayley, Esqr.* (Chichester: J. Seagrave; London: Longman & Co, 1804) [untraced]. Blake thanked Hayley in advance, on 18 December 1804, for the copy which Hayley had evidently said he was sending Blake.

22 William Hayley, *The Life, and Posthumous Writings, of William Cowper, Esqr.* (3 vols.) (London: J. Johnson, 1803, 1804) [untraced]. Blake thanked Hayley on 4 May 1804 for 'Cowper's third volume', and he must have been given the first two as well.

23 William Hayley, *The Triumph of Music; A Poem: In Six Cantos* (Chichester: J. Seagrave; London: T. Payne, J. Johnson, R. H. Evans, and Longman & Co, 1804) [untraced]. Blake's letter of 18 December 1804 seems to indicate from its reference to his 'second and third perusal' of the poem that he had been given a copy of it.

24 William Hayley, *The Triumphs of Temper; A Poem: In Six Cantos*. The Tenth Edition (London: T. Cadell, jun. & W. Davies, 1799) [untraced]. Hayley wrote a poem in the copy of the book, which he gave to Blake, according to J. T. Smith.

25 William Hayley, *The Triumphs of Temper, A Poem: In Six Cantos. The Twelfth*

Edition With New Original Designs, By Maria Flaxman (London: T. Cadell & W. Davies, 1803) [British Library]. A Large Paper copy of the edition with Blake's engravings is inscribed 'To Mrs Blake from the Author 1803'.

26 *The Whole Works of Homer; Prince of Poetts In his Iliads, and Odysses*, Tr. Geo: Chapman (London: Nathaniell Butter [1616]) [untraced]. Linnell bought Blake's copy in 1829.

27 *The Iliad and Odyssey of Homer*, tr. W. Cowper. In Two Volumes (London: J. Johnson, 1791) [untraced]. The subscription list includes 'Mr. W. Blake, Engraver', who must have heard about the work from his friend Henry Fuseli, who was frequently consulted about the translation.

28 The Revd James Hurdis, *Poems*, In Three Volumes (Oxford: J. Parker; London: Rivington and Longman & Co, 1808) [untraced]. The 'Mr. Blake' in the subscription list may well be the poet.

29 Frederick Heinrich Carl Baron de La Motte Fouque, *Sintram and his Companions*: A Romance [Tr. Julius C. Hare] (London: C. & J. Ollier; Edinburgh: William Blackwood, 1820) [untraced]. Blake showed a copy to Crabb Robinson and praised it.

30 John Caspar Lavater, *Aphorisms on Man*. Tr. [Henry Fuseli] (London: J. Johnson, 1788) [Huntington Library]. Blake annotated his copy extensively in 1788.

31 John Locke, *Essay Concerning Human Understanding* [untraced]. Blake annotated 'Locke on Human Understanding' 'when very Young', but we do not know whether he had any of the sixteen editions in print by 1768.

32 *Reliques of Ancient English Poetry: Consisting of Old Heroic Ballads, Songs, and other Pieces of our earlier Poets, (Chiefly of the Lyric kind.) Together with some few of later Date.* [3 vols., ed. Bishop Thomas Percy] (London: J. Dodsley, 1765) [Wellesley College]. Blake inscribed a copy to the wife of John Linnell.

33 *The Works of Sir Joshua Reynolds, Knight; Late President of the Royal Academy: Containing His Discourses, Idlers, A Journey to Flanders and Holland, and His Commentary on Du Fresnoy's Art of Painting. In Three Volumes. To which is Prefixed an Account of the Life and Writings of the Author, By Edmond Malone.* The Second Edition (London: T. Cadell, Jun. & W. Davies, 1798) [British Library]. Blake made extensive annotations in his set during two periods, ?1801–2 and ?1808–9.

34 *The Poetical Works of Will. Shenstone. With the Life of the Author, and A Description of the Leasowes. Embellished with Superb Engravings* (London: C. Cooke [1795]) [Cambridge University Library]. Blake signed his copy with the date 1799.

35 J. G. Spurzheim, *Observations on the Deranged Manifestations of the Mind, or Insanity. With Four Copper Plates* (London: Baldwin, Cradock, & Joy, 1817) [untraced]. Blake made a note on the book on a separate scrap of paper which has disappeared together with the copy of the book he read.

36 J. G. Stedman, *Narrative, of a five years expedition, against the Revolted Negroes of*

Surinam, in Guiana, on the Wild Coast of South America; from the year 1771 to 1777: elucidating the History of that Country, and describing its Productions, Viz. Quadrupedes, Birds, Fishes, Reptiles, Trees, Shrubs, Fruits, & Roots; with an account of the Indians of Guiana, & Negroes of Guinea. Illustrated with 80 elegant Engravings, from drawings made by the Author. [2 vols.] (London: J. Johnson and J. Edwards, 1796) [untraced]. The 'Blake (Mr. Wm.) London' in the subscription list is almost certainly the poet who engraved plates for his friend's book.

37 Emanuel Swedenborg, *A Treatise Concerning Heaven and Hell, and of the Wonderful Things therein, As Heard and Seen, By the Honourable and Learned Emanuel Swedenborg*, Tr. [William Cookworth & Thomas Hartley]. The Second Edition (London: T. Evans, T. Buckland, J. Denis & Son; Manchester: I. Clark; Bristol: T. Mills; Bath: S. Hazard, 1784) [Harvard University]. Blake annotated his copy about 1788.

38 Emanuel Swedenborg, *The Wisdom of Angels, Concerning Divine Love and Divine Wisdom*. Tr. [Dr. N. Tucker] (London: Printed by W. Chalklen, 1788) [British Library]. Blake's sympathetic annotations were made about 1789.

39 Emanuel Swedenborg, *The Wisdom of Angels Concerning the Divine Providence*. Tr. [Dr. N. Tucker] (London: R. Hindmarsh, 1790) [Cambridge University Library]. Blake's indignant annotations were written about 1790.

40 Charles Heathcote Tatham, *Etchings, Representing the Best Examples of Ancient Ornamental Architecture; Drawn from the Originals in Rome, and Other Parts of Italy, During the Years 1794, 1795, and 1796* (London: Printed for the Author, and Sold by Thomas Gardiner, 1799) [untraced]. The 'Mr. William Blake' in the subscription list is probably the poet, who gave *America* (B) to his friend Tatham in 1799.

41 Charles Heathcote Tatham, *Three Designs for the National Monument, Proposed to Be Erected in Commemoration of the Late Glorious Victories of the British Navy* (London: T. Gardiner, 1802) [untraced]. The 'Mr. William Blake' in the subscription list is probably the poet.

42 Joseph Thomas, *Religious Emblems, Being a Series of Engravings on Wood, Executed by the First Artists in that Line, from Designs Drawn on the Blocks Themselves by J. Thurston, Esq. the Descriptions Written by the Rev. J. Thomas* (London: R. Ackerman, 1809) [untraced]. The 'William Blake, Esq.' in the subscription list may well be the poet, for Thurston had bought a number of works from him.

43 Robert John Thornton, *The Lord's Prayer, Newly Translated from the Original Greek, with Critical and Explanatory Notes. With a Frontispiece from a Design by Harlow. Addressed to the Bible Societies for Distribution* (London: Sherwood & Co, Cox, and Dr. Thornton, 1827) [Huntington Library]. Blake annotated his copy furiously in the last six months of his life.

44 [Horace Walpole] *A Catalogue of the Royal and Noble Authors of England, with*

Lists of their Works. In Two Volumes. A New Edition (Edinburgh: Lawrie & Symington, 1792) [Harvard]. Blake wrote his name and the date, 1795, in his copy of each volume.

45 Richard Watson, *An Apology for the Bible, in a Series of Letters, Addressed to Thomas Paine, Author of a Book entitled, The Age of Reason, Part the Second, being an Investigation of True and of Fabulous Theology. Eighth Edition* (London: T. Evans, 1797. Price One Shilling, or Fifty Copies for Two Pounds, stitched) [Huntington Library]. Blake's incandescent annotations were made in 'this year 1798'.

46 [John & Charles Wesley] *Hymns for the Nation, In* 1782. [London, 1782]) [Cambridge University Library]. Blake wrote his name and the date, 1790, in his copy.

47 Abbe [J. J.] Winkelmann, *Reflections on the Painting and Sculpture of the Greeks: with Instructions for the Connoisseur, and An Essay on Grace in Works of Art. Tr. Henry Fusseli* [i.e. Fuseli] (London: Printed for the Translator, and Sold by A. Millar, 1765) [Cambridge University Library]. The poet wrote 'William Blake, Lincoln's Inn' in his copy, presumably when he was an apprentice.

48 [John Wolcot], *The Works of Peter Pindar*, 12mo [untraced]. A set with Blake's signature was sold in 1926, but we do not know which edition: 1794–1801, 1809, 1812, or 1816.

49 William Wordsworth, *The Excursion, Being a Portion of The Recluse, A Poem*. (London: Longman, Hurst, Rees, Orme, & Brown, 1814) [untraced]. Blake copied the Preface from the copy Crabb Robinson lent him.

50 William Wordsworth, *Poems: Including Lyrical Ballads, and the Miscellaneous Pieces of the Author. With Additional Poems, A New Preface, and a Supplementary Essay. In Two Volumes.* (London: Longman, Hurst, Rees, Orme, & Brown, 1815) [Cornell University Library]. Blake made notes in the copy Crabb Robinson lent him.

51 Edward Young, *The Complaint; or, Night Thoughts on Life, Death, and Immortality. To which are added, A Glossary, A Paraphrase on Part of the Book of Job, and A Poem on the Last Day. A New Edition* (London: T. Longman, Dodsley, C. Dilly, F. & C. Rivington, W. Otridge & Son, T. Cadell Jun., & W. Davies, and Bookham & Carpenter, 1796) [untraced]. A copy of Young's *Night Thoughts* (1796) with a 'Note of W. Blake the artist' is recorded by Sotheby's (1893) in a Glasgow edition and by Keynes in his *Bibliography* (1921) in a London edition.

APPENDIX III: FURTHER
CORRESPONDENCE

In 1829, Allan Cunningham applied to a number of artists for information for his biography of Blake (published in 1830). One of the most helpful of his informants was John Varley, who promised to try to get a letter of Blake and who recommended that Cunningham should write to John Linnell. Cunningham did so on 20 July 1829:

> Sir,
>   I have published one volume of the Lives of the Eminent British Painters, and I have another in progress . . . [*which*] will contain amongst others West, Barry, Fuseli Opie, and Blake if I can find suitable materials. Mr Varley from whom I have received much curious information tells me that you can aid me much in this matter.

Apparently Linnell volunteered information which Cunningham did not use, for Linnell wrote to Bernard Barton on 3 April 1830: 'I am sorry Mr Cunningham did not avail himself of the information I offered him'. Linnell also provided a Blake letter for Cunningham, as Varley wrote to Cunningham on 28 December [1829]:

> Dear Sir
>   There has been so much delay in getting Blake's writing that I fear it may arrive too late. I commissioned a friend to get it for me, not being able to find any among my own papers, & he neglected to do so. I have borrowed from Mr Linnell a note which I think will answer your purpose, and will thank you to let me have it again when you have done with it.
>   I am dear Sir
>   Yours truly
>   J. Varley
> Decr 28[1]

28 December [?1829]

Notice that Varley had not received, or at any rate had not kept, any letters from Blake.

Apparently Cunningham neglected to return the Blake letter to Varley (as requested) or to Linnell, for on 28 November 1860 Linnell wrote to Alexander Gilchrist:

---

[1] Quoted from the manuscript in the Pierpont Morgan Library.

I have been terrified at lending anything of Blakes through having lost one[*?*] of his letters which I lent to Allan Cunningham. [*BR*, 375 n. 1]

Cunningham did not quote any 'note' from Blake in his biography, and the only Blake letter he gave, to John Flaxman, was copied from J. T. Smith's life of Blake of 1828. Of the Blake letters to Linnell which survive, all came through the Linnell family from 1918 to 1960[1] except for two very brief ones of 11 October 1819 and [?April 1826]. Perhaps it was the second which Cunningham borrowed and did not return.

---

[1] Save that of 31 March 1826 which Linnell gave in 1830 to Abraham Cooper, after first prudently making a copy of it (*BR*, 378–9).

ADDENDA

AFTER the failure of his exhibition, Blake sank further and further into obscurity. His last public gesture for many years was his engraving of Chaucer's Canterbury Pilgrims. He devoted more than a third of his *Descriptive Catalogue* (1809) to an account of the picture on which it was based, and he issued two prospectuses for it, one entitled 'Blake's Chaucer: *The Canterbury Pilgrims*' (15 May 1809) and the other called 'Blake's Chaucer: An Original Engraving . . .' (1810). In the former, 'The Artist engages to deliver it, finished, in One Year from September next', i. e. in 1810, at £4. 4s. 0d. to subscribers; in the latter the price was reduced to £3. 3s. 0d. In fact, the finished print is dated 8 October 1810.

Blake sent copies of these prospectuses to his friends such as Thomas Butts, and he probably gave a few to dealers. Today they are very uncommon; of the former, only one copy is known, and of the latter only three. One of the dealers to whom he gave the second prospectus was Robert Bowyer, one of the most ambitious print-dealers of his time, along with John Boydell and Thomas Macklin. When he was publishing his great illustrated edition of Hume's *History of England* in 1793–1806, he had a fashionable gallery at 80 Pall Mall, and 'W. Blake' is one of the engravers named in Bowyer's prospectus for it of January 1792. However, Blake was given none of the plates for it, and he was bitterly resentful of being neglected by these great printsellers.

> Was I . . . angry with Macklin or Boydel or Bowyer
> Because they did not say 'O what a Beau ye are'[*?*]
>
> [*Notebook*, p. 23]

And in his letter of 11 December 1805 he wrote:

> I was alive & in health & with the same Talents I now have all the time of Boydells Macklins Bowyers & other Great Works. I was known by them & was lookd upon by them as Incapable of Employment in those Works . . .

However, he evidently swallowed his pride, showed Bowyer the etched state of his Canterbury Pilgrims plate, and asked him for assistance in selling it, for on 20 June 1810 Bowyer wrote to Earl Spencer:

Mr Bowyer begs leave to acquaint Lord Spencer that the Plate of which the enclosed is a prospectus is Engraving in the line manner & of which W: B: has already a very fine Etching & he has reason to believe it will be one of the finest Engravings which has been seen in this country for some Years—[1]

20 June 1810

This solicitation might have had remarkable consequences, for Lord Spencer was one of the most munificent book collectors in Europe, as well as a man with extremely influential connections, and a commission from him could have been agreeably rewarding to Blake. Lord Spencer may already have known of Blake, for on 16 June 1802 Lady Hesketh had sent to Dr Randolph a copy of the first of Hayley's *Designs to A Series of Ballads* illustrated and published by Blake to show to Lord Spencer. Further, about 1815 Lord Spencer acquired copy O of Young's *Night Thoughts* (1797) with Blake's plates splendidly coloured.

So far as we know, Lord Spencer did not subscribe for Blake's Canterbury Pilgrims plate—but he may have done more, partly as a result of this letter with its recommendation of Blake as being capable of producing 'one of the finest Engravings which has been seen in this country for some Years'. At any rate Blake made a very fine engraving after Thomas Phillips's portrait of Earl Spencer. The date and circumstances of the commission are unknown, but it may well have arisen from Bowyer's letter here. Only a few copies of the unpublished print are known, and two of them are on paper watermarked 1811.[2] However, on 12 April 1813 George Cumberland recorded in his notebook that he 'Saw Blake who . . . is Doing I.^d Spencer', so Blake was evidently then working on his engraving of the portrait. Perhaps the engraving was somehow connected with the marriage of Georgiana Charlotte Spencer in 1814.

---

[1] The letter, temporarily numbered 1299, is in a volume now called Althorp G318 among the vast collection of Spencer Papers given to the British Library Department of Manuscripts in 1984 The prospectus is not with the letter, nor is it preserved with Lord Spencer's books which went in 1892 to the John Rylands Library, now part of the University of Manchester. Bowyer's letter is addressed to Lord Spencer at Ryde, Isle of Wight, where he was apparently visiting, and Lord Spencer may not have taken the prospectus home with him.

Note that Bowyer's part here is apparently disinterested, for Blake's prospectus said that subscriptions should be sent to [his brother's house at] 28, Broad Street, and Bowyer was therefore unlikely to receive any commission through his initiative.

[2] See Robert N. Essick, *The Separate Plates of William Blake: A Catalogue* (1983), where the portrait is reproduced as Plate 78.

INDEX

Blake's poems, books, and pictures are entered under their titles; works by others are entered under the maker's name.

Index